SAMUEL JOHNSON
AND NEOCLASSICAL DRAMATIC THEORY

Next to the excursions of fancy are the disquisitions of criticism, which, in my opinion, is only to be ranked among the subordinate and instrumental arts. Arbitrary decision and general exclamation I have carefully avoided, by asserting nothing without a reason, and establishing all my principles of judgment on unalterable and evident truth.

Rambler no. 208

And inasmuch as the life which is both the subject and object of literature, is neither scientific nor yet unprincipled but broadly moral; our criticism will be neither scientific nor impressionistic, but will consist in a free play of the intelligence just as life does. It will be based on general principles, which, though elastic, are broader than the observation of a single case, and which are capable of being explained and justified, as our conduct is, rationally and intelligibly, if nothing more.

Prosser Hall Frye

Samuel Johnson
and
Neoclassical Dramatic
Theory

THE INTELLECTUAL CONTEXT OF THE
PREFACE TO SHAKESPEARE

by

R. D. Stock

UNIVERSITY OF NEBRASKA PRESS · LINCOLN

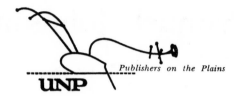

Publishers on the Plains

Copyright © 1973 by the University of Nebraska Press

All rights reserved

Library of Congress Catalog Card Number 72–77194

International Standard Book Number 0–8032–0819–7

Manufactured in the United States of America

To my Mother and Father,
with love and gratitude

Contents

Preface

"Length of duration and continuance of esteem"—Dr. Johnson's two ineluctable standards of literary excellence have long established his own *Preface to Shakespeare* (1765) as a classic. It has frequently been characterized "the greatest neoclassical statement on Shakespeare," but critics have as often called it that to dismiss it as to commend. Little effort has been made to examine in detail Johnson's own words and their historical context; unless we are prepared to do so, we cannot properly determine the quality of Johnson's neoclassicism. Is the *Preface* in fact (as it is often represented to be) a pure distillation of eighteenth-century criticism on Shakespeare: "What oft was thought, but ne'er so well expressed"? Or is it something more—or less—than this? In the present volume some of the materials for an answer are collected. The purpose of this study is twofold: first, it intends to provide the modern reader with a reasonably detailed framework of contemporary thought, enabling him to bring to the *Preface* something of an eighteenth-century perspective; and second, it utilizes the *Preface* as a frame of reference by which to sort and examine eighteenth-century dramatic criticism generally. Thus the *Preface* itself ought to become more intelligible, while at the same time it may be possible to chart more precisely some of the currents in neoclassical criticism.

I have chosen to examine most diligently the years between 1730 and 1770, since it was then that the most decisive developments in eighteenth-century criticism occurred or began to occur. The magazines and journals matured and established themselves; Continental criticism became more diversified and interesting. I shall make references back to Dryden and forward to the Romantics to provide perspective, but the references will be neither extensive nor, I trust, irrelevant. In French criticism only have a number of excursions been made into the 1770s; many things clearly in the atmosphere seem to have precipitated into ink some ten years later than in England. In English criticism I have selected 1770, rather than 1765, as my *terminus ad quem*, and have in fact made occasional but cautious forages beyond. Although the *Preface* appeared in 1765, such works as Mrs. Montagu's *Essay on the Writings and Genius of Shakespeare* (1769) or the anonymous *Cursory Remarks on Tragedy* (1774), despite their dates, are of importance in a contextual study; Mrs. Montagu shows the incipience of new ideas, while the *Cursory Remarks* exhibits the perseverance of the old.

A glance at the table of contents will indicate the categories of ideas around which I have organized this study. In each chapter I shall consider first the criticism in the decades prior to 1770, and against that background examine Johnson's own position. I have given no attention to the final quarter of the *Preface*, where Johnson discusses the relative merits of earlier editions and defends his own editorial techniques. Much useful research might be done here, but it is a problem to be taken up by an historian of textual scholarship; my subject is the development of critical theory. Unlike Arthur Sherbo in his recent analysis of Johnson on Shakespeare,[1] I shall not be concerned with isolating direct influences on Johnson's *Preface*, although whenever the evidence suggests such an influence it will be examined. Nor shall I be as sedulous as Sherbo in attempting to distinguish what is *old* from what is *original* in Johnson. Although the *Preface* may not be revolutionary, neither is it unexciting; for even if every *thing* in it should be discovered somewhere in the background, the merit of the work would remain. The Rambler observes that men more frequently require to be reminded than informed. One of the excellences of the *Preface* is that it reminds us in such a way as to inform as well.[2]

1. Arthur Sherbo, *Samuel Johnson, Editor of Shakespeare. With an Essay on The Adventurer, Illinois Studies in Language and Literature,* vol. 42 (Urbana: University of Illinois Press, 1956).

2. I have laid such stress on context, rather than influence, because Sherbo has done as much in this way as possible; in this study I shall refer the reader to the appropriate sections of his work. Where Johnson has expressed an interesting opinion about any of the critics cited here, I shall include it; but these opinions cannot prove that he read the books, and certainly not that he read them through. Nor can influence be documented simply by identifying certain similarities of ideas: Johnson was after all working in a tradition, and only occasionally did he regard his views as innovative. Finally, the sales catalogue of Johnson's library offers little help. The few critical works it includes were published after the *Preface*: the first volume of Warton's *History of English Poetry* (entry no. 535), Campbell's *Philosophy of Rhetoric* (no. 506), and a "Remarks on Shakespeare, &c." (no. 261). This last entry may

Sherbo's is the only study which presses closely on mine. It is a concise and scholarly analysis of Johnson and his immediate predecessors, placing especial emphasis on Johnson's "Notes to Shakespeare"; but owing to the comprehensiveness of his task, Sherbo is unable to devote extensive critical attention either to the *Preface* itself or to its context. Because of this comprehensiveness and because he is so relentlessly employed in determining direct influence and absolute originality, Sherbo has drawn conclusions about the *Preface* which must certainly be qualified.[3] With one important exception, other book-length surveys of neoclassical dramatic criticism are extremely general.[4]

Complete bibliographical information is provided for each reference the first time it is cited in each chapter. Thereafter, references are abbreviated but may be identified by means of the Selected Bibliography.

---

be the *Cursory Remarks on Tragedy, on Shakespear, and on certain French and Italian Poets* (1774), which I shall cite often as an example of the persistence of reactionary neoclassicism. If so, this is mildly intriguing; but even if the conjecture is correct, there can be no possibility of direct influence.

3. In 1956, in the introduction to his Augustan Reprint Society edition of the *Notes to Shakespeare* (nos. 59–60) Sherbo asserts: "And it is on the notes that his claim to remembrance as a critic of Shakespeare must rest, for the famous Preface is, after all, only rarely an original and personal statement." His more recent edition of the *Preface* and *Notes* for the Yale *Works* nowhere indicates that he has altered his opinion. See Henry K. Miller, review of Sherbo's *Samuel Johnson, Editor of Shakespeare, Philological Quarterly* 36, no. 3 (1957): 378–79 (on the *Preface*). On Sherbo's assessment of Johnson's entire edition, see Arthur M. Eastman, "In Defense of Dr. Johnson," *Shakespeare Quarterly* 8 (1957): 493–500.

4. That exception is Robert Witbeck Babcock's *The Genesis of Shakespeare Idolatry, 1766–1799* (Chapel Hill: University of North Carolina Press, 1931). Had Babcock, whose erudition and acuity are unrivalled, fulfilled his intention of producing a companion volume on the earlier period, there would be less excuse for the present work; as it is, he takes up in detail where I leave off. C. C. Green's *The Neo-Classic Theory of Tragedy in England during the Eighteenth Century* (Cambridge: Harvard University Press, 1934) is a thorough if pedestrian survey; however, it has been superseded in many areas by later scholarship. Furthermore, considering the numerous translations and reviews of contemporary foreign criticism in France and England at this time, it is curious that none of these studies has attempted to draw parallels between mid-century English and Continental criticism. My indebtedness to other more specific studies—notably Jean H. Hagstrum's *Samuel Johnson's Literary Criticism* (Chicago: University of Chicago Press, 1967)—will be apparent.

I must express my gratitude to the librarians of Princeton University and the British Museum for their assistance and cordiality. To the Woodrow Wilson Foundation and the University of Nebraska Research Council I am also greatly obliged for their support and encouragement. But I must particularly thank Professor Louis A. Landa, who recommended the subject and supervised its original production. Without his disciplining and sympathetic attention very little might have been achieved.

Introduction:
The Problem of Reason

*From his writing indeed a system of social
duty may be selected, for he that thinks
reasonably must think morally . . . .*

Preface to Shakespeare

Jean H. Hagstrum, in the preface to his authoritative analysis of
Johnson's literary criticism, describes very well the dilemma that
confronts a contextual study of this sort: "Attempts to affirm or
deny that Johnson was predominantly a humanist, an authoritarian,
a traditionalist, a skeptic are necessarily obfuscating. The terms used
are either too vague or too intimately a part of our own intellectual
battles . . . . I have therefore attempted to confine myself to the
language of exposition and to avoid the language of persuasion."[1]
Yet his solution to the problem has not been universally adopted;
the last few years have seen several attempts to persuade us that
Johnson was an Augustinian, a Hobbist, a Thomist—and these
designations are not obviously more intelligible and less perplexing
than those Hagstrum discommends. Certainly they can all be vague
and imprecise, but it seems very difficult to know how to dispense
with them. Unless we are prepared to devise a new terminology,
which would be equally foreign to everybody, we must use the one
we have; and it may well be, in the interests of clarity and truth,
that we shall have to use it for persuasive as well as expositive
purposes. Now for the most part I shall hope to be expositive. The
primary purpose of the present study is to examine what Johnson
and his contemporaries or immediate predecessors were saying about
the drama generally and about Shakespeare particularly; it is an
investigation at once of the attitudes of Johnson and of the early
and middle eighteenth century. But it is also a study of a man

1. Jean H. Hagstrum, *Samuel Johnson's Literary Criticism* (Chicago: University of Chicago Press, 1967), p. xvi.

reasoning, and here it seems necessary to assume the language of persuasion.

Sometime before the middle of 1731 Pope wrote of Newton:

> Could he, whose rules the rapid Comet bind,
> Describe or fix one movement of his Mind?
> Who saw its fires here rise, and there descend,
> Explain his own beginning, or his end?

The *Essay on Man,* despite its contemporary language, is a fairly traditional poem. And this rhetorical question assumes a very traditional answer—no. Newton's reason can explain the physical universe to us, but it cannot explain the moral universe; it is unable to account for our reason and our lack of reason, nor can it comprehend our origins or our destinies. These are normative questions—questions of value—and Newton's reason is discursive; it is concerned with what is true, but not with what is good, with quantitative data, not with qualitative principles; it is the sort used to solve, not moral problems, but scientific or mathematical propositions. However, Pope, though he wished to be traditional, desired also to be fashionable, much to the distress of some of his more orthodox friends. And so a little over a year later he attributes to his theory of the "ruling passion" (a theory more modestly expressed in the *Essay on Man* and much detested by Johnson) a certitude akin to that which Newton's theory of gravitation was believed to possess. His theory has to do with human behavior, not physical laws, yet when it is properly understood, Pope tells us, even the most extreme aberrations of human conduct will become comprehensible. He then traces the unscrupulous career of the duke of Wharton, and having accounted for it by a ruling passion, proclaims:

> Nature well known, no prodigies remain,
> Comets are regular, and Wharton plain.

Between the *Essay on Man* and the epistle *To Cobham* yawns a capacious philosophical chasm. While Pope had earlier distinguished between the motions of a comet and the mind of a Newton, which in its unfathomable mystery stands for that of Everyman, he now equates them. Pope's ruling passion is represented as a "moral theory of gravitation." By applying the principles of discursive reason to moral problems, we can understand the behavior of men as well as the operations of the stars. In this, Pope is no longer traditional; he has been captivated by a vision first evoked by the speculations of the "Enlightenment" pioneers—Descartes, Hobbes, Locke—and subsequently to entrance many other eighteenth-century thinkers: the desire, as Francis Hutcheson declares in his *Inquiry into the Original of Our Ideas of Beauty and Virtue* (1725), "to introduce a mathematical calculation in subjects of morality." From Descartes's ethical calculus through Locke's pleasure-pain calculus to Bentham's felicific calculus, from Spinoza's *Ethica more geometrico demonstrata* to Wolff's *Jus Gentium methodo scientifica pertractum*, we can follow the attempt of the "new philosophers" to apply discursive and "calculating" reason to those areas of experience not previously regarded as susceptible to it: principally ethics, civics, and—as we shall see—aesthetics. Thus even the humanist Pope was not able to evade the influence, or resist the attractions, of what today we call positivism.

As is well known, rationalism was countered in the late seventeenth century by those who, in conscious reaction against Hobbes's cynical and mechanistic understanding of human nature, emphasized man's benevolence and innate goodness. Of these, the Cambridge Platonists were particularly instrumental in laying the groundwork for Shaftesbury and sentimentalism; for while the rationalists endeavored to include as much of experience as they could within the confines of a narrowed, analytical reason, these tried to escape from those confines by placing ethical issues under the province of sensibility or sentiment. Yet though these two philosophical attitudes seem at odds, many of their disagreements are merely a matter of shading or emphasis. For our purposes it is much more instructive to see the areas where they found common ground. Both the rationalists and the sentimentalists opposed traditional notions of right or normative reason. For the sentimentalist, man behaved in a moral way, not because his reason had apprehended the ethical law—in short, because reason was normative—but because his impulses were sound. Thus the rationalists would have replaced right reason with discursive reason, and their opponents with sentiment. They both questioned existing institutions, the one because they were "irrational"—the product of superstitious ages— and the other because they constrained the expression of man's good instincts. They both were inclined to place the *individual's* opinion, whether it proceeded from his discursive reason or from his instincts, over the collective wisdom of the past. Thus it is not remarkable that these two attitudes should cooperate, indeed, that they should be held simultaneously by the same philosopher. Hutcheson, whom we have seen wishing to devise a mathematical system of morality, was also a disciple of Shaftesbury and one of the chief architects of the "moral sense." Diderot was quite professedly a scientific positivist who viewed a Newtonian system of ethics as the most valuable project a philosopher could contemplate; and yet, although he rejected the moral sense, he was in part a sentimentalist, believing in human goodness and at times defining virtue as an emotional state. Rousseau tried on the one hand to arrive at a strictly rational system of human rights through the myth of the social contract, and on the other situated moral imperatives in the sensibility. In short, the late seventeenth and eighteenth centuries witnessed revolutionary new conceptions of reason and feeling, the rationalists investing in discursive reason, and the sentimentalists in feeling and subjectivity, an authority they had not usually been accorded. Both these philosophies, occasionally opposed but so often joined, have exercised an incalculable influence on the modern world. Rationalism is doubtless one of the ancestors of structural linguistics and the behavioral sciences, and it explains too the high repute of Chardin, in whom the identification of physical with spiritual or moral nature is very close. Sentimentalism is in part responsible for the popularity of situation ethics and civil disobedience, where moral imperatives are defined both subjectively and relatively. Hagstrum is therefore quite correct in seeing the terms he condemns as "intimately a part of our own intellectual battles." But it is precisely this intimacy that makes them difficult to avoid. Surely a study of the past—especially a past so responsible for contemporary thought as the eighteenth century—ought to enable us better to understand our own age; and while this is hardly the main purpose of the present study, it is a purpose to which I have not been indifferent.

How Johnson relates to this context has been the subject of much recent and sometimes acidulous controversy. As Hagstrum points out, after having recovered from nineteenth-century conceptions of Johnson as a hidebound and insensitive old Tory, we in the present century have made some effort to sentimentalize or

pre-Romanticize him. Most recently, however, still another attempt
has been undertaken: to associate Johnson with the Hobbists and
Lockians. This interest proceeds in large measure from a very laud-
able motive—to challenge our image of Johnson the conservative,
Christian humanist, and the like, by showing that in a significant
way his thoughts and values were formed by the rationalists of the
seventeenth century. Now to a degree this is all well and good. No
thoughtful eighteenth-century man could be expected to escape
the influence of such giants as Hobbes and Locke, and particularly
with so empirical and pragmatic a thinker as Johnson, it is ill-
advised to be too complacent over his traditionalism; certainly, *he*
was not complacent over it! At the same time, two of the most
persuasive of these attempts—Robert Voitle's *Samuel Johnson the
Moralist* (1961) and Donald J. Greene's *Politics of Samuel Johnson*
(1960), both of which associate his moral and political principles
with rationalism—have been accused of failing properly to distinguish between right reason and discursive reason, and hence with
failing to understand that Johnson, despite what he *seems* to say
sometimes, is in fact a traditionalist rather than a thoroughgoing
Cartesian, Hobbist, or Lockian.[2] This debate over Johnson's reason
is nowhere better summarized than in a rather unrestrained and
prolonged disagreement between Greene and Peter J. Stanlis which
enlivened the pages of the *Journal of British Studies* a few years
ago; it was precipitated by an article of Greene's on Johnson and
the natural law.[3] The argument, at its inception, was over what
concept of natural law Johnson held, but finally it was over what
sort of reason he used. Was he a traditionalist, employing reason
in its old, broad sense of right reason, normative reason, or was
he using it, like Locke and Hobbes, to mean discursive reason?
In short, was Johnson a real traditionalist, or was he, like Pope,
strongly attracted to certain rationalist principles?

  We have no occasion to enter into the niceties of the controversy,
although in its course both sides found it necessary to refine their

  2. Voitle is so arraigned in *The Burke Newsletter* 3 (Fall 1961): 66–69; Greene
in the *Journal of British Studies* 2 (1963): 76–83.

  3. See: Donald J. Greene, "Samuel Johnson and 'Natural Law,'" *Journal of
British Studies* 2 (1963): 59–75, and Peter J. Stanlis's "Comment," ibid., pp. 76–83.
See also in ibid.: Greene's "Response," 2 (1963): 84–87; Warren Fleischauer's
letter, 3 (1963): 155–58; and further letters by Stanlis, 3 (1963): 158–64; Greene,
3 (1963): 164–67; Stanlis, 4 (1965): 149–57; see finally Francis Oakley, "Greene
and Stanlis on Dr. Johnson and the Natural Law . . . ," ibid. 4 (1964): 1–5.

terms and to be rather more cautious in what they thought Johnson
was thinking. It is not unfair to say that Stanlis fails to prove
his point with respect to natural law: Johnson uses the term, but
with such latitude that there is no more apparent reason to associate him with Saint Thomas than with Cicero. He was simply not
a systematic theologian or political theorist. But it seems equally
apparent that Greene, in denying, as he certainly seems to do, that
Johnson made the traditional distinction between normative and
discursive reason, is demonstrably wrong. A number of passages
can be adduced where Johnson seems clearly to discriminate in this
way.[4] The upshot of the whole controversy is that Johnson, so
far as we can determine, was a traditional Christian accepting that
law which, so Saint Paul tells us, is written into the hearts of
believer and Gentile alike, which illumines the conscience and is
apprehended by reason. As he says in the *Preface*, "He that thinks
reasonably must think morally." To assert that Johnson held some
normative conception of reason is not to say that he was uninfluenced by rationalist thought, nor need it involve us in such more
delicate questions as have agitated Stanlis and Greene. It is to say
that on this point he probably thought pretty much as most traditional Anglicans and Roman Catholics have thought. But Hagstrum has still a right to ask where all this has got us in understanding Johnson.

If we persist in using the terms Hagstrum deplores, in defiance
of his example, we are obliged to create a context for them in which
they work and communicate meaning. In the present study I would
signify by *traditionalist* one who is not an exponent of some variety
of rationalism or sentimentalism. This is not to say, obviously, that
he might not be influenced by both. As a definition, this is loose
but practicable; it can be applied to a number of authors, and
the more often one applies it, the more it can be refined and sub-
tilized. If employed with modesty and deliberation, the term need
not be obfuscating. The opening lines of *Religio Laici*, for example,
express at least one of the traditional attitudes toward reason; we
sense that this will be a "traditional" poem. Throughout Dryden
attempts to move between the excesses of the rationalists, here represented by the Deists, and those of the enthusiastic sectarians; both
place their personal wills—the Deists' reason and the sectarians'

---

4. Warren Fleischauer, cited note 3 above, provides and comments on several
such passages.

zeal—over the collective wisdom of the nation to the destruction of public order and "common quiet." The Deists exalt their more limited, discursive reason, the sectarians their individual consciences, in order to challenge traditional values and beliefs. Dryden opposes both extremities: although we must not despise (discursive) reason, we must recognize that it is unable to produce certitude in ethical matters; nor can such certitude proceed from our private instincts. Salvation is not attendant on our solving all our doubts, and where we cannot satisfy all of them, tradition—the consensus of the ages—is our least fallible mentor.

Swift satirizes the utopian aspirations of the rationalists in the *Voyage to Laputa*, whose "scientific" rulers unite inefficiency with inhumanity. And the "reason" of the Projector in *A Modest Proposal*, while admirably consistent and exquisitely calculating, is the reason of a fanatic, utterly unrelated to political reality and human nature: the ethical calculus of Descartes, Locke, and—prophetically—Bentham reduced to the absurd and the inhumane. Nor is Swift inclined to trust to the benevolence of our emotions. One behaves morally, not because one's sensibility delights in doing good, but because one knows through a combination of faith and reason that it will be to one's advantage to do so—hence the necessity of the doctrine of rewards and punishments. Shaftesbury called this a selfish and degrading belief; but Swift might well have replied, adapting a phrase of Dr. Johnson's, that nothing is too degrading for so degraded a creature as man.[5]

Years later Burke compares the revolutionary rulers of France to the "learned academicians of Laputa and Balnibarbi";[6] he compares them also to Don Quixote, who is not for Burke that courageous and eccentric idealist so beloved in modern times, but a dangerous and irrational fanatic. He charges the revolutionists, as Swift did the Laputan magistrates, with both inefficiency and inhumanity. The "science" of creating a state is not of the Newtonian sort; unlike geometry or mathematics it is "not to be taught *a priori*."[7] Rather, it must comprehend the realities of political and

---

5. For this aspect of Swift's thought, and relevant citations from his works, see James Brown, "Swift as Moralist," *Philological Quarterly* 33 (1954): 368–87.

6. Edmund Burke, *Reflections on the Revolution in France*, ed. H. D. Mahoney (New York: Bobbs-Merrill, 1955), p. 152.

7. Ibid., p. 69.

human nature. He forthrightly repudiates Hutcheson's aspiration "to introduce a mathematical calculation in subjects of morality":

> We know that *we* have made no discoveries, and we think that no discoveries are to be made, in morality, nor many in the great principles of government . . . which were understood long before we were born, altogether as well as they will be after the grave has heaped its mold upon our presumption and the silent tomb shall have imposed its law on our pert loquacity.[8]

At the same time, although conscious of the value of instinct and sentiment, he opposes Roussellian primitivism: art is man's nature. Man's "natural" state is not that of primitivism or anarchistic liberty, but of civilization, whose institutions do not so much obstruct his instincts as channel them in valuable directions.

My intent is very far from making Dryden, Swift, and Burke of one cut. Dryden's opposition to the Deists does not parallel exactly Swift's to the projectors or Burke's to the revolutionists. Quite the contrary, a more thorough consideration would reveal the diverse "traditions" which serve to distinguish them both as artists and individuals.[9] And yet it remains that we first think of them all as "traditionalists," and when we look into the matter, we find that our first thoughts are sound; their shaping of experience is so unmistakably similar as to suggest certain commonly held values and modes of reasoning.[10] Once we build a context around the word,

8. Ibid., p. 97.

9. More thorough studies discriminate more nicely than I have been able to do. For Swift and Dryden, see Phillip Harth's two books: *Swift and Anglican Rationalism* (Chicago: University of Chicago Press, 1961) and *Contexts of Dryden's Thought* (Chicago: University of Chicago Press, 1968). For theories of rationalism, sentimentalism, and ethics generally, see Louis I. Bredvold's two concise studies: *The Brave New World of the Enlightenment* (Ann Arbor: University of Michigan Press, 1962) and *The Natural History of Sensibility* (Detroit: Wayne State University Press, 1962); and for more detailed analyses, consult Lester G. Crocker's *An Age of Crisis: Man and World in Eighteenth-Century Thought* (Baltimore: Johns Hopkins Press, 1959) and *Nature and Culture: Ethical Thought in the French Enlightenment* (Baltimore: Johns Hopkins Press, 1963). Peter Gay's many books and articles portray the antitraditionalists more favorably than Bredvold's and Crocker's; for a brief and provocative statement of his views see *The Bridge of Criticism* (New York: Harper and Row, 1970).

10. The truth of this is superbly documented by Paul Fussell, *The Rhetorical World of Augustan Humanism: Ethics and Imagery from Swift to Burke* (Oxford: Oxford University Press, 1965).

it can become intelligible and useful. It is my contention that in this very latitudinarian and not very complicated sense Johnson is traditional, and that in his criticism, and specifically in the *Preface to Shakespeare*, one can discern qualities of reasoning not unlike those that I have so cursorily sketched here. The aesthetic thoughts of an age cannot be distinguished absolutely from its other thoughts: who, for example, could have conceived of structural linguistics or descriptive grammar without being acquainted as well with the tenets of scientific positivism? The common assumptions and values of an age—the "patterns of thought" or "climates of opinion" our positivist would say—not only manifest themselves in all its branches of learning, but to a degree determine *which* branches of learning it decides to explore. The "persuasive" portions of this study, then, will be to this end: that Johnson regarded literary criticism, like reason itself, as a subordinate and instrumental art; it is not on the one hand merely a matter of mood or sentiment, nor on the other a highway to positive and scientific certitude. Like Burke's political "science," it is not to be taught a priori; like Dryden's reason, though it may indicate where the truth lies, it cannot of itself guide us there. If his principles are established "upon unalterable and evident truth," that is because they are rooted in consensus and traditional wisdom. As Dryden and Swift move between the extremes of subjective sectarianism and inhuman rationalism, and Burke between the sentimental popularizers of Rousseau and the experimental philosophers of the Revolution, so Johnson, in his critical principles and judgments, preserves the art of criticism against those who would reduce it to a feeling or exalt it to a science. In its way no less than the *Reflections on the Revolution in France*, the *Preface to Shakespeare* dramatizes the conflict between the older values yet current, and the newer ones just appearing. To this belief, at any rate, I shall endeavor to persuade, with the hope that the terms employed will not obfuscate, but illuminate, the intellectual context of Johnson's reasoning.

SAMUEL JOHNSON
AND NEOCLASSICAL DRAMATIC THEORY

Chapter I

The Principles of Literary Criticism:

Length of Duration and Continuance of Esteem

Time is the judge; Time has nor friend nor foe;
False fame *must* wither, and the true *will* grow.

Edward Young, *Two Epistles to Mr. Pope*

... the People's Voice is odd,
It is, and it is not, the voice of God.

Alexander Pope, *The First Epistle of
the Second Book of Horace*

In 1944 T. S. Eliot, addressing the Virgil Society on "What Is a Classic?", concluded that the English language has neither experienced a classic age nor produced a classic poet. Only Pope, he argues, most closely approaches that union of qualities worthy of the term: maturity of mind, of manners, and of language; yet even he wants the fourth necessity: comprehensiveness. But by 1765 Shakespeare—who for Eliot is deficient in the category of manners—had survived by half again that minimum of one hundred years which less fastidious critics have proposed as the criterion for a "classic." Nevertheless, Eliot is correct in requiring more than merely temporal endurance; and neither Edward Young's sanguine assurance nor Pope's teasing equivocation advances us profoundly into the mysteries of artistic greatness. In the opening paragraphs of his *Preface* Johnson concedes that the merit of a work must necessarily be tested by time, but he complains that its antiquity is too often reverenced "not from reason, but from prejudice."[1] Johnson quite understands the importance of the test of time and a *consensus gentium*, but he is also aware of the imperfection of "human judgment," and hence of the necessity for undertaking critical investigations to remedy possible errors. Although Johnson would perhaps agree with Young, therefore, that false fame *must* wither and the true *will* grow, he would contend that such a botanical economy is not to be achieved without rather more conscientious gardening than Young suggests. Although Johnson does not here use the word, he is in fact concerned with the problem of *taste*, a problem which was much debated among his contemporaries and which posed the fundamental question: how do we know whether or not a work of art is great? It is probably true, as J. T. Boulton has remarked, that in the eighteenth century "to define 'taste' was to define one's aesthetic presuppositions." Before examining Shakespeare's merit as an author, Johnson here establishes several critical principles and presuppositions which we in turn, before examining Johnson on Shakespeare, must understand.

R. W. Babcock was deterred, by the simple magnitude of the task, from including a chapter on taste in his *Genesis of Shakespeare Idolatry, 1766–1799*. Although the present study concerns Shakespeare criticism in the years before Babcock takes it up, it would be equally presumptuous to expect to cover the ground.[2]

---

1. *The Yale Edition of the Works of Samuel Johnson*, 8 vols. (New Haven: Yale University Press, 1958–69), 7: 59 (hereafter cited as *Works*). All quotations from Johnson's Shakespeare criticism, and from the *Rambler, Idler*, and *Adventurer*, are from this edition. Cf. *Idler* no. 59: "That which is to be loved long must be loved with reason rather than with passion" (ibid., 2: 184).

2. Good general discussions of the word may be found in: E. N. Hooker, "The Discussion of Taste from 1750 to 1770 and the New Trends in Literary Criticism," *PMLA* 49 (1934): 577–92; supplemented by R. W. Babcock, "The Idea of Taste in the Eighteenth-Century," ibid. 50 (1935): 922–26. See also: Gordon McKenzie, *Critical Responsiveness* (Los Angeles: University of California Press, 1949), pp. 85–116; M. H. Abrams, *The Mirror and The Lamp* (Oxford: Oxford University Press, 1953), pp. 12–13, 18–19, 104; René Wellek, *A History of Modern Criticism: 1750–1950*, vol. 1, *The Later Eighteenth Century* (New Haven: Yale University Press, 1955), pp. 24, 107–9; and, for other early eighteenth-century citations, Edward Niles Hooker's annotation in John Dennis, *Critical Works*, 2 vols. (Baltimore: Johns Hopkins Press, 1939–43), 1: 458–59. Finally, for Johnson and taste, see Jean H. Hagstrum, *Samuel Johnson's Literary Criticism* (Chicago: University of Chicago Press, 1967), pp. 26–27, and chap. 2 passim.

But the general lines of thought, and the patterns they had formed by 1765, must be indicated before one can determine Johnson's position precisely. Like many ethical philosophers of the time, the philosophers of taste can be roughly grouped into the sentiment-alists and the rationalists, although—as with the moralists—the same critic may be so dexterous as to embrace simultaneously both positions. For the sentimentalists, taste may be in all of the people, or in only a few; but regardless, the test of time is an empirical demonstration of the subtle, if at times rather mechanical, opera-tion of taste. By the more zealous critics of this persuasion taste was held to be the only sure test of a work of art, a test against which critical principles could be marshaled in vain. Of all the English and Continental critics, the Abbé Dubos (1719) is one of the earliest and most explicit adherents of this notion. Theoretical analysis for him is highly suspect: consensus of taste—the empirical test—is the only relevant criterion. And this taste will exert itself in the general public quite independently of any rationalistic scheme or specialized critical knowledge: "Ce n'est point en raison-nant qu'on juge des ouvrages faits pour toucher & pour plaire. On en juge par un mouvement intérieur qu'on ne sçauroit bien expliquer."[3] But Dubos was only putting more plainly what ear-lier French critics had assumed. The two Gallic commentators on Longinus, Boileau and Dacier, endorse and develop Longinus's own opinion that a work may be said certainly to contain the marvelous or sublime "when a great Number of Persons, of different Professions and Ages, having no manner of Relation to each other . . . shall be equally touch'd with any Part of a Discourse."[4] "Indeed [says Boileau] there's nothing but the Approbation of Posterity than can Establish the true Merit of Writings." An author may be praised in his lifetime and condemned in the next generation (e.g., Ronsard). But if writers have been admired many ages, one is foolish and tasteless to doubt their value. More than any other early critic, Boileau clearly anticipates Johnson in recognizing that length of duration alone is inadequate; a real *consensus gentium* must be formed: "The Antiquity of a Writer is a certain Sign of

3. Jean Baptiste Dubos, *Réflexions critiques sur la poésie et sur la peinture,* 2 vols. (Paris, 1719), 2: 303–13. This work was most influential both on the Continent and in England; a translation was provided by Thomas Nugent in 1748.

4. Nicolas Boileau-Despréaux, *The Works,* 2 vols. (London, 1712), 2: 21.

his Merit; but the Antique and Constant Admiration, which his Works have always been in, is a sure and infallible Proof that they ought to be admir'd." But unlike Johnson he sees no very compelling necessity for a reasoned reappraisal of ancient works; the uniform taste of successive generations is enough. This opinion of Longinus's is sanctioned as well by Dacier and in England, as late as 1752, by Johnson's acquaintance, the notorious and unfortunate Dr. Dodd.[5] The thought prevails in French criticism for more than a century after Boileau.[6]

Sentimental theories of taste find fewer partisans in England. Oliver Goldsmith, possibly influenced by Adam Smith's theories of sympathy and sentiment, promotes such views in his rather immature *Enquiry into the Present State of Polite Learning* (1759), where criticism is almost invariably denounced as inimical to taste and genius: "Of all misfortunes . . . in the commonwealth of letters, this of judging from rule, and not from feeling, is the most severe. At such a tribunal, no work of original merit can please."[7] His understanding of taste is quite relativistic, however; each nation has its own genius, and any rules we may devise must refer to the specific taste of a country. Thus Goldsmith's whole theory tends to give priority to individual feeling over universal laws.[8] William Melmoth's popular *Letters of Fitzosborne* (1742–47), although somewhat self-contradictory, reflects the sentimental view. Our sense of beauty is just *naturally* delighted with certain forms, and one of the criteria of fine taste is derived from those works which have been long admired: "For whatever, thro' a long series of ages, has

5. Ibid., 2: 113–16, 145; William Dodd, *The Beauties of Shakespeare* (London, 1821), p. vii.

6. See L. Sébastien Mercier, *Du théâtre: ou, nouvel essay sur l'art dramatique* (Amsterdam, 1773), p. 211, and also his *De la littérature et des littérateurs* (Yverdon, 1778), p. 99. And see also Denis Diderot, *Oeuvres de théâtre . . . avec un discours sur la poésie dramatique*, 2 vols. (Amsterdam, 1772), 2: 424.

7. Oliver Goldsmith, *An Enquiry into the Present State of Polite Learning* (London, 1774), p. 112. On p. 117 he slightly modifies his position: "The public in general set the whole piece in the proper point of view; the critic lays his eye close to all its minuteness, and condemns or approves in detail." Smith's influence is proposed by Ricardo Quintana, *Oliver Goldsmith* (New York: Macmillan, 1967), pp. 32–33; for Quintana's entire and extremely sympathetic analysis of the *Enquiry*, see pp. 28–41.

8. This theory is developed in chap. 7 of the 1759 edition, which, curiously, was largely dropped from the 1774 edition.

been universally esteemed as beautiful, cannot but be conformable
to our just and natural ideas of beauty." [9] He explicitly approves
Longinus's principle of consensus. Even the more skeptical Richard
Hurd will occasionally assume this position and regard sentiment
as the ultimate standard against which no appeal can be made.[10]
The tendency of all these critics is to justify the importance placed
on consensus—the continued admiration of ancient works—by
appealing to taste, a natural sense of beauty which is essentially the
same in all ages, shared by most educated people, and generally
opposed to the lifeless and analytical systems of criticism. One
would search long in these works to find any penetrating analysis
of taste and its operations; it is simply offered as a satisfactory if
ambiguous explanation of the survival of ancient works. Such an
explanation may be reduced not unfairly to the proposition that
we ought to like the things that last, for these things have lasted
because our ancestors liked them. Thus, we have little more for our
pains than Pope's *vox populi, vox Dei.*

By the middle of the century not a few voices had been raised
in protest against such a circular philosophy of aesthetics. A correspondent to the *Gentleman's Magazine* who has read Goldsmith's
Enquiry agrees that works of genius "should be judged by *feeling,*
and not by *rule,*" but questions whether the two are really irrecon-
cilable: "nor yet does it seem probable [he continues] that a genius
able to exact the approbation of our feeling will lose this power

9. William Melmoth, *Letters . . . by . . . Sir Thomas Fitzosborne*, 7th ed.
(London, 1768), p. 186. But Melmoth does suggest (pp. 20–22) that the ancients
are perhaps too thoughtlessly esteemed. Neither Goldsmith nor Melmoth is a
naïve advocate of the sentimentalist position; yet the emphasis is in this
direction.

10. Richard Hurd, ed., *Q. Horatii Flacci epistolae ad Pisones et Augustum,*
4th ed., 3 vols. (London, 1766), 2: 108: "The *pathos* in tragic, humour in
comic . . . and of every other *species* of excellence in universal poetry, is the
object not of *reason,* but sentiment; and can be estimated only from its *impression* on the mind, not by any speculative or general *rules.*" This is one of the
richest and most interesting of mid-century critical works. Although I am
using the 1766 edition, much of the material cited in this study had appeared
in the earlier, less complete editions published from 1749 to 1757. John
Gregory's *Comparative View of the State and Faculties of Man* (London, 1765),
pp. 125–27, attacks criticism as inimical to the free exercise of taste; and a
review of Moor's *End of Tragedy* is decidedly "anticritical" (*Critical Review*
18 [December 1764]: 480). J. G. Cooper's *Letters concerning Taste* (London,
1755) defines the word on sentimentalist principles.

by a conformity to rule." The writer then produces what is a fairly representative mid-century account of the relationship of taste to criticism:

> Criticism may shew what rules have been violated, when true taste, without knowing the rule . . . has been disgusted. It may also shew what rules have been fulfilled, when true taste has been gratified. Thus a standard may be established to a certain degree, and those who write under the direction of true taste may, by a knowledge of the rules, know how far it has carried them right by a shorter way, and where, it having failed them, they have wandered out of the path.[11]

Furthermore, many began to suspect that the test of time may not be infallible; and this debate often centered around Shakespeare himself. One of Voltaire's more frequent criticisms of the dramatist is that his very faults, repeatedly encountered and endured, become accepted: "Time, which alone is capable of establishing the reputation of authors, serves at length to consecrate their very defects." [12] And even his archfoe Mrs. Montagu, in an uncharacteristic lapse from patriotism, prefers the more critical France to England, where Shakespeare's "very faults pass . . . unquestioned." She is concerned that Shakespeare

> is now in danger of incurring the fate of the heroes of the fabulous ages, on whom the vanity of their country, and the superstition of the times, bestowed an apotheosis founded on pretensions to achievement beyond human capacity, by which they lost in a more sceptical and critical age, the glory that was due to them for what they had really done; and all the veneration they had obtained, was ascribed to ignorant credulity, and national prepossession.

Although she is confident that as the taste of the nation becomes refined, Shakespeare's reputation will grow, she nevertheless emphasizes that "unprejudiced and candid judgment will be the surest basis of his fame."[13] Johnson himself declares the necessity of

11. *Gentleman's Magazine* 29 (April 1759): 170–71.

12. Voltaire, *Works*, 38 vols. (London, 1778–81), 13: 134 (hereafter this English translation will be cited as *Works*).

13. Elizabeth Montagu, *An Essay on the Writings and Genius of Shakespeare* (London, 1769), pp. 1–10. Some fifteen years before, Dr. John Armstrong (*Miscellanies*, 2 vols. [London, 1770], 1: 134–36) attacks the certainty of taste and

critical judgment: "The faults of a writer of acknowledged excellence are more dangerous, because the influence of his example is more extensive; and the interest of learning requires that they should be discovered and stigmatized, before they have the sanction of antiquity conferred upon them, and become precedents of indisputable authority." [14] By mid-century, then, both the absolute supremacy of taste and the certitude accorded to consensus had been questioned; it was a logical next step to disenfranchise the general public. Taste, if it exists at all, is the property of the few, who may or may not be fit for purifying the national taste. In 1758 Dr. John Armstrong, always vigorously antisentimentalist, contends that in aesthetic matters the public are commonly led by a few who for some reason or other are respected as judges.[15] Fielding observes that few agree as to the nature of taste, and "as for the Bulk of Mankind, they are clearly void of any Degree of [it]."[16] The test of time was also challenged. In France the great "modern" and enemy of Voltaire, Houdart de La Motte, complains of the peoples' excessive fear of criticizing the great masters: if the masters fail to please us, they have no right to be great; this attack on consensus was sustained throughout the century.[17] Eng-

---

the test of time. He urges that one not be the "dupe of Names." Shakespeare, to be sure, is the "great stupendous genius" of drama, yet this "Boast of our island, pride of human-kind,/ Had faults to which the boxes are not blind." Nor is he willing to agree "That every work which lasts, in prose or song,/ Two thousand years, deserves to last so long/ . . . Tasteless, implicit, indolent and tame,/ At second-hand we chiefly praise or blame."

14. *Rambler* no. 93 (*Works*, 4: 134). Cf. no. 86 (4: 88) where he remarks, justifying his criticism of *Paradise Lost:* "There are in every age, new errors to be rectify'd, and new prejudices to be opposed. False taste is always busy to mislead those that are entering upon the regions of learning. . . ." See also no. 156 (5: 66): "The accidental prescriptions of authority, when time has procured them veneration, are often confounded with the laws of nature, and those rules are supposed coeval with reason, of which the first rise cannot be discovered."

15. Armstrong, *Miscellanies,* 2: 138. But Armstrong does believe in an innate good taste which even the uneducated may possess.

16. *The Covent-Garden Journal,* ed. G. E. Jensen, 2 vols. (New Haven: Yale University Press, 1915), 1: 196 (no. 10, 4 February 1752).

17. Houdart de La Motte, *Oeuvres de théâtre . . . avec plusiers discours sur la tragédie,* 2 vols. (Paris, 1730), 1: 13. See Alexandre de Méhégan, *Considérations sur les révolutions des arts . . .* (Paris, 1755), p. xix: the republic of letters is a democracy, and no author is so great as to be above re-examination. This is

land in the 1750s was no less inclined to challenge the autocracy
of the ancients and to affirm the necessity for judicial criticism:
"Nothing is more absurd or useless [exclaims Thomas Warton in
1754] than the panegyrical comments of those, who criticise from
the imagination rather than from the judgment, who exert their
admiration instead of their reason, and discover more of enthusiasm than discernment." As is apparent, Warton's emphasis is
quite different from Goldsmith's, and he is but one of several dis-
sentient voices denying that such confidence should be reposed
in a faculty so impressionistic and whimsical as taste.[18]

These critics were not necessarily "moderns" of the late seven-
teenth-century variety. Although occasionally they will attack the
ancients in behalf of the moderns, their skepticism seems to stem
rather from a general dissatisfaction with the ambiguities and
inutility of the school of taste. The solution which a number of
critics found was to define the aesthetic or psychological principles
which lay behind the word; in mid-century criticism Alexander
Gerard, Lord Kames, and other Scottish critics stand foremost
among the rationalizers of taste, though some groundwork had been
laid in France earlier. Charles Rollin's *Taste, an Essay*, translated
in 1732 by James Usher, is instructive by virtue of its deficiencies.
At first, much in Rollin's dissertation seems to anticipate the Scottish school. Taste is more the product of judgment than of genius,
"and is a kind of natural reason brought to perfection by study";
much is said about certain "unalterable principles" upon which
taste is founded and which are the same in all ages. One is soon
lost in generalities, however, and the book remains an example of
much verbiage and little enlightenment. Rollin was a distinguished

---

echoed by Mercier, *De la littérature*, p. 89. Even the archclassicist Voltaire warns,
a year after his arrival in England, that our "just Respect" for the ancients may
degenerate into "meer Superstition" (*Essay upon the Civil Wars of France* . . .
[London, 1727], p. 46).

18. Thomas Warton, *Observations on the "Fairy Queen,"* 2d ed., 2 vols.
(London, 1762), 2: 263. See also William Warburton in his "Preface to Shakespeare" (1747) who, echoing Pope, *Essay on Criticism*, line 101, calls on the
critics to teach the people not just to admire, but "how *with reason to
admire* . . ." (*Eighteenth-Century Essays on Shakespeare*, ed. D. Nichol Smith
[Oxford: Oxford University Press, 1963], pp. 96–97). Gerard in 1759 censures
that uncritical veneration for antiquity which "often stamps a value on its
productions, disproportioned to their intrinsic merit" (Alexander Gerard, *An
Essay on Taste*, ed. W. J. Hipple [Gainesville: Scholars' Facsimiles & Reprints,
1963], p. 130).

educator, but in this work, at least, there is prolonged discussion, but little identification, of principles. It is a gentlemanly essay, with no obstinate questioning, and as such, it could not long content. Abbé Batteux's influential *Les beaux arts réduits à un même principe* (1747) is hardly more satisfactory. "Imitons," he urges, "les vrais Physiciens, qui amassent des expériences, & fondent ensuite sur elles un systême qui les réduit en principe." But as M. H. Abrams has observed, Batteux only calls principles what the earlier critics had called the rules.[19] From these works we may conclude that in France intent outran achievement for a number of years. Aestheticians resented the ambiguity of taste, but could escape only into the rules, which themselves were increasingly suspected. It is in a work by the famous *philosophe* and mathematician d'Alembert, oddly ignored by historical critics nowadays, that we find really interesting anticipations of Gerard and the Scottish school: *Reflections on the Use and Abuse of Philosophy in Matters That Are Properly Relative to Taste,* read before the French Academy in 1757 and translated by Gerard seven years later. Basically, d'Alembert urges that the "philosophical spirit," already allowed in matters of science, be admitted into those of taste: "It will justify our esteem of the antients by rendering that esteem rational, and reducing it within its proper bounds; it will prevent our admiring them in their defects; it will show us their equals in several of our modern writers." He aligns himself with those who would reason about taste and not reduce it "to mere feeling and perception." It is not an arbitrary thing, but "must be founded on fixed and evident principles, by the application of which, we may form a decisive judgment of all the various productions of art." He is confident that analytical discussion will not unweave rainbows; rather, artistic beauties "gain in proportion as they are attentively examined."[20]

19. Charles Rollin, *Taste, an Essay* (London, 1732), pp. 2 ff.; Charles Batteux, *Les beaux arts réduits à un même principe* (Paris, 1747), pp. i–ii; Abrams, *Mirror and the Lamp,* pp. 12–13. The Abbé Le Blanc, *Letters on the English and French Nations,* 2 vols. (Dublin, 1747), 1: 177–78, is similarly obscure; although he seeks and fails to find an absolute beauty underlying apparent varieties of taste, he refuses to consider taste merely arbitrary. If it were so, he candidly inquires, "why should France be the leader of Europe in every thing relating to it?"

20. Jean le Rond d'Alembert, *Miscellaneous Pieces* . . . (London, 1764), pp. 178–80, 193. He admits we cannot hope to arrive at first principles, but we must exercise our judgment as well as our sensibility.

Alexander Gerard's *Essay on Taste* was published in 1759 and awarded the prize as the "best essay on Taste" by the Select Society of Edinburgh; he shows plainly the influence of d'Alembert and other French critics whose work he had translated. Although the premises of this dissertation are obvious enough in the original edition, they become quite explicit in part 4, section 4, which Gerard added some twenty-two years later, where the test of time is forthrightly rejected as failing to provide a standard of taste: more penetrating principles are required than this one. Gerard opens his discussion by summarizing the earlier views that the "judgment of sentiment gradually gets the better of the judgment of criticism," but he finds this generality unsatisfying and suggests that "a more precise standard may be derived from philosophy." For, he observes, it does not seem that any work has truly received universal approbation; one can appeal, in fact, only to the European nations for evidence, and such a limited consensus Gerard declares insufficient. Excellence must be determined by "criticism or philosophy." Moreover, some works of real merit, because of their originality, will not be esteemed by the people as they ought; such works require "the instructions of the true critic, unfolding their uncommon beauties, and forming the general taste to the perception of them." At length Gerard plainly sets forth what many had been saying partly or vaguely:

> Though general or universal approbation be assigned as the test of excellence, it really amounts to no more than the approbation of a very few. Multitudes are excluded from the right of suffrage, as being in one respect or another unfit to judge; the select few take the lead; what pleases their vigorous and improved taste, ought to please all; whoever dissents, ought to impute it solely to his own want of taste.

It is through the influence of the few that "the admiration of Shakespear has been heightened, extended, and justified." Gerard proceeds in the next section to argue that the standard of taste must be more accurate than that produced by "mere sentiment." We are justified in looking into the psychological causes of our feelings, he says, so long as his assumption is correct that "principles of science form the most accurate standard of excellence in the fine arts." These principles "admit as indubitable certainty, and as great precision, as those of any science." Between Gerard and Goldsmith, who are separated not at all in time, a considerable aesthetic chasm opens. From the same premise—that taste is a relative concept and any real consensus difficult to find—Goldsmith exalts the individual sensibility as all the more an ultimate standard, while Gerard seeks certitude in the schematizations of science. Like the French critics, he is not denying, but redefining taste. To begin with, he has dissolved its alliance with the test of time. Taste is not used as an hypothesis to justify the consensus of the ages (as such critics as Goldsmith and Melmoth tended to use it); quite the contrary, taste is an entity of itself which takes precedence over the test of time: the latter serves only to document the proper operation of the former. This is a radical departure, not only from Goldsmith's procedure, but also from Johnson's, as we shall see. Gerard senses no conflict between taste and criticism, "the opposition which is studiously, but without reason, stated between the critic and the man of taste." Nor does he find sentiment and reflection at odds; they are joined in a true critic—"he who not only feels strongly, but is also capable of reflecting on his feelings, of accounting for them, of distinguishing their objects, and tracing out their causes." What Gerard wants is a *taste methodized*, a system which does not need to abide the test of time, but can determine immediately and accurately the value of modern as well as ancient works. Thus he commends Blair's *Critical Dissertation* on Ossian as the work of a critic who establishes sound principles and proceeds to apply them to a newly discovered poem, and who is therefore able to demonstrate the excellence of that epic without waiting for a consensus to be established.[21]

The subtitle to Hogarth's *Analysis of Beauty* (1753) proclaims its intention "of fixing the fluctuating Ideas of Taste." The 1750s and 1760s saw several such attempts besides those of Hogarth and Gerard.[22] Burke's "Essay on Taste," prefixed to the second edition

21. Gerard, *Essay on Taste*, pp. 240–44, 273–74; for his entire discussion of consensus, see pp. 225–45. See also Hipple's introduction (pp. v–xxiv), and Marjorie Grene's ingenious article, "Gerard's *Essay on Taste*," *Modern Philology* 41 (1943): 45–58. Hume saw Gerard's essay through the press.

22. William Hogarth, *Analysis of Beauty* (London, 1753); he maintains (p. 3) that a perfect knowledge of the elegant and beautiful is to be acquired by considering them "in a systematical, but . . . familiar way." John Upton, *Critical Observations on Shakespeare*, 2d ed. (London, 1748), p. v, admits that to try to reduce the irregular art of criticism to any precision may be an impractical scheme, but still, one ought to inquire "whether or no, there really is in nature any foundation" for a standard of taste. Gregory, *Comparative View*,

of his *Philosophical Enquiry into the Origin of Our Ideas of the Sublime and Beautiful* (1759) is singularly disappointing, even considering it as the work of a young man; as his editor J. T. Boulton rightly remarks, his is not a very significant contribution to the debate. Although Burke is less rationalistic than Gerard or d'Alembert, he believes that taste can be improved "exactly as we improve our judgment, by extending our knowledge, by a steady attention to our object, and by frequent exercise." And he concludes optimistically: "The logic of Taste, if I may be allowed the expression, might very possibly be as well digested, and we might come to discuss matters of this nature with as much certainty, as those which seem more immediately within the province of mere reason." [23] The method of Lord Kames's *Elements of Criticism* (1762), a work regarded by Johnson as "pretty," though largely chimerical,[24] rests entirely upon his assumption that criticism is "a regular science, governed by just principles"; critics so governed are contrasted with "the man who resigns himself entirely to sentiment or feeling." By studying human nature, the critic can construct a "foundation for judging of taste, and for reasoning upon it . . . . Thus the fine arts, like morals, become a rational science; and, like morals, may be cultivated to a high degree of refinement." Kames's chapter on the standard of taste is, however, disappointingly general. We take our standard from the consensus of the most sensitive readers: the differences concerning taste are usually over trifles, or if not, then there must simply be a "depraved Taste" in one of the arguers. Kames, like other methodizers of taste, accounts for diversity of opinion,

---

p. 75, maintains that it is "the business of Philosophy to analyse and ascertain the Principles of every Art where Taste is concerned."

23. Edmund Burke, *A Philosophical Enquiry into the Origin of Our Ideas of the Sublime and Beautiful*, ed. J. T. Boulton (London: Routledge and Paul, 1958), pp. 11–12, 26. For a more detailed account of Burke's aesthetics see Boulton's introduction and Neal Wood, "Burke on Power," *Burke Newsletter* 5, nos. 3 and 4 (1964): 311–26. For the relationship between his aesthetic, moral, and political thought: Neal Wood, "The Aesthetic Dimension of Burke's Political Thought," *Journal of British Studies* 4 (1964): 41–65; Peter J. Stanlis, *Burke and the Natural Law* (Ann Arbor: University of Michigan Press, 1965), pp. 170–73.

24. James Boswell, *Life of Johnson*, ed. G. B. Hill, rev. L. F. Powell, 6 vols. (Oxford: Oxford University Press, 1934–50), 1: 393–94 (hereafter cited as *Life*). But cf. *Life*, 2: 89–90: "The Scotchman has taken the right method in his 'Elements of Criticism' [Johnson says]. I do not mean he has taught us any thing; but he has told us old things in a new way."

first by minimizing the importance of the diversity, and then by invoking the unanswerable specter of a depraved taste.[25] I have not been concerned with the *methods* of these critics, but with their assumptions; in this chapter I deal entirely with presuppositions rather than procedures. It would be wrong to divide mid-century criticism too rigorously into those critics who sought to explain taste by sentiment and those who looked to science or psychology; but as a provisional and tentative distinction, it is not inutile.

Before attempting to form a generalization about the problem of taste in the middle eighteenth century, the contribution of one more author must be examined, whose work is certainly the most elegant, and possibly the most interesting, of all the pieces on this subject. Hume's essay "Of the Standard of Taste," published in 1757, can claim neither the subtlety of Gerard nor the *furor systematicus* of Kames; it remains, however, the most intelligent concise treatment, the finest attempt (as Hume says) "to mingle some light of understanding with the feelings of sentiment." And it is also, as Jean H. Hagstrum has noted, "eminently Johnsonian."

Hume first acknowledges how dissimilar tastes seem to be; yet it is natural for us to seek a standard by which to reconcile the various sentiments of men. He provides a résumé of that "species of philosophy" which would remove sentiment completely from the domain of judgment, and agrees that it seems taste is entirely relative. In point of fact, however, our own experience contradicts any theory of relativism. We immediately reject the taste of one who would equate Ogilby with Milton or Bunyan with Addison.[26] Hume proceeds to classify works of art with the "practical sciences," since the rules and laws of both are drawn from experience; and these he contrasts with "geometrical truth and exactness." The latter are neither to prevail in poetry nor to determine the laws of criticism, for although poetry ought to be bound by rules discovered "by genius or observation," it can "never submit to exact truth." Because this is so, and because all men do not respond in the same way to a work of art (their dispositions being variable), one can identify true taste "not so much from the operation of each par-

25. Henry Home [Lord Kames], *Elements of Criticism*, 3 vols. (Edinburgh, 1762), 1: 8, 241; 3: 351–74.

26. Cf. Burke, *Philosophical Enquiry*, p. 21, who cites a preference for Bunyan as evidence of an undeveloped taste.

ticular beauty, as from the durable admiration, which attends those works, that have survived all the caprices of mode and fashion, all the mistakes of ignorance and envy." Hume then moves to a traditional exposition of the test of time. Bad works may be accorded a temporary vogue, but will not survive, while "a real genius, the longer his works endure, and the more wide they are spread, the more sincere is the admiration which he meets with." This suggests that there are indeed "certain general principles of approbation or blame," although taste, like any other sensory organ, may well be defective in various individuals. Beauty or deformity are not qualities *in* objects, Hume maintains, but describe instead the operations of taste; yet these operations ought to be methodized, formulated as general principles, so as to enable us to refine imperfect taste and to persuade a faulty critic that he is mistaken. Returning full circle, Hume then argues that the best way of so fixing or ascertaining delicacy of taste "is to appeal to those models and principles, which have been established by the uniform approbation and experience of nations and ages." Taste, Hume continues, is strengthened through exercise. One refines it through distinguishing beauties and faults in various works and then deliberating on them. Such a procedure inevitably involves making comparisons, before which no judgment can be rendered.

> A man who has had no opportunity of comparing the different kinds of beauty, is indeed totally unqualified to pronounce an opinion with regard to any object presented to him. By comparison alone we fix the epithets of praise or blame . . . . A man, who has had opportunities of seeing, and examining and weighing the several performances, admired in different ages and nations, can alone rate the merits of a work exhibited to his view, and assign its proper rank among the productions of genius.

The true critic must have delicacy of sentiment, experience in comparing, and freedom from prejudice. Such a man, if he exists, can be of the greatest value to the majority, whose taste is defective and who are therefore unqualified to make aesthetic discriminations.[27]

Thus Hume defends both the test of time and taste while also conceding that certainty of the geometrical sort is not to be expected,

27. David Hume, *Essays and Treatises on Several Subjects*, 2 vols. (London, 1768), 1: 260–69.

that few men have a genuinely delicate taste, and that taste itself may be improved through experience in comparing and judging. He has steered between the more extreme sentimentalists and rationalists; he is prepared to reason about the "feelings of sentiment," but not to claim for such reasoning the certitude of a "science." And yet if Hume succeeds in avoiding extreme positions, he succeeds largely through ambiguity and paradox: taste can be philosophized about, but ultimately we must rely on consensus; it can be methodized to a degree and improved in individuals, but true taste is to be identified not from "each particular beauty" but from those works which survive many changes in fashion. For all of his subtlety and charm, Hume teaches us little: some works are long admired, and this suggests that principles of taste exist; these principles we may try to discover, although what they are it is difficult to say. It would be highly unjust to dismiss Hume's essay as Johnson dismissed the *Essay on Man* ("never before were penury of thought and vulgarity of sentiment so happily disguised"); but it must be suspected that some later critics have thought they were praising Hume's ingenuity when in fact they were admiring his manner.

It should be sufficiently apparent by now that the question of taste, when Johnson approached the subject in 1765, had been much argued and not at all decided. Generally, there is a movement away from simple appeals to taste (Dubos, Goldsmith) to more systematic attempts to explain it or to uncover aesthetic principles which underlie it (d'Alembert, Gerard, Kames). And yet, just as sentimentalist and positivist ethical theories are joined in such philosophers as Diderot and Rousseau, so in aesthetics it is not uncommon to find the notion that taste is a mysterious and instinctive response connected with the somewhat inconsistent theory that taste may be methodized and the art of criticism reduced to a genuine science. Thus Goldsmith, having been at great pains to demonstrate the relativity and spontaneity of taste, makes no inconsiderable claims for it at the end of his *Enquiry*: we have nothing permanent by which to compare our ancestors with us but taste, and "in taste, we have standing evidence, we can, with precision, compare the literary performances of our fathers with our own, and from their excellence, or defects, determine the moral, as well as the literary merits of either." And Melmoth, who is as reticent about the principles of taste as he can be, suggests: "Perhaps the principles of criticism are as certain and indisputable, even as those of mathematics." That we prefer harmony to dissonance is as certain a truth as the mathematical proposition that the whole is greater than any of its parts. "And in both cases, the propositions which rest upon these plain and obvious maxims seem equally capable of the same demonstration." [28] Even the young Burke, as Boulton points out, is at once a follower of Dubos in laying stress on the sensibility and the subjective aspects of taste, and a "Newtonian" in his experimental method and his search for "scientific principles" of beauty.

Thus at the end of the 1750s we encounter a cluster of notable and intelligent attempts to solve the problem of taste. Hume's tentative essay appears in 1757, Goldsmith's, Gerard's and Burke's all in 1759, and Lord Kames's in 1762.[29] And yet, as the two literary reviews of the day indicate, these essays settled no controversy. The *Critical Review* in 1759 is skeptical of Gerard's—or anyone's—success in establishing a standard of taste.

> After all, though we acknowledge the erudition and genius of Mr. Gerard, we think his Essay has reflected no great light upon his subject. . . . Men's feelings will ever be as various as their faces. We cannot therefore blame the ingenious author, for not having drawn general conclusions from principles so vague and uncertain, nor for having erected a limited theory, where it will be impossible to rear one universal and without exception, till all men's ideas are reduced to one certain standard.[30]

On the other hand, William Rose's opinion of Gerard in the *Monthly Review* is generally favorable: "Mr. Gerard has treated his subject, not in a loose and superficial manner, but has entered into it with the spirit and abilities of a philosopher. . . . those of

28. Goldsmith, *Enquiry into Polite Learning*, pp. 155–56; Melmoth, *Letters of Fitzosborne*, pp. 184–85. Cf. Jean Terrasson: "No man who does not think in questions of literature as Descartes told us to think in questions of Physics is worthy of the present age" (quoted in Jacques Maritain, *Three Reformers* [New York: Thomas Y. Crowell, 1970], pp. 87–88).

29. Gerard's may well have been written in 1757; and Burke's may have been a reply to the faintly incredulous essay of Hume's. Reynolds's *Idler* papers, also in 1759, discuss the question rather skeptically, and may be a response to Gerard and Burke.

30. *Critical Review* 7 (May 1759): 446–47; this review has been attributed to Goldsmith.

a philosophical turn will, we doubt not, read it with pleasure, and readily allow that the author has given a distinct and accurate analysis of the principles of taste." [31] The debate at mid-century is conveniently dramatized by another disagreement between the *Monthly* and the *Critical*, this time over the *Elements of Criticism*. Owen Ruffhead in the *Monthly* is extremely incredulous, dismissing Kames's discussion of the standard of taste as "vague and unsettled": "Criticism, taken in its enlarged signification, is improperly termed an art; for the principles of Criticism, which constitute a part of our sensitive nature, are not to be acquired by rule." Continuing the argument in a later issue, he states:

> To tell us that the Standard of Taste is to be found among judges of a good natural taste . . . is, with deference to his Lordship, saying no more than that, "Taste is to be found among people of taste." It is explaining the difficulty by the term to be defined: for we are still at a loss to determine what are the essential properties which constitute what is called Taste: and till they are known, it is vain to reason about a common standard, which, in truth, is much easier conceived than expressed.[32]

But the *Critical* has nothing but bouquets; they believe that his remarks on the standard of taste are "more decisive than all that has ever been contained in the numberless volumes written upon the subject." A month earlier they asserted:

> Lord Kaymis hath clearly demonstrated, to our apprehension, from a beautiful investigation of the passions, what objects will necessarily excite certain feelings and emotions; whence he deduces an infallible rule for judging of works of art, by referring to the effects they produce. . . . Hence he has united philosophy with taste, exhibited a just standard of fine composition, and shown what is beautiful, fit, and

31. *Monthly Review* 20 (June 1759): 545.

32. Ibid. 26 (June 1762): 413–14; 27 (August 1762), 115–16. Ruffhead continues: "When we come to establish an universal standard of Taste, we are involved in endless contradictions and perplexities: and nothing can be a stronger proof of the intricacy of this inquiry, than that even Lord Kaims has not been able to ascertain the standard in question, in a clear and satisfactory manner." His conclusion is not equivocal: "Perhaps the Standard of Taste . . . is founded more on authority, custom, or fashion, than on principles of nature. . . . what is called the Taste of a nation . . . is perhaps nothing more than the caprice of one man, who . . . has acquired such reputation and influnce, as to make a peculiarity of his own become by degrees a reigning principle."

becoming in the arts, with the same precision as if he had been treating of ethics.

These reviewers are confident, furthermore, that his work may "supersede the critical labours of the stagyrite," and that Kames is in criticism "what Bacon, Locke, and Newton, are in philosophy—the parent of regulated taste, the creator of metaphysical criticism, the first interpretor of our feelings, and of the voice of nature, and the lawgiver of capricious genius, upon principles too evident to be controverted." [33] Their confidence had been anticipated, however, by Johnson's friend and colleague in Grubstreet William Guthrie, who proclaimed, possibly as early as 1747, and at any rate before Lord Kames's work: "Thus dramatic poetry stands upon the same footing with our noble system of Newtonian philosophy. . . . It is not derived from any hypothesis which experiments are tortured to serve, but the result of repeated effects from certain causes." [34]

With the controversy thus undetermined in the fifties and sixties, Johnson's own contribution has especial interest. W. R. Keast, in his remarkable essay on Johnson's criticism, quotes Trilling's opinion that Johnson drew his critical principles from sensibility rather than judgment, and then comments: "To distinguish so sharply between sensibility and principles as the guaranty of critical judgment is a modern habit, and it is common in our time, when this distinction is made, to prefer sensibility to principles." When one considers the protestations of the sentimentalists against formal criticism, one must hesitate to reserve for modernity such a "habit" as Keast describes; however, he is quite correct in objecting to this view of Johnson and in arguing that although he may have distrusted systematic theorizing, he did not play "entirely or even primarily by ear." [35] In the introduction to his edition of Gerard,

33. *Critical Review* 13 (May 1762): 377; 13 (April 1762): 285, 302–3. Joshua Reynolds, *Discourse VII* (1776), celebrates confidently the "introduction of philosophy into the regions of taste" (*Discourses on Art*, ed. S. O. Mitchell [New York: Bobbs-Merrill, 1965], pp. 117–18). However, resistance to such a notion may be found, by implication, in Daniel Webb, *Observations on the Correspondence between Poetry and Music* (London, 1769), p. 38; and in Adam Smith, *The Theory of Moral Sentiments* (London, 1774), pp. 294 ff.

34. William Guthrie, *An Essay upon English Tragedy* (London, [1747?]), p. 6.

35. W. R. Keast, "The Theoretical Foundations of Johnson's Criticism," in *Critics and Criticism*, ed. R. S. Crane (Chicago: University of Chicago Press, 1952), pp. 389, 391.

W. J. Hipple dismisses Johnson's analysis as a rather superficial reflection of the tendency of neoclassical criticism to move from the acceptance of consensus as a standard of taste to the search for aesthetic and psychological principles.[36] But this, too, needs serious qualification. Johnson's discussion is to be distinguished from all of those examined here, not excluding Hume's.

Johnson begins with a defense of the test of time: not all ancients are truly great, to be sure, and we may well admire them for the wrong reasons; still, to time must the final appeal be made. The third paragraph, as it is crucial to Johnson's argument, must be quoted entire:

> To works, however, of which the excellence is not absolute and definite, but gradual and comparative; to works not raised upon principles demonstrative and scientifick, but appealing wholly to observation and experience, no other test can be applied than length of duration and continuance of esteem. What mankind have long possessed they have often examined and compared, and if they persist to value the possession, it is because frequent comparisons have confirmed opinion in its favour. As among the works of nature no man can properly call a river deep or a mountain high, without the knowledge of many mountains and many rivers; so in the productions of genius, nothing can be stiled excellent till it has been compared with other works of the same kind. Demonstration immediately displays its power, and has nothing to hope or fear from the flux of years; but works tentative and experimental must be estimated by their proportion to the general and collective ability of man, as it is discovered in a long succession of endeavours. Of the first building that was raised, it might be with certainty determined that it was round or square, but whether it was spacious or lofty must have been referred to time. The Pythagorean scale of numbers was at once discovered to be perfect; but the poems of Homer we yet know not to transcend the common limits of human

36. "Earlier efforts to ground a standard on the consensus of nations and ages gave place . . . to reasonings drawn from general principles of human nature. The change can be seen in microcosm in Johnson's preface to Shakespeare, where the initial argument from consensus ('no other test can be applied than length of duration and continuance of esteem') gives way to the more philosophic principle, 'Nothing can please many and please long, but just representations of general nature.' Yet Johnson's argument is simple, compared with those of more philosophic critics like Kames and Gerard" (Gerard, *Essay on Taste*, p. xxii). In general terms, this is an adequate summary of the evidence presented in this chapter. I shall consider its specific applicability to Johnson in the pages that follow.

intelligence, but by remarking, that nation after nation, and century after century, has been able to do little more than transpose his incidents, new name his characters, and paraphrase his sentiments.[37]

Here Johnson states, first, the nature of literary excellence (tentative and experimental), and next, the sort of procedure which must therefore be used to estimate it (comparative). It is quite true that neither observation is original; Hume's essay clearly establishes both of them. Moreover, each has antecedents which have never been collected and examined. Johnson's distinction between literature and those works dependant on "principles demonstrative and scientifick" was affirmed by others than Hume. Even so early and unprepossessing a critic as Leonard Welsted, for example, distinguishes in 1724 between *poetical reason,* as he terms it, and *mathematical reason.* But his distinction is really only a quantitative one; poetry is more complicated than scientific propositions are, and thus more taste (an entire *je ne sais quoi* for Welsted) is required properly to relish it.[38] Later and far more penetrating aestheticians make this distinction for essentially the same reason.[39] And three years before the *Preface* the reviewer of Daniel Webb's *Remarks on the Beauties of Poetry* argues: "The imitative arts alone are the province of genius. The objects of other sciences may be explored by demonstrative reasoning, and their heights attained by industrious speculation; but these have no bounds except those of nature." [40] By mid-century the lines of argument were being more clearly drawn, but their clarity did not free the critic from a difficult dilemma. The absolute distinction between taste and criticism, of

37. *Works,* 7: 59–60.

38. Leonard Welsted, *Works in Prose and Verse* (London, 1787), p. 131 especially. There are other early tentatives in this direction: see *Gentleman's Magazine* 9 (December 1739): 640.

39. See: Gerard, *Essay on Taste,* p. 178; William Duff, *An Essay on Original Genius,* ed. J. L. Mahoney (Gainesville: Scholars' Facsimiles & Reprints, 1964), pp. 11–17; Gregory, *Comparative View,* pp. 125–27; Voltaire (quoted in Wellek, *History of Modern Criticism,* 1: 38). These critics, even Gerard for all his love of system, emphasize the necessity for taste to preside in the arts lest they should become as systematized (and therefore rigidified) as scientific subjects.

40. *Monthly Review* 26 (April 1762): 282. Cf. Reynolds, *Discourses on Art,* p. 103: "Many wise and learned men, who have accustomed their minds to admit nothing but what can be proved by mathematical demonstration, have seldom any relish for those arts which address themselves to the fancy, the . . . truth of which is known by another kind of proof."

which Dubos and Goldsmith were so fond, seemed now too elementary. At the same time, attempts to systematize taste, and hence to make it a term acceptable to criticism, seemed possibly too presumptuous. Fearing the confining dogmas of some hypothetical system, and convinced that art is somehow different from science or mathematics, they resisted the more audacious campaigns to rationalize taste; but for the most part they had no other defense than the old one of Goldsmith, that the sanctity of taste must be preserved inviolable from the incursions of reason. Johnson makes the distinction between art and science more confidently and more clearly than anyone of the time except Hume; and yet, unlike the others including Hume, he never employs the word *taste.*

Johnson's second observation—that works must be compared to be judged—is also not new. Gerard makes much of the value of comparing a "present object with others of the kind" in order to form a just estimation of a performance; "many things which might be tolerable, if viewed by themselves, will disgust when set in competition with others." A good taste must be qualified, by practice, for making comparisons.[41] In France, some effort was made to assert a sort of absolute or *real* excellence, and yet to admit that there was another excellence which could be subjected to comparison and analysis—an interesting attempt to preserve the holiness of taste while extending the range of criticism.[42] Finally, Owen Ruffhead's review of Brumoy's *Greek Theatre,* just five years before the *Preface,* affirms the comparative nature of aesthetic judgment and employs an architectural metaphor not unlike Johnson's. If we compare Aeschylus and Corneille the *men,* Ruffhead argues, the genius of the former, considering all the advantages of Corneille, will be found superior; but it is another matter if we consider their *works,* since the ancient is much inferior to the modern: "The merit of the self-taught Artist, who first planned a house for the

41. Gerard, *Essay on Taste,* pp. 107–8.

42. Dubos (*Réflexions critiques,* 2: 398) so distinguishes. Brumoy's discussion of Greek comedy, translated by Johnson for Mrs. Lennox's edition, defines two types of beauty, one stable and permanent, the other mutable (*The Greek Theatre of Father Brumoy,* trans. Charlotte Lennox, 3 vols. [London, 1759], 3: 147). See also Batteux, *Les beaux arts,* pp. 117–22, who categorizes the several types of comparisons involved in judging a work; anticipating Arnold's theory of touchstones, Batteux recommends that we read all the most excellent works in the various genres and make "un heureux mélange des qualités uniques de ces grands Hommes" which we may use as a standard for comparison.

habitation of man, if abstractly considered, is probably superior to that of the vast Architect of St. Paul's; yet no one will venture to compare that superb edifice with the first rude structure of untutored genius."[43] For Ruffhead, as for Johnson, our final estimation of art, whether manifested in poems or buildings, must be the result of comparison; no other procedure is suited to Johnson's empirical definition of literary excellence.

In what ways, then, does Johnson concur or differ with his contemporaries? Far too skeptical to accept the test of time unquestioningly, he was too skeptical as well to accept the supposition upon which the Scottish critics, despite their own occasional protestations to the contrary, seemed to rely: that one might develop a Newtonian system of criticism which would enable one to determine literary excellence immediately. Such a possibility is prevented by his initial definition of artistic excellence as comparative in nature. It is important to recognize that Johnson's distinction between art and science is precisely Hume's; he is not opposing art to *science* in its modern sense, but rather, like Hume, groups art with the "practical sciences" and opposes both to "geometrical truth." An examination of the central paragraph quoted above will demonstrate that this is really Johnson's distinction. *Round* or *square* are qualities which may be decided "upon principles demonstrative and scientifick," while *deep* and *high, spacious* and *lofty*, are "gradual and comparative" qualities which, he would agree with Hume, are not *in* objects, but are mental determinations arrived at through experience and comparison.[44] That this is a fundamental principle of Johnson's criticism its frequent iteration in his works will confirm. In *Rambler* no. 92 he defines beauty as "relative and comparative" and alludes to Pascal, approvingly, on the difference between beauty, which is not subject to reason, and mathematical demonstration: "[Beauty] is, indeed, so little subject to the examinations of reason, that Paschal supposes it to end where demonstration begins, and maintains that without incon-

43. *Monthly Review* 23 (December 1760): 462.

44. Keast fails to observe this distinction and uses *science* just as Johnson does, with no qualification (e.g., his essay cited note 35 above, *Critics and Criticism*, p. 398). Hagstrum, reviewing Keast in *Philological Quarterly* 32, no. 3 (1953): 278, makes the proper distinction: "The most basic antithesis in Johnson's thought lies between the deductive, *a priori* reason used in mathematics and logic, and the inductive, investigative reason, used in both literature and empirical science."

gruity and absurdity we cannot speak of 'geometrical beauty.' " And in the next number he contrasts literary beauty with "the batteries of Euclid or Archimedes." [45] In number 121 he distinguishes between science, which is "fixed and limited," and the "boundless regions of possibility, which fiction claims for her dominion"; and in number 158 he denies that criticism has attained the "certainty and stability of science" with the implication that there is little chance of its doing so.[46] He observes of Addison's criticism that it "is condemned as tentative or experimental rather than scientifick, and he is considered as deciding by taste rather than by principles," but he proceeds to defend Addison as just the sort of critic wanted by the age, a critic lacking "all the pomp and severity of science." [47] Repeatedly Johnson opposes oversystematizing and asserts the necessity of empirical observation.[48] He is the most eloquent of all in the *Preface* itself.

> The first care of the builder of a new system, is to demolish the fabricks which are standing. The chief desire of him that comments an authour, is to shew how much other commentators have corrupted and obscured him. The opinions prevalent in one age, as truths above the reach of controversy, are confuted and rejected in another, and rise again to reception in remoter times. Thus the human mind is kept in motion without progress. Thus sometimes truth and errour, and sometimes contrarieties of errour, take each others place by reciprocal invasion. The tide of seeming knowledge which is poured over one generation, retires and leaves another naked and barren; the sudden

45. *Works*, 4: 121, 131.

46. *Works*, 4: 282; 5: 76.

47. Samuel Johnson, *The Lives of the English Poets*, ed. G. B. Hill, 3 vols. (Oxford: Oxford University Press, 1905), 2: 145–46 (hereafter cited as *Lives*). Hagstrum, *Johnson's Literary Criticism*, p. 27, seems to imply that Johnson is defending Addison from this charge by stressing the importance of principles, however liberal they may be, over uncertain taste; as I see it, he is defending Addison by *minimizing* the relative importance of scientific rules in criticism. Throughout his discussion, Hagstrum associates Johnson more with the "rationalists" in this matter than I do.

48. "Human experience, which is constantly contradicting theory, is the great test of truth. A system, built upon the discoveries of a great many minds, is always of more strength, than what is produced by the mere workings of any one mind, which, of itself, can do little" (*Life*, 1: 454). And for a whimsical version: "Hurd, Sir, is one of a set of men who account for every thing systematically; for instance, it has been a fashion to wear scarlet breeches; these men would tell you, that according to causes and effects, no other wear could at that time have been chosen" (*Life*, 4: 189).

meteors of intelligence which for a while appear to shoot their beams into the regions of obscurity, on a sudden withdraw their lustre, and leave mortals again to grope their way.[49]

Johnson's rejection of aesthetic systems is interesting but predictable; more interesting is his refusal to avail himself of that unaccountable entity taste. For him, empirical observation—the act of comparison, and time in which to do it—is the final and really only means of estimating a literary work. Indeed, comparison is the cornerstone of Johnson's entire epistemology, and receives, fittingly, its most solemn and generalized form in *Rasselas*: "To judge rightly of the present we must oppose it to the past; for all judgment is comparative, and of the future nothing can be known." [50] So important, in fact, was this activity for Johnson, that it is proposed in the *Preface* as the only explanation of just *why* consensus, the test of time, is valid; the whole question of taste is avoided. Works of such tentative nature must be compared against other works and against the "general and collective ability of man, as it is discovered in a long succession of endeavours." Time is the ultimate judge simply because "what has been longest known has been most considered, and what is most considered is best understood." Welsted in his rudimentary way, Gerard, Duff, and several Continental critics distinguished between art and science only to emphasize the operation of taste in the former; and of course even Hume is primarily concerned with the possibility of a standard of taste. But in the *Preface* Johnson offers no discussion of taste, innate sensibility, or of any of the psychological principles which Gerard and Kames formulated to explain them. Rather, he sets the whole matter into a context which eludes both the subjective incertitudes of the school of taste and the excessive hypothesizing of rationalism. To be sure, his discussion rests upon assumptions shared by most of the others: that human nature is the same, that what *has* pleased *will* please, and the like. But in using a different set of emphases, in making consensus pre-eminent, which was so often regarded by fellow critics (e.g., Gerard, Duff, Goldsmith) as merely one of the

49. *Works*, 7: 99.

50. *The Works*, 9 vols. (Oxford, 1825), 1: 264 (hereafter cited as *Oxford Works*). In the *Lives of the Poets* Johnson refers to artistic works as "things admitting of gradation and comparison," and later describes critical determinations as "depending not on rules, but on experience and comparison" (1: 14; 2: 47—these citations are given in Keast's "Theoretical Foundations," in *Critics and Criticism*).

demonstrations of the operation of taste, he has set forth a position singularly different from theirs. The test of time is not justified by invoking a word which itself must then be defined and explained; it is simply that time is necessary for the collective wisdom of mankind to come to a determination about such "tentative" problems as artistic worth. Of all the critics examined here, Hume is closest to Johnson in his distinction between artistic and geometrical truth, in his emphasis on comparison, and in his recognition that it is as foolish to remonstrate against the *vox populi*, on the one hand, as it is dangerous to relinquish all critical principles on the other. But it is impossible to determine whether or not Johnson was influenced by Hume. His empiricism is more unrelenting, and if he does not bring us much closer to a solution, he at least has avoided confusing us by appealing to certain "standards of taste" about which little can be said. Despite his equivocations, Hume is seeking a kind of certitude in matters of taste which Johnson seems to rule out in the *Preface*; Hume's discussion may be eminently, but it is not wholly, Johnsonian.

Hipple's suggestion, therefore, (see note 36) seems inexact that in the *Preface* the "initial argument from consensus" gives way to the enumeration of principles by which Johnson will judge Shakespeare. In these paragraphs there is no epitome of the development of eighteenth-century criticism from Dubos to Lord Kames. The principles which follow, and with which the rest of this study will be occupied, are far from those of a Gerard. They are not such as pretend to assure a certitude independent of time and consensus; Johnson, one supposes, would have been highly amused to observe his "unprincipled" ridicule of the pretensions of Ossian vindicated by time, while Gerard's enthusiasm for Blair's systematic demonstration of Ossian's excellence now diverts us as an aesthetic eccentricity. Johnson does not "move on" to abandon the test of time in favor of the search for principles. He never denies it, as the Scottish school tended to do, and he always exalts it over criticism as the final test.[51] One might summarize Gerard's position thus: the test

51. E.g., *Rambler* no. 3 where, when concerned with difficult problems, criticism is advised to refer the cause to time (*Works*, 3: 17–18). In no. 23 he expresses confidence in the verdict of the public, "which is never corrupted" (3: 128). And he advises Mrs. Thrale: "Never let criticisms operate upon your face or your mind; it is very rarely that an author is hurt by his criticks. The blaze of reputation cannot be blown out, but it often dies in the socket" (*The Letters*, ed. R. W. Chapman, 3 vols. [Oxford: Oxford University Press, 1952], 2: 351).

of time is invalid, *so*, let us seek for certainty in principles. But Johnson's is rather: the test of time is the ultimate appeal, *but*, let us seek for tentative principles, not to erect a system, but to correct the inevitable vagaries of time. In a more complicated way, these paragraphs in the *Preface* mirror the movement in *Rambler* number 92, where Johnson defines beauty as relative and comparative and accepts the test of time, but where he is no less resolute in asserting the task of criticism: "to establish principles; to improve opinion into knowledge; and to distinguish those means of pleasing which depend upon known causes and rational deduction, from the nameless and inexplicable elegancies which appeal wholly to the fancy." Or as he was later to phrase it more memorably: the writer, like the critic, must first endeavor "to distinguish nature from custom, or that which is established because it is right, from that which is right only because it is established." [52]

One cannot, of course, be satisfied with such elementary principles of literary excellence as length of duration and continuance of esteem; Johnson, and most other neoclassical critics, knew that one must go beyond them.[53] But after all they are elementary in the sense that they are fundamental; and they are the only criteria which lie wholly outside the individual; they constitute the collective wisdom to which deference must be made. If one resorts to "taste" to explain either the achieving or the appreciating of artistic merit, one has opened the way to rampant impressionism; taste is its own justification, and, as we have seen, an entity almost exquisitely recalcitrant to analysis or discussion. A thoroughgoing aesthetic of taste is either a denial of the art of criticism, or a reducing it to mere feeling, which is the same.[54] But Johnson was aware that the

---

52. *Works*, 4: 122; 5: 70 (*Rambler* no. 156). Cf. *Rambler* no. 158 (5: 76).

53. Contrary to A. O. Lovejoy's opinion, *The Great Chain of Being* (New York: Harper and Row, 1960), p. 292, that neoclassical critics unthinkingly accepted the test of time as ultimate and were unprepared to reason about it. Lovejoy's section on eighteenth-century "universalism," which he contrasts so unfavorably with Romantic "diversitarianism," must be considerably qualified.

54. See Paul Ramsey's excellent discussion of this subject in *The Lively and the Just* (Tuscaloosa: University of Alabama Press, 1962), pp. 24–27. And concerning the opposite extremity, the presumptuous extension of criticism into a science, see Prosser Hall Frye, *Literary Reviews and Criticisms* (New York and London: G. P. Putnam's Sons, 1908), pp. 257–62. On the whole question of a standard of taste, see Paul Elmer More, "The Demon of the Absolute," *New Shelburne Essays*, vol. 1 (Princeton: Princeton University Press, 1928).

most pretentious systems may be as subjective and transient as the vagaries of taste, and that both the "feeler" and the systematizer impose on us their individual sensibilities, whether they invoke taste or Newton as their motive. Johnson will proceed to "establish principles," but these will be principles suited both to the gradual and comparative nature of his subject—an assessment of William Shakespeare as a classic—and to the subordinate and instrumental nature of the art he is practicing.

Chapter II

The Poet of Nature

Whatever T. S. Eliot's criteria, Johnson's initial qualifications for a classic have been met: Shakespeare has "gained and kept the favour of his countrymen." But it is one thing to demonstrate Shakespeare's popularity, another to identify the reasons for it. Johnson addresses himself next to two primary aesthetic concerns: the nature of Shakespeare's characters, and the nature of the works in which they exist. Johnson describes the characters as species rather than individuals, although he also praises the nicety with which they are distinguished from each other. The plays he calls tragicomedies, and defends them because they are "like life." In discussing both topics, Johnson appeals to *nature*; but in his account of dramatic character he apparently uses the word in its general or ideal sense, while in his analysis of tragicomedy he certainly uses it to mean sublunary or *real* (earthly) nature. My concern here is *nature* as it is employed in the *Preface*. Since Johnson, having now determined a consensus, resorts frequently to this word—one which, however ambiguous, is fundamental to eighteenth-century thought— it is appropriate that a study of his aesthetic principles should begin with its examination. Both sections of this chapter will be occupied with the disintegration of neoclassical dramatic theory and the appearance of new theories which, if not strictly pre-Romantic, anticipate Romanticism in their interest in sympathy and sentiment. In the first section I shall examine the effects of this development on traditional conceptions of dramatic character, particularly the tragic hero, whereas in the second section I shall be more concerned with tragicomedy and its eighteenth-century descendant (or mutant), domestic tragedy. But it will be proper to remember that the two subjects cannot be distinguished precisely; the division is for convenience, and merely tentative.

DRAMATIC CHARACTER: JUST REPRESENTATION
OF GENERAL NATURE

> As poetry has to do rather with the passions
> of men, which are uniform, than their customs,
> which are changeable, the varieties, which time
> or place can furnish, will be inconsiderable.
>
> *Rambler* no. 36

As the eighteenth century wore on, dramatic characters came increasingly to be regarded as corporeal human beings possessed of their own inner life and susceptible to feelings not necessarily disclosed to us by the dramatist directly. This attitude is explicitly promoted, for example, in Maurice Morgann's revolutionary *Essay on the Dramatic Character of Falstaff* (1777) and in William Richardson's series of essays on Shakespeare's dramatic characters in the seventies and eighties; Coleridge and Hazlitt continue the tradition, which culminates in the agile and ingenious criticism of A. C. Bradley. During the Age of Johnson *character* assumed the position which *plot* had hitherto occupied as the "soul of tragedy"; and by character was understood, not a merely dramatic construction, but a psychological being—a personality. Falstaff is no longer a *dramatic* character manipulated by Shakespeare for histrionic, structural, or thematic purposes; he is an actual entity whose interior life is as amenable to psychological conjecture as that of our neighbors. Behind this shift in emphasis lies a growing interest in *particular* nature, the specific images, with all their associations, which were believed to form elementary and personal mental patterns; and accompanying this preoccupation was a diminishing interest in abstract, general, or ideal nature. Blake's exasperated exclamation, "To generalize is to be an idiot," allowing for that element of oversimplification appropriate to such an outburst, is a logical consequence of the new aesthetic theories. Now it is obvious that the way in which a critic conceives of dramatic character must influence conspicuously his notion of how characters ought to appear and behave in plays, in short, what a good dramatic character is to be *like*. To understand Johnson's commendation of Shakespearean characters as "just representations of general nature," it is desirable first to understand the conflict between *ideal* and *particular* conceptions. That Johnson should be found with Blake's idiots will be neither surprising nor necessarily regrettable; but as I shall hope to show, his position is idiosyncratic and in some ways destructive of the tenets upon which neoclassicism rests.

The various theories of the ideal in post-Renaissance criticism have been thoroughly and amply documented;[1] I shall only summarize them briefly and indicate their survival and vitality up through 1765. Though theories of generality have been identified with Platonism, one of their major sources is Aristotle's distinction between poetry and history: history is "real nature," life as it is in its imperfect and confused mundane state, whereas poetry is selected nature, nature so arranged and ordered as to reveal more clearly the divine plan, the moral *substance* of life which lies behind its physical *accidents*; at least, so the neoclassicists understood Aristotle. Sir William Davenant's commentary is instructive: "Wise Poets think it more worthy to seek out truth in the Passions, than to record the truth of Actions . . . it being nobler to contemplate the general History of Nature, than a selected Diary of Fortune."[2] Poetry is the history of human nature, of life as apprehended by the intellect and the moral consciousness; history, however selective it may be, is a mere diary of *fortune*, recording necessarily and without judgment the daily events of life. But to what purpose is poetic judgment directed? Thomas Rymer is clear: the poet "must have judgment to select what is noble or beautiful, and proper for his occasion. He must by a particular Chymistry extract the essence of things, without soiling his Wit with the gross and

1. See especially: M. H. Abrams, *The Mirror and the Lamp* (Oxford: Oxford University Press, 1953), pp. 35–42; C. C. Green, *The Neo-Classic Theory of Tragedy in England during the Eighteenth Century* (Cambridge: Harvard University Press, 1934), pp. 34–35, 150–65; L. I. Bredvold, "The Tendency toward Platonism in Neo-Classical Esthetics," *ELH* 1 (1934): 91–119; Arthur Sherbo, *Samuel Johnson, Editor of Shakespeare, With an Essay on The Adventurer, Illinois Studies in Language and Literature*, vol. 42 (Urbana: University of Illinois Press, 1956), pp. 53–56; Ernest Tuveson, *The Imagination as a Means of Grace* (Berkeley: University of California Press, 1960), pp. 114–18; Scott Elledge, "Background and Development in English Criticism of the Theories of Generality and Particularity," *PMLA* 62 (1947): 147–82. On the kind of nature in Johnson, see Jean H. Hagstrum, *Samuel Johnson's Literary Criticism* (Chicago: University of Chicago Press, 1967), chap. 4 passim, also pp. 83–89, and his long note, p. 190; my own analysis should be compared with his, especially his conclusion that Johnson's "nature was *la vrai nature*, never *la belle nature*."

2. Preface to *Gondibert* (quoted in John Dryden, *Essays*, ed. W. P. Ker, 2 vols. [Oxford: Oxford University Press, 1926], 1: 285n.)

trumpery." [3] As Abbé Terrasson was to express it more than half a century later: "L'Histoire, dans ses Circonstances, n'est souvent qu'une suite d'Erreurs de fait: Et la Poësie . . . une suite de vérités Morales." [4] The distinction is as fundamental to English as to French neoclassicism. The historian, says Dr. Johnson, "has facts ready to his hand; so there is no exercise of invention. Imagination is not required in any high degree; only about as much as is used in the lower kinds of poetry." [5] History is unstructured nature, the *rudis indigestaque moles* of real life.

The selectivity of poetic imitation produces a copy of nature which is ideal, general, or "wrought up." We may take René Rapin (1674) for our *locus classicus*: a poet does not simply copy nature; rather, "he must choose in *her* what is *beautiful*, from what is *not*: *She* has her *secret Graces* in *Subjects* which *he* must *discover*." [6] Not long before Rapin, Dryden had written: "A play . . . to be like Nature, is to be set above it; as statues which are placed on high are made greater than the life, that they may descend to the sight in their just proportion." Protean a critic as he may be, Dryden is quite consistent in affirming that tragedy is "Nature wrought up to an higher pitch." [7] And with a few variations, Dryden's opinion

3. Thomas Rymer, *The Critical Works*, ed. C. A. Zimansky (New Haven: Yale University Press, 1956), p. 7 (preface to Rapin).

4. Jean Terrasson, *La philosophie applicable à tous les objets de l'esprit et de la raison* . . . (Paris, 1754), p. 153. Jean-François Marmontel draws similar distinctions, sometimes using science in place of history, since neither is able to transcend mere fact: "Voir n'est rien; discerner est tout." See his *Poétique françoise*, 2 vols. (Paris, 1763), 1: 85, 104, 342, and on poetic selectivity, 1: 118. See also: Corneille's *Sur la tragédie*, passim; Jean Racine, *Principes de la tragédie*, ed. E. Vinaver (Manchester: Manchester University Press, 1944), p. 16; André Dacier, *Aristotle's Art of Poetry* (London, 1705), pp. 142–43 and passim; René Rapin, *Reflections on Aristotle's Treatise of Poesie*, trans. Thomas Rymer (London, 1694), p. 87; Charles Batteux, *Les beaux arts réduits à un même principe* (Paris, 1747), p. 25; C. J. F. Hénault, *Nouveau théâtre françois* (Paris, 1747), sig. A2ᵛ.

5. *Life*, 1: 424. On this distinction in English criticism, see also: Gerard, *An Essay on Taste*, ed. W. J. Hipple (Gainesville: Scholars' Facsimiles & Reprints, 1963), p. 282; Elizabeth Montagu, *An Essay on the Writings and Genius of Shakespeare* (London, 1769), p. 276; Richard Hurd, ed., *Q. Horatii Flacci epistolae ad Pisones, et Augustum*, 3 vols. (London, 1766), 3: 75–79; *London Magazine* 35 (December 1766): 64.

6. Rapin, *Aristotle's Treatise of Poesie*, p. 57; cf. pp. 37–38.

7. Dryden, *Essays*, 1: 102, 100 (*Essay of Dramatic Poesy*); cf. 1: 144, 148, 185; 2: 137. As late as 1777 Joseph Baretti, *Discours sur Shakespeare et sur Monsieur*

was to prevail as uninterruptedly in English criticism as in the French.[8] The purpose of poetry, Richard Hurd is still advising us at mid-century, is

> not to delineate truth simply, but to present it in the most taking forms; not to reflect the real face of things, but to illustrate and adorn it; not to represent the fairest objects only, but to represent them in the fairest lights, and to heighten all their beauties up to the possibility of their natures; nay, to *outstrip* nature.[9]

At about the same time Lord Chesterfield writes: "Tragedy must be bigger than life, or it would not affect us. In nature, the most violent passions are silent; in tragedy they must speak, and speak with dignity too." Seven years before Johnson's *Preface*, the *Critical Review* remarks that just as we ought to praise, not condemn, classical statues because they are more perfect than any human being, so "we ought to judge of the poet, who has certainly lost his labour, if he does not exhibit figures and characters better than life." [10] Thus, having run through nearly a century of neoclassicism, we are brought back to Dryden's statues once again.

In the eighteenth century, *nature* was used to designate human nature especially; and the rather granitic view of dramatic character

---

de Voltaire (London and Paris, 1777), p. 36, compares Shakespeare's characters to the statues at Rome and Florence which are not of any particular men or women.

8. In French criticism, see: Batteux, *Les beaux arts*, pp. 9, 17, 38 (and chap. 5 passim); Louis Racine, *Remarques sur les tragédies de Jean Racine*, 2 vols. (Paris, 1752), 1: 19–20; Marmontel, *Poétique françoise*, 1: 321 ff.; L. Sébastien Mercier, *De la littérature et des littérateurs* (Yverdon, 1778), p. 154; J. B. A. Suard, *Variétés littéraires*, vol. 1 (Paris, 1768), p. 146.

9. Hurd, *Horatii epistolae*, 2: 140–41; cf. 1: 254: "In deviating from particular and partial, the poet more faithfully imitates *universal* truth."

10. Chesterfield, *Letters to His Son*, ed. O. H. Leigh, 2 vols. (New York: n.p., [1937]), 2: 57 (23 January 1752); *Critical Review* 6 (December 1758): 465. See also: Thomas Wilkes, *A General View of the Stage* (London, 1759), p. 229; Daniel Webb, *An Inquiry into the Beauties of Painting* (London, 1760), pp. 40–41; Oliver Goldsmith, *Miscellaneous Works*, ed. J. Aikin, 5 vols. (Baltimore, 1809), 4: 174; Earl of Shaftesbury, *Characteristicks*, 5th ed., 3 vols. (London, 1732), 1: 145; Bernard Mandeville, *Fable of the Bees*, ed. F. B. Kaye, 2 vols. (Oxford: Oxford University Press, 1924), 2: 33–34; James Harris, *Three Treatises* (London, 1744), pp. 216–27; Joshua Reynolds, *Discourses on Art*, ed. S. O. Mitchell (New York: Bobbs-Merrill, 1965), pp. 7, 40 ff., 99, 160–61, and *Discourse III*, passim.

produced by idealistic theories is not ineptly illustrated by such statues. Charles Gildon, usually representative if nothing else, is sufficiently plain: "The Poet is not oblig'd to relate things just as they happen, but as they might, or ought to have happen'd: that is, the Action ought to be general and allegorical, not particular, for particular Actions can have no general Influence." Tragedy, he continues, gives true names to its characters in order to preserve credibility, "the Persons still remaining general and allegoric." Furthermore, if the character is to be general and allegorical, he must follow the decorum of his type. In Thomas Rymer we can see how this notion of decorum arises directly from idealistic pre-suppositions. Rymer criticizes the king drolling and quibbling in *A King and No King*, and, anticipating Johnson's apology for such low actions, contends: "This too is *natural*, some will say. There are in nature many things which Historians are asham'd to mention, as below the dignity of an History: Shall we then suffer a *Tom Coriat* in *Poetry?*" For Rymer, the logic is inescapable: if poetry is concerned with ideal nature, then the characters in poetry must themselves be idealized. For example, according to natural history woman is modest; thus, "tragedy cannot represent a woman without modesty as natural and essential to her." Rapin agrees, and of them all Dacier is perhaps the most explicit. The poet directs his attention to generals so that he can delve into causes and effects with which the historian is unable to cope:

> Thus when *Homer* wrote the Action of *Achilles*, he had no design to describe that Man alone who bore that Name, but to set before our Eyes, what Violence and Anger could make all Men of that Character, say, or do. *Achilles* is then an Universal Person, General and Allegorical; it is so of the Hero's of Tragedy.

Although individual names may be provided, the poet does not make the characters "speak truly," but "probably"; he makes them "speak and do, all that Men of the same Character would say or do in the same Circumstances, either of necessity, or according to the rules of verisimilitude." John Dennis gives the argument even more of a Platonic turn, but the results are the same. Horace's injunction to follow nature, he says, means "not to draw after particular Men, who are but Copies and Imperfect Copies of the great universal Pattern; but to consult that innate Original, and that universal Ideal, which the Creator has fix'd in the minds of

ev'ry reasonable Creature, and so to make a true and just Draught."
It is from such a position that Dennis, in a passage criticized by
Johnson in the *Preface*, censures Menenius in *Coriolanus*: "Witness
Menenius . . . whom he has made an errant Buffoon, which is a
great Absurdity. For he might as well have imagin'd a grave majestick *Jack-Pudding*, as a Buffoon in a *Roman* Senator."[11] In France,
of course, the insistence on decorum is even more strenuous, especially in Voltaire, whom Johnson rebukes along with Dennis in
this particular.[12] But in England, the debate over dramatic decorum
through 1765 is unexciting; most critics endorse it, but ritualistically
and without passion. Shakespeare is almost invariably censured for
lowering his characters, the gravediggers' scene in *Hamlet* receiving
the severest criticism.[13]

Along with decorum, critics insisted that the social rank itself
of the principal personages must be exalted. Dacier may be our
locus classicus here, for his interpretation of the *Poetics* 5 is typical.
He reads Aristotle as recommending that a tragedy be an "imitation of the Actions of the greatest Persons," rather than the possible reading that it be an "Imitation of great illustrious actions";
and he glosses the passage so as to make his meaning quite clear:
"The most notable Action of a Citizen, can never be made the
Subject of an *Epick Poem*, when the most indifferent one of a King,
or General of an Army, will be such, and always with Success."
Dacier is representative of early neoclassicism in placing the sense of
Aristotle's *exalted* entirely on the social position of the characters,

11. Charles Gildon, *An Essay on the Art, Rise, and Progress of the Stage*,
in *The Works of . . . Shakespear*, vol. 7 (London, 1710), p. xxxii; Rymer, *Critical Works*, pp. 44, 64; Rapin, *Aristotle's Treatise of Poesie*, pp. 39–44; Dacier,
Aristotle's Art of Poetry, p. 144; John Dennis, *Critical Works*, ed. Edward Niles
Hooker, 2 vols. (Baltimore: Johns Hopkins Press, 1939–43), 1: 418; 2: 5.

12. See Voltaire, *Oeuvres complètes*, 70 vols. (Paris, 1785–89), 49: 314, and his
edition of *Théâtre de Corneille*, 12 vols. ([Geneva], 1764), 1: 132. See also the
Abbé Le Blanc, *Letters on the English and French Nations*, 2 vols. (Dublin,
1747), 1: 219–20: he rebukes Shakespeare for introducing Caesar onto the stage
in his nightcap, hence violating the rule that "no hero wears a nightgown."
Le Blanc concludes with astonishment: "In some of his plays, he makes his
[heroes] appear in deshabille: and sometimes he even represents them drunk."

13. The author of the *Miscellaneous Observations on the Tragedy of Hamlet*
(London, 1752), p. viii, is notably mild: "Tho *Shakespeare* has for the most
Part caused his Kings and Heroes to maintain their Dignity, without stooping
into vulgar Phrase, yet he sometimes makes them descend from their Characters, and use the Language of a Buffoon."

and not at all on the events themselves.[14] Corneille asserts that the characters in a tragedy must at least be illustrious and extraordinary; and in his edition of Corneille, Voltaire adds a note declaring that the characters should be noble, not only because the destiny of states resides with them, but because the misfortunes of people of a rank so public "font sur nous une impression plus profonde que les infortunes du vulgaire."[15] In the period between Corneille and Voltaire's commentary upon him, French criticism is fairly consistent. It is the highest kind of respect—admiration (in its Latin sense)—that we are principally to feel for the main dramatic characters.[16] Noble characters, then, are to be used in tragedy because they are in exalted positions and hence suitable to the dignity of that genre (or so says Aristotle as revealed by Dacier), because what befalls them has a public as well as merely private significance, and above all because we admire them.

This interpretation of Aristotle does not prevail so widely in English criticism after the days of Rymer, Dennis, and Gildon, though it is found as late as Goldsmith's celebrated and splendidly reactionary *Essay on the Theatre* (1773): "The distresses of the Mean by no means affect us so strongly as the Calamities of the Great." When a great man falls, "our pity is increased in proportion to the height from whence he fell." But we do not pity or sympathize with those of humble birth, nor in fact can such people fall very far. Delightedly, he quotes the comment of a friend of his who was sitting unmoved at a sentimental comedy: " 'Why, truly,' says he, 'as the Hero is but a Tradesman, it is indifferent to me whether he be turned out of his Countinghouse on Fish-street Hill, since he will still have enough left to open shop in St. Giles's.' "[17]

14. Dacier, *Aristotle's Art of Poetry*, p. 64.

15. *Théâtre de Corneille*, 2: 561.

16. See Jean Racine, *Oeuvres*, 3 vols. (Paris, 1755–60), 2: 72. Cf. his *Principes de la tragédie*, p. 11, and Vinaver's note in this work, p. 57; Batteux, *Les beaux arts*, p. 226; Jean Baptiste Boyer, *Réflexions historiques et critiques sur le goût* (Amsterdam, 1743), p. 127. Pope's Prologue to *Cato* is an especially fine expression of this view. Even the liberal La Motte, many years after Racine, is emphatic: "Ainsi les Héros qui s'immolent pour leur Patrie, sont sûrs de nôtre admiration, parce que, au jugement de la raison, le bonheur de tout un People est préférable à celui d'un seul homme" *(Oeuvres de théâtre . . . , 2 vols.* [Paris, 1730], 1: 28).

17. Oliver Goldsmith, *Essays and Criticisms*, 3 vols. (London, 1798), 3: 59, 62. See also the anonymous *Some Remarks on the Tragedy of Hamlet* (London, 1736), p. 55.

Goldsmith's hypothetical and acrimonious friend, however, was most decidedly in the minority by the early 1770s. Six years before Johnson's *Preface* Adam Smith defends the orthodox view, but he defends it in a manner which must have seemed extraordinary to a conservative neoclassicist. Persons of high rank are appropriate to a tragedy, he argues, because we regard their condition as perfectly happy, and hence sympathize with them all the more:

> We favour all their inclinations. . . . What pity, we think, that any thing should spoil and corrupt so agreeable a situation! . . . Every calamity that befals them, every injury that is done them, excites in the breast of the spectator ten times more compassion and resentment than he would have felt, had the same things happened to other men. It is the misfortunes of Kings only which afford the proper subjects for tragedy. . . . To disturb, or to put an end to such perfect enjoyment, seems to be the most atrocious of injuries.[18]

For Smith, tragedy must tell sad tales of kings, not because we admire them more and are impressed with the importance and responsibilities of their rank, but because we sympathize with them more; not because we are struck with terror at their descent (fearing the downfall of the state as well), but because we pity them more than we do ordinary people. Smith thus defends a critical commonplace in a singular way.

As early as Rowe in his prologue to *The Fair Penitent* (1703), however, critics with as much taste for sympathy as Adam Smith had broken with the older theory of decorum and were calling for a more democratic variety of drama.

> Long has the fate of kings and empires been
> The common business of the tragic scene,
> As if misfortune made the throne her seat,
> And none could be unhappy, but the great.

Half a century later, in his preface to Mrs. Lennox's edition of Brumoy, the earl of Orrery reproaches English dramatists for their exalted subjects: "We deal almost solely in the fate of kings and princes, as if misfortunes were chiefly peculiar to the great." And his next comment transforms Rowe's complaint into a psychological principle: "We feel not so intensely the sorrows of the higher

18. Adam Smith, *The Theory of Moral Sentiments* (London, 1774), pp. 87–88.

powers, as we feel the miseries of those who are nearer upon a level with ourselves." With domestic tragedy now beginning to flourish, critics kindly disposed to it availed themselves often of this justification. Both Orrery and Smith believe that it is sympathy, rather than admiration, which tragedy is to evoke; but mid-century critics found Orrery more persuasive than Smith. The mimic Samuel Foote, for example, in his *Roman and English Comedy* (1747) challenges Steele's assertion that some distresses are too vulgar for tragedy: "Did Tragedy owe its Essence to the Adventures and Misfortunes of People in High Life only, Sir *Richard's* Argument might have some Weight: But it is the Distresses, not the Situations of Mankind, that are truly interesting, and the Story affecting[,] the Rank and Quality of the Personae are of no great Consequence." Thus Foote neatly reverses Dacier's dramatic theory: the emphasis is now on the *distresses* rather than the *situations* of mankind; on what the characters feel, not on the rank in which they are placed. An event, if it is truly touching, is exalted, regardless of how humble the protagonists may be. The periodicals of the 1750s indicate to what extent distress, instead of dignity, has become the capital quality of a tragic hero. The *London Chronicle* praises a revival of *The Fair Penitent*, commenting that the drama "shews us how greatly those Critics are mistaken, who insist that the Subject of Tragedy should always be some illustrious Action depending among [*sic!*] great and exalted Personages." Of John Home's *Agis* the *Critical Review* observes:

> Stories of domestic distress affect the hearts of all mankind, although the persons should be obscured and unknown. But the struggles of patriots for laws and institutions, that bear little similitude to our own; and with which the bulk of the audience is entirely unacquainted, cannot be supposed to rouze or interest them to any degree.

Thus the reviewers find the play rather less moving than might have been expected from the pathetic author of *Douglas*.[19]

This erosion of classical values at mid-century is displayed most pointedly in William Mason's "rigorously classical" drama *Elfrida*

19. *The Greek Theatre of Father Brumoy*, trans. Charlotte Lennox, 3 vols. (London, 1759), 1: xxvi; Samuel Foote, *The Roman and English Comedy Consider'd and Compar'd* (London, 1747), pp. 6–7; *London Chronicle*, no. 30 (8–10 March 1757); *Critical Review* 5 (March 1758): 237. See also: *London Chronicle* no. 302; Arthur Murphy, *The Gray's-Inn Journal*, 2 vols. (London, 1756), 1: 144.

(1752). Mason, the elegant friend of Gray and Hurd, describes his play on the title page as "a Dramatic Poem, Written on the Model of the Antient Greek Tragedy" and makes much of his courageous stand against a barbarous and licentious modernism; in point of fact, *Elfrida* frankly exploits the sentimental vogue. In the letters prefixed to the play, Mason maintains that he drew his characters "as nearly approaching to private ones, as Tragic dignity would permit; and affections rais'd rather from the impulse of common humanity, than the distresses of royalty and the fate of kingdoms." The anonymous and suspiciously enthusiastic *Remarks on Mr. Mason's Elfrida*, attributed, erroneously one hopes, to Gray, also praises the play for

> having great Personages for Actors in it, to make it *important*, and answerable to the Dignity of Tragedy; and at the same Time it is so far domestic, as to be closely *interesting* and affecting to the private Reader. I would have you take the Word *domestic* here in the same Sense, in which the Fable of *the Orphan* may be called a domestic one, inasmuch as it is taken from common Life.

The Reverend Thomas Francklyn, in his *Dissertation on Antient Tragedy* (1760), praises Euripides for his excellence in tender and pathetic emotions, adding in a footnote: "One of the greatest advantages of modern tragedy over the antient is perhaps it's judicious descent from the adventures of demi-gods, kings, and heroes, into the humbler walk of private life, which is much more interesting to the generality of mankind." By the 1750s, then, a considerable heap of criticism has accumulated which is favorable to domestic tragedy; it is not remarkable that by 1774 William Richardson should come out so emphatically for the genre: "The hero in distress is beholden with calm and composed concern, but the man of misery and anguish excites the most compassionate sympathy; it is a brother, it is a second self that extorts our tears." [20]

20. William Mason, *Elfrida, a Dramatic Poem* (London, 1752), p. ii; *Remarks on Mr. Mason's Elfrida* (London, 1752), p. 5; Thomas Francklyn, *A Dissertation on Antient Tragedy* (London, 1760), p. 55–57; William Richardson, *Cursory Remarks on Tragedy* . . . (London, 1774), p. 101 (this work has also been attributed to Edward Taylor, but for purposes of convenience I shall refer to it throughout as by Richardson). Sentimental critics were in disagreement, however, over whether or not the Greek dramatists had suitably humble characters. Tom Davies argues (*Dramatic Miscellanies*, 3 vols. [Dublin, 1784], 2: 318–19):

Thus the inclination of much mid-century criticism was to depress the social position of the primary characters so that they might affect us more immediately than those of royal rank. This humiliation of the dramatic character had two immediate and related consequences: more importance came to be attached to the domestic life of the protagonist (logical enough, since a shopkeeper could not properly be said to have a public life), and more emphasis came to be placed on the protagonist as a particular individual with his own exceptional difficulties and desires. As the merit of domestic tragedy began to be reckoned more highly, comedy was increasingly praised for the same reasons.[21] For Voltaire and the conservatives, if a tragedy dwelt too long on the domestic life of even a king, it had degenerated into a mere comedy.[22] But the characters in comedy had always been low, and in a sense were more *particular* than those in tragedy; hence, critics less rigorous than Voltaire began

---

"The Greek tragedians who deal much in demi-gods, too often raise their heroes above humanity." But Johnson's friend Guthrie believes that unlike the French and English, the "antients always brought the same men upon the stage, which they saw in the world." He contrasts *Cato* unfavorably with *Hamlet* and observes that when we have recourse to models of greatness "the language of the world drowns the whispers of the heart . . . the distress which rises is not that of a man, but of a hero; the elevation is that of state, but not of sentiment" (*An Essay upon English Tragedy* [London, (1747?)], pp. 20–27).

21. The changing attitudes toward dramatic character and tragicomedy described in this chapter, and toward morality and the drama taken up in the next, point, more generally, to the changing conceptions of society, the purpose of drama, the nature and function of comedy and humor. See particularly John Loftis, *Comedy and Society from Congreve to Fielding* (Stanford: Stanford University Press, 1959), and Stuart M. Tave, *The Amiable Humorist* (Chicago: University of Chicago Press, 1960). The premises and conclusions of Arthur Sherbo's *English Sentimental Drama* (East Lansing: Michigan State University Press, 1957) have been seriously challenged by Loftis. Finally, Prosser Hall Frye's account of the ethos responsible for Romantic "tragedy of character" remains superlatively incisive; see his *Romance and Tragedy* (Lincoln: University of Nebraska Press, 1961), pp. 53–54, 230–31, 247–49.

22. Voltaire (*Works*, 38 vols. [London, 1778–81], 25: 116–17) says that the plots of tragedies may be founded "either on the interests of a whole nation, or the private interests of the sovereign." But in the second case, "all the interest is confin'd to the hero of the piece and his family: all turns upon such passions as the vulgar feel equally with princes, the plot . . . may be as proper for comedy as for tragedy: for take away the names only, and *Mithridates* is not more than *an old fellow in love with a young girl*." As in Dacier, the emphasis is placed entirely on the rank of the characters, instead of on the events themselves.

to esteem comedy both for its lowness and its apparent particularity.[23] In 1750 the actor John Hippisley admits that comedy is inferior to tragedy in dignity, but argues that it is superior in its influence on mankind; "its Examples are taken from familiar Life, and are such as . . . come home to Men's Business and Bosoms." John Aikin asserts that sentimental comedies, because they "move the heart by tender and interesting situations" are "much more affecting than our modern Tragedies, which are formed upon nearly the same plan, but labour under the disadvantage of a formal stately stile, and manners removed too far from the rank of common life." If those tragedies are most affecting which are least grand and heroic, then it is logical to think that the lowness and particularity of comedies should render them equally affective. By 1750 sentimental comedy and domestic tragedy are praised for the same reasons and often by the same critic. Similarly, the opponents of the one, if they cared to be consistent, must have been opponents of the other; for the rigorously generic approach enforces a distinction between tragedy, which is to arouse pity, fear, and admiration, and comedy, which is not to evoke tears, but to ridicule vices and foibles. The newer attitude resulted not only in a depression of the rank of characters, but in a conscious vulgarizing of style, diction, and sentiments. In 1753 the *Gentleman's Magazine* thus concludes a commendatory review of a fashionable play:

This is the dramatic action . . . of the *Gamster*, which if it is not worked up with the force, and the elegance of poetry, is yet heighten'd with many tender incidents, and, as the dialect is perfectly colloquial, it probably produced a greater effect upon the majority of the audience than if it had been decorated with beauties which they cannot miss, at the expense of that plainness without which they cannot understand.

23. Traditionally, the characters in comedy had been regarded as more *general* than those in tragedy (see Dennis, *Critical Works*, 1: 187; Hurd, *Horatii epistolae*, 2: 183, 185–86). G. E. Lessing, *Hamburgische Dramaturgie*, 2 vols. (Hamburg, 1769), st. 87–95, quotes Hurd's discussion at length—but only to argue that characters in tragedy are no more particular than those in comedy. But comic characters, in their mode of behavior, habits, speech, etc., often seemed to be more *particularly* drawn and individualized than tragic characters. For other citations, see Hooker's note in Dennis, *Critical Works*, 1: 496–97; and for the distinction between individuals and types in French criticism, see: Marmontel, *Poétique françois*, 2: 372; L. Sébastien Mercier, *Du théâtre . . .* (Amsterdam, 1773), pp. 69–70; Denis Diderot, *Oeuvres de théâtre . . .*, 2 vols. (Amsterdam, 1772), 1: 243.

How remote now seems Dryden's "A play . . . to be like Nature, is to be set above it." [24]

Continental criticism by the middle of the century had become equally infected by sentimentalism. Even in Dacier's time it was asked how we can sympathize with the misfortunes of kings if, as Aristotle says, we are affected only by people like ourselves. Dacier's rhetorical evasion seems to have satisfied for a while. The poet, he observes, gives his characters eminent names "to render the Action the more noble and credible . . . however . . . 'tis a common Man that Acts under the Name of a Prince, or King. Thus *Aristotle* had reason to call Kings and Princes *like our Selves*; for the aim of the Poet is, not to imitate the Actions of Kings, but of mankind." [25] In the light of Dacier's earlier remark about the importance of social rank in *arousing* our interest, this distinction between the title and the man seems at least inconsistent, and very probably specious. A work by Voltaire's friend Jean-François Marmontel, published two years before Johnson's *Preface*, indicates to what extent even orthodox neoclassicism had shifted (or yielded) its ground. The second volume of his *Poëtique françoise* contains one of the most thoughtful discussions of heroic and domestic tragedy in the period. He very adequately summarizes the favorable attitude toward domestic tragedy but, like Dacier, rebuts the insistence that we cannot sympathize with people above us in rank. We *do* weep for Hecuba or Clytemnestra: "Un Roi dans le bonheur est pour nous un Roi; dans le malheur il est pour nous un homme." Because the victim of a passion is illustrious does not make less general the lesson his fate enforces: we share with him the emotions he suffers; the moral is the same for those in all conditions of life.

24. John Hippisley, *A Dissertation on Comedy* (London, 1750), p. 6; J. Aikin and A. L. Aikin, *Miscellaneous Pieces in Prose* (London, 1773), p. 21; *Gentleman's Magazine* 23 (February 1753): 61. Cf. the review in the next year (24: 84) of Morgan's *Philoclea*: "The language, though it is measured, is scarcely elevated into poetry; but as all dialogue in verse is a deviation from nature, this defect . . . could not much lessen its effect upon the spectators." Thus Dryden's defense of rhyme and heightened language is quite rejected: we are not to admire a play as an imitation of "nature wrought up," but are instead to be taken in by its verisimilitude. Donald J. Greene has made the tantalizing suggestion, arguing mainly from internal evidence, that this review is Johnson's; see his "Was Johnson Theatrical Critic of the *Gentleman's Magazine?*" *Review of English Studies*, n.s. 3 (1952): 161.

25. Dacier, *Aristotle's Art of Poetry*, p. 210.

To think that exalted titles are necessary to move us, he believes, slanders the human heart. As a good classicist, Marmontel is disposed favorably to heroic tragedy, whose grandeur simply cannot be denied; but he defends at great length the desirable pathos of the domestic variety.[26] In effect, he develops more candidly and sensitively what Dacier had quietly confessed, that tragic effect may not depend ultimately on the rank of the protagonist. Foote, as we have seen, had done just this sixteen years before, but for a respectable Academician, this is something; and what Marmontel is willing to concede is given extreme form a few years later by the popular writer of domestic *drames*, L. Sébastien Mercier, and the Shakespeare translator, P. F. Le Tourneur.[27]

In mid-century criticism, both English and French, the classical conception of poetry as an imitation of moral or ideal nature is yielding to the notion that it is principally an affective form of art. The interest is turning from *what* it represents to the *sentiments* aroused by what it represents. The admiration which was of such importance for Corneille, Dacier, and Voltaire is being replaced by the softer passion of sympathy. And while a later neoclassicist like Marmontel may argue that we can sympathize with the *man* beneath the hero's robes of state, his argument is a fatal concession to the newer aesthetic theories, an admission that sympathy *is* an important and fundamental part of our aesthetic response. For with this much conceded, what remains but to inquire why, if we sympathize with the man beneath the royal robes, we should be hindered by the robes at all? Marmontel and Adam Smith, within four years of each other, aspired to have their sentiment and royalty too; but this fusion was too implausible to endure. Neoclassical dramatic

26. Marmontel, *Poétique françoise*, 2: 143–50. Cf. *Greek Theatre of Brumoy*, 1: cv. Marmontel is in a sense Richard Hurd's opposite number in France. Like Hurd, he is an intelligent critic the bulk of whose writings appeared shortly before Johnson's *Preface*, and, like Hurd's essays and commentary in *Horatii epistolae*, his two volumes of criticism represent mid-century neoclassicism at its most flexible: generally conservative, but strongly marked by newer tendencies and interests. Hume recommended his works (in vain) to Blair.

27. Mercier, *Du théâtre*, passim (but see especially p. 42) is forthright in his rejection of heroes and heroic actions as unable to rouse our sympathy; he continues this attack in *De la littérature*: classical heroes cannot interest us. P. F. Le Tourneur, *Shakespeare traduit de l'anglois*, vol. 1 (Paris, 1776), lxxv-lxxvi, praises Shakespeare extravagantly for his refusal to create heroes and imaginary demigods.

theory could not long resist the intrusion of such alien values as commonness, realism, particularity. Mere history—that "diary of Fortune" so disdained by a Davenant—is now exalted into the realm of art. Though not about drama, Joseph Warton's *Essay on the Genius and Writings of Pope* (1756) provides the most remarkable indication of what these new interests portended for dramatic theory. To begin with, the book is a long defense of particular against general nature. He defends Homer's use of *"natural, little circumstances"* against "those who are fond of *generalities"*; he defends Shakespeare's particularity against Voltaire, who cannot appreciate the dramatist's "little touches of nature" because he wants them himself; he defends *"true* and *lively,* and *minute* representations of Nature" as not being beneath the dignity of a tragedy or epic. But what is most interesting for us is his distinction between history and poetry: "A minute and particular enumeration of circumstances judiciously selected, is what chiefly discriminates poetry from history, and renders the former, for that reason, a more close and faithful representation of nature than the latter." The neoclassical distinction is almost, but not quite, reversed; although Warton preserves the judicious selection, he denounces the emphasis on generalization. Poetry has now become involved with those particularities that had hitherto been the province of mere history.[28]

But the traditional understanding of poetry as nature "wrought up," and the emerging desire for the particulars of common life, jostle each other almost promiscuously in the 1750s and 1760s; from the evidence of the books and periodicals surveyed here, it is not probable that a critic who argued vehemently for the classical or the sentimentalist position would fear that he had exposed himself to popular derision as an extremist. But although things were in flux, the sentimentalist view was to gain ground, and we may now consider the ways in which this view was to alter the critical treatment of Shakespeare's characters. Dryden and subsequent critics

28. Joseph Warton, *Essay on the Genius and Writings of Pope,* 4th ed., 2 vols. (London, 1782), 2: 166, 171–2; 1: 48, cf. 1: 335; 2: 393. Some of my citations are taken from material added to editions after 1756; but the first part, which was published that year, praises particularity as much as the later sections; the distinction between history and poetry is made in this part. A few years later Lord Kames [Henry Home], *Elements of Criticism,* 3 vols. (Edinburgh, 1762), 3: 198–200, defends the particularity of Shakespeare's style; and cf. 3: 174: even the slightest circumstance "cannot be described too minutely" in order to convince the audience of the reality of the spectacle.

had acclaimed Shakespeare's delicate delineation of his characters; and the priority now placed on common and particular characters gave a new emphasis—indeed, a new meaning—to this praise. Earlier, Lewis Theobald had commended him for his "Variety of Originals." Other artists draw fools similarly, but "*Shakespeare's* Clowns and Fops come all of a different House: they are no farther allied to one another than as Man to Man, Members of the same Species: but as different in Features and Lineaments of Character, as we are from one another in Face, or Complexion." Pope, in a passage to which Johnson refers in the *Preface*, also praised this quality of Shakespeare's:

> . . . every single character in *Shakespear* is as much an Individual as those in Life itself; it is as impossible to find any two alike; and such as from their relation or affinity in any respect appear most to be Twins, will upon comparison be found remarkably distinct.

Remarks of this nature are plentiful in the first half of the century.[29] But although both Pope and Theobald appeal to "life" in their defense of Shakespeare's characters, the context is not that of sentimentalism; rather, it reflects an attitude toward dramatic character which still involves traditional notions of decorum. This is especially evident in Joseph Trapp's definition: "Per *Characterem* . . . intelligimus, universam congeriem eorum omnium quae quamlibet Personam a caeteris discriminant; ut Aetas, Fortitudo, Mores, Indoles." The characteristics which Trapp enumerates here, and the description of characters which follows (Senex, Juvenis, Rex, Servus) indicate that Trapp has in mind character *types*: these types must be distinguished from each other, and they ought to be consistent within themselves, but they remain idealized. There is nothing in the neoclassical doctrine of character discrimination to suggest that the characters are *really* to be like that diversified mankind

29. Theobald's Preface to Shakespeare, in *Eighteenth-Century Essays on Shakespeare*, ed. Nichol Smith (Oxford: Oxford University Press, 1963), p. 60; Pope's preface in ibid., p. 45. See also Peter Whalley, *An Enquiry into the Learning of Shakespeare* (London, 1748), p. 21, and Dennis, *Critical Works*, 2: 424–25, where Hooker demonstrates how traditional such observations were. However, he also comments: "Here [in Steele, Hughes, Theobald, and Warburton], rather than in the second half of the eighteenth century, do we see the real beginnings of the romantic criticism of Shakespeare's characters." But as I shall endeavor presently to indicate, the *real* beginnings are not found significantly among these critics.

which the actual world affords; or if there is, the early neoclassicists were unaware of it. The "as we are" in Theobald and the "Life itself" in Pope are, I suggest, merely metaphorical and cannot confidently be cited as anticipations of realism.[30]

But by Mrs. Montagu's time the attitude had begun to change. When *she* praises Shakespeare's characters for their individuality, it is not because they conform accurately to the decorum of their type, but because they are realistic and more easily win our sympathy. In her long and remarkable defense of Shakespeare against Voltaire, published four years after Johnson's *Preface* (but dismissed very contemptuously by Johnson himself), the newer theories of dramatic character are conspicuous; and they are skilfully argued as well. Mrs. Montagu defends Shakespeare by claiming that he copied "nature, as he found it, in the busy walks of human life, he drew from an original, with which the Literati are seldom well acquainted." Unlike Dryden, she does not compare tragic characters to statues; quite the contrary, she is more than happy to concede that Shakespeare's are very different from the "celebrated forms preserved in the learned museums." The important question is, do they resemble the real persons after whom they were drawn?

> Among these connoisseurs, whose acquaintance with the characters of men is formed in the library, not in the street, the camp, or village, whatever is unpolished and uncouth passes for fantastic and absurd, though, in fact, it is a faithful representation of a really existing character.

A subsequent passage reveals how far we have come from the heroes of Corneille and Dryden, the ideal if individualized types of Trapp, Gildon, or Pope.

30. Joseph Trapp, *Praelectiones poeticae*, 3d ed., 2 vols. (London, 1736), 2: 170–71. Both Gildon (*Works of . . . Shakespear*, 7: xli, li) and John Upton (*Critical Observations on Shakespeare*, 2d ed. [London, 1748], pp. 68 ff.) make this double emphasis. Both assert that the characters must be general and allegorical, but both stress the necessity that they be individualized. Notice in Upton especially: each of Shakespeare's characters is "strongly marked and manner'd" so that the audience will "know how he will behave, and what part he will take on any emergency." This consistency relies upon conventional notions of decorum and is very far from the sentimental praise of *particular* characters.

Shakespear's dramatis personae are men, frail by constitution, hurt by ill habits, faulty and unequal. But they speak with human voices, are actuated by human passions, and are engaged in the common affairs of human life. We are interested in what they do, or say, by feeling every moment, that they are of the same nature as ourselves.

Here it is obvious that the appeal to "real life" is not metaphorical. Shakespeare's characters are individuals because they are like particular men in the streets, and *because* they are like men in the streets, we are interested in them. Four years before, Dr. Johnson had written: "[Shakespeare's] story requires Romans or kings, but he thinks only on men"—meaning to compliment the poet for not encumbering himself with trivial particulars. But for Mrs. Montagu the poet who is describing another country must make us sympathize with its very strangeness, and this he does by familiarizing us in detail with its differences. Of *Julius Caesar* she exults: "To the very scene, to the very time, therefore, does our Poet transport us: at Rome, we become Romans; we are affected by their manners; we are caught by their enthusiasm." And she adds: "This is truly Imitation, when the poet gives us the just copies of all circumstances that accompanied the action he represents." What sort of imitation Mrs. Montagu prizes, her next sentence makes clear: "Corneille's drama's are fantastic compositions, void of historical truth, imitation of character, or representation of manners." But Mrs. Montagu only expresses more strongly the desire which many were feeling for particular and historical truth.[31]

In the French critics Diderot and Mercier the break with neoclassical theories of dramatic character becomes decisive. Only the gods, Diderot believes, can create truly ideal types; it is therefore better that mortal artists depict men as they are. A year later, Mercier praises Shakespeare for the variety and individuality of his

---

31. Montagu, *Essay on Shakespeare*, pp. 17–18, 81, 248, 254. See also Hurd, *Horatii epistolae*, 2: 193; Daniel Webb, *Remarks on the Beauties of Poetry* (London, 1762), pp. 98–99; *Gentleman's Magazine* 8 (January 1738): 4. Wilkes in his *General View of the Stage*, p. 29, urges that the passions ought to be blended in characters "so that they may be real pictures of man as he is, not as he ought to be." Cf. Gerard, *Essay on Taste*, p. 51: "Imperfect and mixt characters are, in all kinds of writing, preferred to faultless ones, as being juster copies of real nature." The earlier justification of mixed or impure characters on the basis of poetic justice (if the hero must fall, the hero must not be faultless) has given way to arguments from realism.

characters, their unique and realistic Englishness, and exclaims: "Tous ses héros sont hommes, & cet alliage du simple & de l'héroïsme ajoute à l'intérêt." [32] But there is little more than a verbal similarity between Mercier's "Tous ses héros sont hommes" and Johnson's "Shakespeare has no heroes; his scenes are occupied only by men."

> Nothing can please many, and please long [says Johnson], but just representations of general nature. Particular manners can be known to few, and therefore few only can judge how nearly they are copied. . . .
> Shakespeare is above all writers . . . the poet of nature; the poet that holds up to his readers a faithful mirrour of manners and of life. His characters are not modified by the customs of particular places, unpractised by the rest of the world; by the peculiarities of studies or professions, which can operate but upon small numbers; or by the accidents of transient fashions or temporary opinions: they are the genuine progeny of common humanity, such as the world will always supply, and observation will always find. His persons act and speak by the influence of those general passions and principles by which all minds are agitated, and the whole system of life is continued in motion. In the writings of other poets a character is too often an individual; in those of Shakespeare it is commonly a species.[33]

That art properly imitate general nature: after the initial test of consensus, this is the first of Johnson's standards of excellence. Shakespeare meets this requirement, too; his characters are just representations of general (human) nature. A few paragraphs further, however, Johnson approves of Shakespeare's character discrimination, but at the same time he objects to Pope's praise as too exaggerated: the characters are well distinguished from each other, but not so perfectly as Pope suggests. He comments that other dramatists rely on extremes of characterization ("unexampled excellence or depravity"), but "Shakespeare has no heroes; his scenes are occupied only by men, who act and speak as the reader thinks he

32. Diderot, *Oeuvres de théâtre* . . . , 1: 274, 435; with some variations, he reiterates these theories in his *Essais sur la peinture* (Paris, [1795]); Mercier, *Du théâtre,* p. 206. Marmontel, *Poétique françoise,* 1: 343–66, censures Louis Racine's definition of ideal nature as too rigid and exclusive and suggests that *la belle nature* may vary according to the intent of the poet and his subject matter; Marmontel's relativism is remarkable for the time.

33. Johnson, *Works,* 7: 61–62; all ensuing references in this chapter will be from these and the next several pages.

should himself have spoken or acted on the same occasion." [34] Thus, Shakespeare's drama is the "mirror of life"; but this fidelity to general nature "has exposed him to the censure of criticks, who form their judgments upon narrower principles." To the supporters of decorum (Rymer, Dennis, Voltaire) he replies: "Shakespeare always makes nature predominate over accident; and if he preserves the essential character, is not very careful of distinctions superinduced and adventitious. His story requires Romans or kings, but he thinks only on men." Kings and senators, he argues, can be drunkards and buffoons like other men, and those who criticize Shakespeare's characters because they are indecorous are expressing merely the "petty cavils of petty minds; a poet overlooks the casual distinction of country and condition, as a painter, satisfied with the figure, neglects the drapery." Thus Johnson identifies Shakespeare's characters as "just representations of general nature," but at the same time praises them as the "genuine progeny of common humanity"; they are species, not individuals, but they are distinct characters as well; in them "nature predominates over accident," yet they are also men like ourselves, not heroes. To what degree is Johnson a traditional neoclassicist who admires Shakespeare for his imitation of the general and universal; or to what extent has he been influenced by newer critical trends to prefer particular and common men? Johnson's discussion is more complicated than it may appear; his defense of Shakespeare against Voltaire, while in its vocabulary most neoclassical, seems in its mode of argument very like that of Mrs. Montagu four years later.

Two problems require examination: Johnson's rejection of one of the keystones of neoclassical theory, decorum, and his belief that the characters, although general, are well discriminated. The first problem is by far the more significant. Arthur Sherbo suggests that Johnson

> is taking a stand against the doctrine of decorum, not the decorum that demanded nothing but soldierly actions from a soldier, but the diluted, and hence more insidious because less obvious, kind which insisted that Shakespeare's characters were so individualized that no speech could

34. It should be remembered, in the following discussion, that in contrasting Shakespeare's men with heroes, Johnson was probably contrasting them with the extravagant characters of heroic drama.

appropriately be spoken by any character other than the one for whom it was intended.[35]

But in fact Johnson *is* attacking the first type of decorum that Sherbo describes, and it is an argument which turns the ideal theory of imitation against that inference which so many drew from it. As for the "diluted" and "insidious" kind (the kind believed in by Pope), Johnson surely objects to it, but his is a temperate, and not even a complete, objection.[36] Throughout his analysis of dramatic character, Johnson opposes general nature to "particular manners," the "customs of particular places." He opens his discussion with this contrast, and his conclusion, attacking artificial decorum, rests on the same foundation: general nature is concerned with the emotions and passions of all men and must not be restricted by false or superficial notions of what a king is supposed to be like. He is plainer, perhaps, in his dedication (1753) to Mrs. Lennox's *Shakespear Illustrated*: Shakespeare's "*Heroes* are *Men* . . . the Love and Hatred . . . are . . . common to other human Beings, and not like those which later Times have exhibited, peculiar Phantoms that strut upon the Stage." It is not Johnson's point that Shakespeare's heroes are men, and hence we can identify sympathetically with them; it is rather that they experience universal, instead of eccentric or private, passions. The distinction between *nature* and *manners* was a favorite of Johnson's. Fielding, he says elsewhere, was concerned with characters of manners, Richardson with characters of nature; the former "are to be understood by a more superficial observer, than characters of nature, where a man must dive into the recesses of the human heart." And, contrasting Dryden and Pope, Johnson finds that "Dryden knew more of man in his general nature, and Pope in his local manners. The notions of Dryden were formed by comprehensive speculation, and those of Pope by minute attention. There is more dignity in the knowledge of Dryden, and more certainty in that of Pope." [37] So far, then, Johnson is simply asserting in the *Preface* one of those "truths too important to be new." Neoclassicism commonly distinguished between those general characteristics shared by all men, and those local man-

35. Sherbo, *Samuel Johnson, Editor of Shakespeare*, p. 55.

36. See *Works*, 7: 64.

37. Charlotte Lennox, *Shakespear Illustrated* . . . , 3 vols. (London, 1753–54), 1: x; Boswell, *Life*, 2: 48–49; Johnson, *Lives*, 3: 222.

ners which are found only among men of a specific age or nationality. But what Johnson proceeds to do in the *Preface* is remarkable: he identifies decorum with manners, the merely particular, and hence dismisses it as too specific.

The trappings of decorum are rejected because they *are* trappings, the "casual distinctions of country and condition," the "drapery." Formerly justified by idealistic theories, decorum is now condemned on the basis of another interpretation of the same theory, an interpretation which is possibly more sophisticated, and certainly more idiosyncratic. To compare Johnson's attack on decorum with two slightly earlier ones—the only ones that I have discovered prior to 1765—will make the singularity of his argument more apparent. Discussing the power of jealousy over Othello, an essayist in the *Museum* for 1747 observes that "whenever Poets attempt to paint a Man under its Influence, they seldom regard his *Rank*, his *Character*, or his *Temper*; but confounding all Rules of Decency and Decorum, shew him, however great or elevated his Station, as brutal as one of the lowest Mob." The writer wonders whether or not poets are justified in doing this. He decides that they are and appeals to history for real examples of the extreme passion which poets depict. He criticizes Rymer, "of wrangling Memory," as a "merciless Critick," and to defend *Othello* against his strictures relates at length an incident from Sampietro's life to show that jealousy can *really* operate this way. He concludes that Shakespeare "has copied faithfully, without exceeding or exaggerating; and has frighted us . . . not with an imaginary Scene, but with a real Spectacle of a wise and worthy Man made mad by Jealousy."[38] It is true, of course, that the author is not directly attacking decorum; yet it is clear that he conceives of Othello as a psychological entity the authenticity of which is to be determined, not by comparing it to a character type or by inquiring whether it is decorous for one in Othello's position to be so jealous, but by appealing to the real experience of historical beings. At about this same time—possibly the same year—William Guthrie repudiates a French criticism that the parley between Brutus and Cassius, Octavius and Antony, is too gross. Guthrie argues that there is no modern ribaldry too coarse or indecorous for the Romans:

38. *Museum* 3 (1747): 437–42.

This is a character stamped upon that people by their own historians. . . . Salust, the finest gentleman in Rome abuses Caesar in the most gross terms; and Cicero, the fountain of eloquence and address, has . . . discharged against the greatest men in Rome, torrents of abuse, which would pollute the stile even of our Billingsgate.[39]

Both the contributor to the *Museum* and Guthrie, in wishing to escape from a decorum they felt too straitening, appeal to supposed historical fact, in short, to real and particular life, to justify what Rymer or Dennis would have condemned as a poetic extravagance. From the same realistic premises Mrs. Montagu defends Shakespeare as copying from the paths of life, and the French bourgeois dramatists Diderot and Mercier extol the verisimilitude of Shakespeare's characters. Now in a sense Johnson's argument is not unlike theirs; he does tacitly appeal to the "real world" to show that "kings love their wine like other men," that senate houses *do* contain buffoons. But Johnson's terminology is very far from that of the realistic critics. He does not say, these things occur in real life, hence the poet may imitate them. That kings love wine is an observation which is not simply to be vindicated by producing an historical Claudius; it is defended by affirming that it is a general human appetite, natural rather than accidental, essential, not adventitious, the figure as against the drapery. Thus Johnson *is* attacking that sort of decorum "that demanded nothing but soldierly actions from a soldier"—and attacking it using the vocabulary, not of realism, but of generality.[40]

Nevertheless, although Johnson uses the vocabulary, he does not assume the position of conservative neoclassicists. William Richardson nine years later agrees with Johnson that kings may love wine, but in art a "consistency of passion, emotion, and sentiment" is to be observed: "whatsoever indulgence may be shown to the statesmen and courtiers of real life, those of the drama must be of an uniform and consistent conduct." Voltaire, replying in the *Dictionnaire philosophique* to Johnson's censure, rejects his application of the "drapery" metaphor to matters of decorum and suggests: "La com-

39. Guthrie, *Essay upon English Tragedy*, pp. 32–33.

40. The drapery metaphor is conventional. See Reynolds, *Discourses on Art*, pp. 103, 157, and especially 40–41, 44. Upton, *Critical Observations on Shakespeare*, p. 93, and Webb, *Inquiry into the Beauties of Painting*, pp. 49–50, also use *drapery* to represent those transient configurations which conceal natural form.

paraison serait plus just s'il parlait d'un peintre qui, dans un sujet
noble, introduirait des grotesques ridicules." [41] Both Richardson
and Voltaire are orthodox neoclassicists; both believe that there
must be a uniformity and regularity in poetry beyond that which
real life may afford; art is more than a diary of fortune. Voltaire
seems as much surprised as indignant at Johnson's rebuttal, and his
surprise is proper. The Merciers and Montagus, after all, should
occasion the intelligent neoclassicist little perplexity, for he can
readily identify their error in confounding life with art. But
Johnson, without appealing to real life—indeed, by appealing to
the values of idealistic aesthetics—denies the orthodox opinion.
Voltaire, whose exasperation was excited by so many trivialities, is
here justified: to criticize decorum because it is not general nature
is a devious and—for a neoclassicist—an ungentlemanly maneuver.
If as Richardson and Voltaire believe, decorum truly preserves
unity of tone in a work, it can hardly be dismissed as mere drapery.

Johnson's preference of men to heroes rests on the same distinction. *Heroes* are the exaggerated, the unnatural; unlike Racine and
Corneille, he does not see them as heightened, ideal types, but as
monsters opposed to men who "act and speak as the reader thinks
that he should himself have spoken or acted." Being a hero in this
way is the same as being a "decorous" king: both are the product of
an excessively rigid conception of character drawing. There must
be a man beneath both the hero and the king or we shall not be
able to learn anything from them applicable to ourselves. But the
common man is not to be an individual or an *eccentric* (for this is
what Johnson means by *individual*); this, too, would be to fall prey
to the particular. The common man is man in general, while the
man in the street (like the hero or king) is a particular man. It is
not Johnson's rhetoric alone that distinguishes him from Mrs.
Montagu; though he may tacitly appeal to real life to attack heroes
and decorum, the values which he attaches to that reality are quite
different from hers. One praises Shakespeare's men, not because
one identifies with them, but because one *learns* from them. Shakespeare produces scenes "from which a hermit may estimate the
transactions of the world, and a confessor predict the progress of

41. Richardson, *Cursory Remarks on Tragedy*, p. 141; Voltaire, quoted in
Life, 1: 499n.

the passions."[42] I do not intend to petrify Johnson's ideas. It is quite true that elsewhere, especially in his "Notes to Shakespeare," he recognizes some sort of sympathetic identification. Particularly revealing is his "General Observation on *Lear*," where he approves of Arthur Murphy's argument that the cruelty of Lear's daughters constitutes his primary distress: "[Murphy] observes with great justness, that Lear would move our compassion but little, did we not rather consider the injured father than the degraded king."[43] But in the *Preface* this is not Johnson's concern; rather, he is interested in knowing the general nature of man. He is a classicist in the best sense, concerned with intellectual comprehension, not emotional exercise. We learn more about ourselves by seeing characters in the grip of passions which are general (i.e., which we all feel); Johnson makes no mention of our sympathizing with them.

His radical disagreement with fashionable aesthetic theories on this point was perceived from the beginning. In a remarkable passage in her *Anecdotes* Mrs. Thrale is concerned with demonstrating, among other less admirable qualities, Johnson's "extreme distance from those notions which the world has agreed, I know not very well why, to call romantic." Proceeding to her first example, she comments:

> It is indeed observable in his preface to Shakespeare, that while other critics expatiate on the creative powers and vivid imagination of that matchless poet, Dr. Johnson commends him for giving so just a representation of human manners, "that from his scenes a hermit might estimate the value of society, and a confessor predict the progress of the passions." I have not the book with me here, but am pretty sure that such is his expression.[44]

Thus it is Shakespeare the instructor in human nature that attracts Johnson. Although he breaks with neoclassical theories of decorum,

42. Johnson, in his dedication to Mrs. Lennox's *Shakespear Illustrated*, 1: x, had written: "These Characters are so copiously diversified, and some of them so justly pursued, that his Works may be considered as a Map of Life, a faithful Miniature of human Transactions, and he that has read *Shakespear* with Attention, will perhaps find little new in the crouded World." Cf. George Lyttelton, *Dialogues of the Dead* (1760): "If human nature were destroyed, and no monument left of it except [Shakespeare's] works, other beings might know *what man was* from these writings" (*The Works* [London, 1774], p. 403).

43. *Works*, 8: 705. See also: *Works*, 8: 745; *Lives*, 1: 245, 2: 69.

44. *Johnsonian Miscellanies*, ed. G. B. Hill, 2 vols. (Oxford, 1897), 1: 313.

his persistence in using neoclassical vocabulary, while admittedly idiosyncratic, is not merely idiosyncratic. His heart is no more with Mrs. Montagu than with Voltaire; essentially, he is working within the contexts of neoclassicism. In this same section, his concern for the internal consistency of Shakespeare's supernatural characters, and his repudiation of love as too specific and limited an emotion for the stage (rather than too low or immoral), make even more conspicuous his "extreme distance" from Romantic notions.[45]

It remains to be determined whether or not Johnson's designation of the characters as species is inconsistent with his belief that they are nicely discriminated. A similar problem is presented in the famous tenth chapter of *Rasselas*, where Imlac first requires that a poet observe carefully both physical and human nature, and then, in the "tulip" passage, sets forth an idealistic theory of aesthetics. There is nothing very contradictory here: the poet, as preparation for his craft, must observe delicately, even minutely. When he writes, however, he selects only those predominant characteristics which will call the rest to mind. Similarly in the *Preface*, Johnson believes that important differences between characters should naturally be preserved. But to preserve distinctions does not mean to dwell on minute details; species may be distinguished from species as well as individuals from individuals. As Johnson says explicitly, it is just Shakespeare's virtue that he *could* discriminate while preserving his characters generalized. The most zealous classicists from Horace to Hurd advocated character discrimination, but they were not compelled on this account to embrace realistic theories of poetry. There is no reason not to read Johnson's comments in the same way that I have suggested we read Theobald's, Pope's, and Trapp's: as orthodox neoclassicism.[46] To call Shakespeare's characters discriminated, even to call them originals or like nature, is

45. On the consistency of Shakespeare's supernatural beings, and love in the drama, see Appendices A and B.

46. Such scholars as Hooker (see note 29 above) and David Lovett, "Shakespeare as a Poet of Realism in the Eighteenth Century," *ELH* 2 (1935): 268, 275, see in these early critics a growing realistic trend in Shakespearean criticism; but the context of their statements must be taken more into account, as well as their conceptions of "nature." Though Sherbo is correct in seeing Romantic tendencies in Johnson's notes, it is striking how frequently Johnson comments on Shakespeare's ability to generalize about the operation of the passions. The following seem to me more or less to demonstrate this concern: *Works*, 7: 422, 425, 441–42; 8: 553, 897, 902, 1019.

not necessarily to say they are realistic; it *is* to say that those distinctions which reside in general human nature have been preserved. Now in such aestheticians as Mrs. Montagu and Guthrie, Mercier and Diderot, realism *is* clearly being invested with a priority of value foreign to neoclassicism. These authors represent a movement which received its first influential and sophisticated expression in Morgann's *Essay on the Dramatic Character of Falstaff*, where, despite his title, Morgann often regards Shakespeare's characters from a realistic, rather than a dramatic, perspective. It is not with this group that Johnson is to be placed, although, particularly in his notes, he shows its influence. For him, the common man is the essential man, not the man in the street, and he would very probably have suspected of cant those later artists and social engineers who confounded the two.

Johnson's criticism of Shakespeare's dramatic characters is at its most confidently individualistic, ready to erupt from a system which threatened to reduce dramatic characterization to the production of artificial types, but little influenced by those newer theories which failed to distinguish properly between artistic and living creatures, and which, in laying such stress on emotional response, threatened to reduce drama itself to a mode of sensual stimulus. If the tendency of "decorous" critics was to make dramatic characters mere puppets, the sentimentalist inclination was to make the audience precisely that. Between the Richardsons and the Voltaires, the Montagus and the Diderots, Johnson stands pretty much alone, his eye on the main principle of neoclassicism—that art imitate general nature—even while upsetting another principle of neoclassicism that many regarded as equally fundamental, and indeed synonymous, with the first. It is only through a proper understanding of Johnson's attack on decorum that we can truly see what he means by this "general nature." A. O. Lovejoy, for example, records Johnson as preferring generic types to individuals and remarks "how preposterously Dr. Johnson, under the influence of this principle, mispraised Shakespeare, on the ground that his Romans are not particularly Romans nor his kings especially kinglike." [47] But Johnson is actually speaking *against* that type-char-

47. Arthur O. Lovejoy, *The Great Chain of Being* (New York: Harper and Row, 1960), p. 291. Paul Ramsey (*The Lively and the Just* [Tuscaloosa: University of Alabama Press, 1962], pp. 8–9) discusses this aspect of Johnson and is a good corrective to Lovejoy.

acter—the type of the Roman or king—which Lovejoy disapproves of as well. He is distinguishing, not between general types and individuals, but between valid and invalid kinds of generality, between true types and stereotypes. The true generality is not an abstraction, but a character enduring universal passions. It is precisely because Othello is not a stereotyped tyrant, but a man suffering from an emotion we have all experienced in some degree, that he is a just representation of general nature. He is thus a *common* man from whom we may learn something about our own condition, whereas mere individuals, whether in streets or palaces, may endure eccentric and peculiar passions, and hence are not suited to that art which would genuinely represent human nature.[48]

TRAGICOMEDY:
THE REAL STATE OF SUBLUNARY NATURE

> The great source of pleasure is variety. Uniformity must tire at last, though it be uniformity of excellence.
>
> *Life of Butler*

Tragicomedy, that obstinate thorn in the side of generic critics, was accorded the customary academic disapproval and public approbation throughout most of the period; but by the end of the century its descendant, domestic tragedy, had prevailed in the critical camp as well, and the dawning age of republics was able to weep for the distress of citizens as well as to wonder at the fate of kings. It would be an oversimplification to say that a study of critical

---

48. I have deliberately avoided trying to develop Hagstrum's distinction (p. 83) between *la vraie* and *la belle nature*. His analysis is sensitive, and may help to explain how Johnson can use such terms as *drapery, adventitious*, etc., words associated with idealistic aesthetics, and at the same time attack decorum. And yet not only Johnson, but a number of other critics cited in this chapter, both English and French, speak in terms of *la belle nature* when they seem to mean what Hagstrum calls *la vraie nature*. I have found none who consciously distinguishes between theories of generality and Platonism. This is not to say that Hagstrum's distinction is specious or should not be made; it is to say that the distinction is delicate and largely ignored by eighteenth-century critics and modern scholars like Bredvold. When speaking of Platonism in aesthetic matters, they use the term in a most latitudinarian sense; admittedly, I have done the same.

opinion on the subject is confined to those who approved and those who did not; both verdicts were rendered for a number of reasons; and several critics, from Dryden to Johnson himself, assumed at one time or another both sides of the question. Johnson's final pronouncement in favor of tragicomedy has been hailed by Sherbo as one of the few original aspects of the *Preface*.

> . . . here, far more than in the discussion of the unities, Johnson's voice was one of the very few that prepared the way for an acceptance of a new critical position. The four paragraphs in the Preface that re-examine the objections to the "mingled drama" make up the most comprehensive, vigorous, and sane appraisal of the problem up to that time.[49]

Sherbo's opinion is cogent, but Johnson's view is, again, quite individualistic, and the supporters of tragicomedy who succeeded him, like those later critics who praised Shakespeare's characters as real men, had reasons which Johnson might well have found impertinent. To the extent, however, that critics favorable to tragicomedy reasoned from realistic premises, to that extent Johnson does indeed agree with, and largely anticipate, them. Whatever ambiguity there may be about his use of *nature* in his discussion of character, here at least it is certainly sublunary nature to which criticism is appealing.

In the first two-thirds of the century opposition to tragicomedy is determined; its foes ranging from Grubstreet critics like Ralph and Gildon to such subtler aestheticians as Kames, Hurd, and William Richardson. Milton, in 1671, disapproves on conventional grounds of "the Poets error of intermixing Comic stuff with Tragic sadness and gravity; of introducing trivial and vulgar persons, which by all judicious hath bin absurd; and brought in without discretion, corruptly to gratifie the people." He makes two of the capital points used by opponents of tragicomedy: that it confounds the genres and hence is absurd, and that it exists only because the tasteless mob have required it. In addition, it was charged that the comic elements (to use Dryden's words) "will divert the people, and utterly make void" the dramatist's ultimate purpose of arousing terror and pity. Among earlier critics, excepting the mutable Dryden, opinion is next to unanimous and is well stated by Addison:

49. Sherbo, *Samuel Johnson, Editor of Shakespeare*, p. 60.

"The Tragi-Comedy, which is the Product of the *English* Theatre, is one of the most monstrous Inventions that ever enter'd into a Poet's Thoughts. An author might as well think of weaving the Adventures of *Æneas* and *Hudibras* into one Poem, as of writing such a motly Piece of Mirth and Sorrow." Such a form, like those plays with double plots, diverts the concern of the audience "for the principal Action, and breaks the Tide of Sorrow, by throwing it into different Channels." [50]

Almost from the beginning, however, the more sophisticated critics were not content with a mere appeal to decorum, Aristotle, or even to nature. In the apparent need for emotional continuity they believed they had a sufficient psychological motive for their repudiation of the mingled drama. Trapp's *Praelectiones poeticae* employs both generic and psychological arguments. He first condemns tragicomedy because it is not a distinct species, it cannot be located within the authorized generic scheme; but then proceeds to ridicule the entire notion that "Passiones contrariae" can be represented successfully in a single play. Hurd at mid-century expresses intelligently the conservative view. He is confident that "good sense will acknowledge no work of art but such as is composed according to the laws of its *kind*." These kinds have their foundation in nature and should not be mixed or confounded: "true taste requires chaste, severe, and simple pleasures." Thus in tragedy a solemn tone must prevail. Shakespeare has broken this, as he has "almost every other rule, of just criticism"; and his defenders, with "idolatrous admiration," therefore assert that tragedy may at times be gay, even as comedy may sometimes be serious. But this is a false conclusion. Since the end of comedy is painting the manners (*ethos*), it may take on either the pleasant or serious character. But "the end of tragedy being *to excite the stronger passions*, this discordancy in the subject breaks the flow of those passions, and so prevents, or lessens at least, the very effect which this drama primarily intends." Hurd, following almost exactly in Dryden's footsteps eighty years before, argues that the *end* of the form must

50. John Milton, *Works*, vol. 1 (New York: Columbia University Press, 1931), pt. 2, p. 332; Dryden, *Essays*, 1: 208; Joseph Addison and Richard Steele, *The Spectator*, ed. Donald F. Bond, 5 vols. (Oxford: Oxford University Press, 1965), 1: 170–71 (no. 40). See also: Dennis, *Critical Works*, 2: 22, 440; Rowe in *Eighteenth Century Essays on Shakespeare*, pp. 9–10 (and repeated by Giles Jacob, *The Poetical Register*, 2 vols. [London, 1723], 2: 228–29); Gildon, *Works of . . . Shakespear*, 7: 280, vii; James Ralph, *The Touch-Stone* (London, 1728), p. 56.

be considered, and that only those elements may be allowed which conduce to that end.[51] Opposition of a similar, if usually less elegant, quality is undertaken by the magazines of the late forties and fifties. And in the very year of Johnson's *Preface*, the *Critical Review* rejects on traditional grounds Horace Walpole's defense of tragicomedy in the second edition of *The Castle of Otranto*.[52]

From the sixties to a decade or more after the *Preface*, the mixed drama continued to be heavily attacked. Goldsmith, as part of his campaign against sentimental comedy, maintains a strict distinction between the two genres. Although he is concerned with sentimental comedy, not tragicomedy as such, his arguments are precisely those of his predecessors: they are extraordinarily mechanical, punctuated with ritualistic appeals to Aristotle and Boileau. His essay indicates very clearly that the old-fashioned tragicomedy, and the newer sentimental plays, were regarded in the same light by conservative critics. In 1775 William Cooke draws a firm distinction between tragedy and comedy on the basis of subject matter and rank of character. Tragicomedy and sentimental comedy are alike rejected because they want unity of action; and, echoing Dryden a century earlier, Cooke asserts that mirth and low humor are absolutely incompatible with "so refined and exalted a sensation" as compassion.[53] The opponents of both tragicomedy and sentimental tragedy (or comedy) are remarkably consistent for the century from Milton and Dryden through Cooke and Richardson; both forms are accused of breaking down generic distinctions, catering for the unrefined taste of the mob, and disrupting the proper dramatic

51. Trapp, *Praelectiones poeticae*, 2: 142; Hurd, *Horatii epistolae*, 2: 154–55, 103–5 (see also 2: 176, 208–12, 223–25, 238, 240; he usually makes the same objections to domestic tragedy as to tragicomedy). The author of *Some Remarks on Hamlet*, pp. 23–24, argues similarly.

52. *Critical Review* 19 (June 1765): 469. See: *Museum* 3 (1747): 373–77; *Gentleman's Magazine* 22 (April 1752): 163; *London Chronicle*, no. 24 and 147 (1757); *Critical Review* 8 (December 1759): 480.

53. Goldsmith, *Essays and Criticisms*, 3: 58; William Cooke, *The Elements of Dramatic Criticism* (London, 1775), pp. 115–20. See also: Kames, *Elements of Criticism*, 1: 159–60, 375–76; Paul Hiffernan, *Dramatic Genius* (London, 1770), p. 96; Aikin, *Miscellaneous Pieces*, pp. 4–5; William Richardson, *Essays on Shakespeare's Dramatic Characters* (London, 1784), pp. 128 ff.; Frances Burney, *Diary and Letters of Madame D'Arblay*, 2d ed., 7 vols. (London, 1854), 1: 126. In French criticism: Voltaire, *Works*, 32: 123–24; *Greek Theatre of Brumoy*, 3: 153; Terrasson, *Philosophie de l'esprit*, p. 182; Le Blanc, *Letters on the English and French Nations*, 1: 216; 2: 8, 103–4.

effect. With respect to this last point, the argument shifts slightly. While critics like Dryden and Addison feared that comic ingredients would dissipate pity and fear, later critics, moving away from Aristotle and toward Romanticism, were concerned that they might destroy a continuity of emotional tone, a unity of feeling which ought to prevail in serious works. But these two criteria, although belonging to rather different critical traditions, are similar, and hence many conservative and progressive critics found themselves united in their denunciation of the mingled drama.

Of the earlier critics, only Dryden, who later criticized tragicomedy so severely, has left us an extended defense of that form. In the *Essay of Dramatic Poesy* (1668) Lisideius makes the old objection that mirth and compassion are incompatible and that the poet "must of necessity destroy the former by intermingling of the latter." Neander counters, maintaining that the mind *is* capable of passing quickly from one emotion to another; and to demonstrate this flexibility of the mind, he appeals to sensory experience.

> Does not the eye pass from an unpleasant object to a pleasant in a much shorter time than is required to this? and does not the unpleasantness of the first commend the beauty of the latter? . . . contraries, when placed near, set off each other. A continued gravity keeps the spirit too much bent; we must refresh it sometimes, as we bait in a journey, that we may go on with greater ease. A scene of mirth, mixed with tragedy, has the same effect upon us which our music has between the acts. . . . I must therefore have stronger arguments, ere I am convinced that compassion and mirth in the same subject destroy each other.[54]

Dryden makes two of the main arguments to be relied upon by subsequent defenders: he denies outright that the emotions are incompatible, and he asserts that a succession of different emotions, on the contrary, relaxes or refreshes us. And yet Dryden's visual example is unconvincing, as even Gildon perceived. The soul, Gildon argues, cannot pass quickly from one emotion to another: it can do so only by degrees. This inability does not reveal heaviness of soul, as Dryden suggests; indeed, that soul is heavy which is so little engaged in any emotion that it *can* pass easily from one to another. "There is no Agreement," Gildon continues, "betwixt the Passage of the Eye from one Object to another of different,

54. Dryden *Essays*, 1: 69–70.

nay contrary Kinds" and the capacity of the soul to move rapidly from one sentiment to another. And yet even if we take Dryden's simile seriously, "if the Eye be fixt with Pleasure on a grave and serious Object, suppose the taking of our Saviour from the Cross by *Jordan of Antwerp*, the Eye thus attach'd will neither soon nor easily remove it self to look on a droll-piece of *Hemskirk*, &c." Thus Dryden not only misunderstood the nature of the soul, but his simile itself is to no purpose (though in fact, Gildon concedes, most tragicomedies are so feeble as to engage the soul very little one way or another).[55]

Because of the ineptitude of Dryden's argument, and perhaps also because of his later recantation, few followed his lead in defending tragicomedy. Indeed, it is especially perplexing to know how to discuss the "intellectual context" of an idea that is practically nonexistent before its appearance in Johnson's *Preface*; this is not, I think, putting the matter too strongly.[56] But if we cannot balance with defenses the denunciations already surveyed, we can at least trace, in the twenty odd years before 1765, the development of certain ideas which were later used to vindicate the form. As Arthur Sherbo has pointed out, John Upton's *Critical Observations on Shakespeare* (1746) more closely anticipates Johnson's argument than any other earlier work. But although Upton's discussion is more liberal than most, he is defending, not tragicomedy, but the presence of a few comic elements in tragedy. He regards Shakespeare's tragedies as "dramatic heroic poems" whose unity of action is not disturbed by comic passages. He admits that such a mixture is not the happiest for arousing the "tragic passions," but Shakespeare merely throws together some serious and comic characters,

> not two different stories, the one tragic, the other comic . . . as in the Spanish Fryar, and Oroonoko; but the unity of the fable being preserved, several ludicrous characters are interspersed, as in a heroic poem. Nor does the mind from hence suffer any violence, being only accidentally called off from the serious story, to which it soon returns again, and perhaps better prepared by this little refreshment.[57]

55. Gildon, *Works of Shakespear*, 7: 432–34.

56. On tragicomedy, see Green, *Neo-Classic Theory of Tragedy*, pp. 166–80; though he says that Johnson "only precipitated a feeling that was already in the atmosphere," he has uncovered no more defenses than I prior to 1765.

57. Upton, *Critical Observations on Shakespeare*, pp. 95–96.

As we can see, this is very far from the energetic apology which Johnson was to undertake; along with the opponents of tragicomedy, Upton unhesitatingly condemns such productions as *The Spanish Friar* or *Oroonoko*. Yet in effect Upton does what Johnson was to do: he denies that Shakespeare's plays are to be classified as tragedies, and he defends them as a "distinct kind"; like Johnson later and Dryden before him, he finds them less reprehensible because more "refreshing." Some six years later Henry Fielding makes an observation which, although he does not apply it to tragicomedy, has serious implications. He argues in the *Covent-Garden Journal* that the passions are not in themselves comic or tragic, and that the difference lies rather in the manner of treatment.

> It is the same Ambition which raises our Horror in Macbeth, and our Laughter at the drunken Sailors in the Tempest; the same Avarice which causes the dreadful Incidents in the Fatal Curiosity of Lillo, and in the Miser of Moliere; the same Jealousy which forms an Othello, or a Suspicious Husband. No Passion or Humour of the Mind is absolutely either Tragic or Comic in itself. Nero had the Art of making Vanity the Object of Horror, and Domitian, in one Instance, at least, made Cruelty ridiculous.[58]

Once credited, such a theory could undermine the two most persuasive objections to tragicomedy—that it disrupts the genres and that it aspires to combine discordant emotions. If the emotions themselves are relative, there is no reason why they should not be compatible and aroused by the same play. By locating the source of emotional response in treatment rather than the emotions themselves, he has significantly, if inadvertently, challenged the pretensions of generic critics. But Fielding was unwilling to crusade for tragicomedy, and while other mid-century writers—notably those inclined toward psychology like Hartley and Gerard—began to suspect that the emotions were not so mutually exclusive, they were no more prepared than he to conduct an elaborate defense.[59]

It is not until the year of Johnson's *Preface* that we have anything close to a convincing apology for tragicomedy, and this by a man hardly disposed to martyrdom. In the preface to the first

58. Fielding, *The Covent-Garden Journal*, ed. G. E. Jensen, 2 vols. (New Haven: Yale University Press, 1915), 2: 63 (18 July 1752).

59. See David Hartley, *Observations on Man*, 3 vols. (London, 1791), 1: 431, and Gerard, *Essay on Taste*, p. 73.

edition of *The Castle of Otranto* (published Christmas Eve, 1764) Horace Walpole defends his inclusion of domestics, who may be considered "too little serious for the general cast of the story"; they oppose, and contrast with, the principal characters, he contends, and they materially advance the plot. In the preface to the second edition (1765), he again defends his use of such low people, arguing "my rule was nature"—and, a few sentences later: "That great master of nature, Shakespeare, was the model I copied." He believes that the contrast between the sublime sentiments of heroes and the naïve passions of domestics increases our pity for the former. He approves of Shakespeare's gravediggers, the buffoonery of Polonius, and the Roman mob in *Coriolanus*. The speeches of Antony and Brutus are rendered more effective by the contrast with "the rude bursts of nature from the mouths of their auditors." He then takes exception to Voltaire and inquires why, if the French critic allows comedy to have a mixture of the serious, tragedy cannot include comic elements; after all, it is a "picture of human life." [60] Now it will not do to accuse Walpole of democratic sympathies: the domestics, we notice, serve only to augment our pity for the heroes, and their naïveté contributes to our admiration of the heroes' wisdom; Antony's speech, contrasted with that of the mob, is enhanced. But it is significant that two defenses of tragicomedy and of Shakespeare's comic scenes which appeal to sublunary nature should appear in 1765; tragedy is to be a picture of human life. Four years later Mrs. Montagu forthrightly praises Shakespeare for breaking down "the barriers that had before confined the dramatic writers to the regions of comedy, or tragedy" and favors tragicomedy because it makes available to the poet a wider range of material:

60. Walpole, *The Castle of Otranto* (London, 1811), pp. ix–xii. Voltaire, in his account of comedy, sounds very like Johnson on tragicomedy: Comedy "contains that mixture of gravity and mirth, that succession of ridiculous and pathetic events, with which the life of man is variegated. . . . The same person has often laughed and cried at the same thing, in the space of a quarter of an hour" (*Critical Essays on Dramatic Poetry* [London, 1761], pp. 227–28). In certain simple, pathetic passages, he continues, "tragedy and comedy seem to meet. It is here alone that their limits are confounded together. They afterwards return, each to its natural sphere. The one assumes the comic tone; the other the sublime" (p. 229). Hurd approves of Voltaire's opinion, but Walpole's criticism is just; Voltaire, in allowing any compatibility of the emotions whatever, has conceded too much. Clearly the archclassicist is trying at once to accommodate certain increasingly fashionable aesthetic values, and to preserve tragedy in its purity.

Shakespeare "perceived the fertility of the subjects that lay between the two extreams." [61] After 1770 tragicomedy rapidly became fashionable even in criticism, and its supporters no longer needed the courage of their convictions to express them.[62]

The ascendancy of the bourgeois drama in France required her critics to devote much time to the nature and validity of the genre. I shall examine only two of them to indicate what had developed between the mid-forties and the early seventies. In his *Discours sur le théâtre anglois* (1746), the first of eight volumes containing synopses of ten Shakespeare plays and some Restoration dramas, the Abbé La Place, translator of *Tom Jones* and *David Simple*, displays an intelligent orthodoxy confronted with an attractive heresy. One day, he says, he reproached "a famous Englishman," for disparaging the Tuileries and praising Versailles. The Englishman replies at length, comparing the regularity of the Tuileries with the diversity of Versailles. Although the one is symmetrical, the other perpetually surprises; the one is regular, but reveals all at a glance. Such is the French theater. It follows the rules, but the rules by their austerity may deprive one of pleasures; and after all, says the Englishman, "Je préfère la licence qui me réveille, à l'exactitude qui m'endort." This answer, says La Place, and Pope's preface to his edition of Shakespeare, convinced him that he should undertake the project of acquainting his countrymen with the English dramatist. In the discussion that follows, he is remarkably sympathetic with the form of Shakespeare's tragedies, although he is unwilling to approve of tragicomedy. La Place maintains the superiority of the French form, but he concedes that English pieces which follow the rules often want variety and seem cold, and that French taste is "peut-être trop délicat." Tragicomedy is contrary to reason, to nature, and to sentiment, but it pleases the English, who are less fond of regularity than the French and demand more realism. La Place, then, is a good and consistent neoclassicist; he appeals to ideal nature to reject the improper realism of tragicomedy. But by embracing a

---

61. Montagu, *Essay on Shakespeare*, p. 66.

62. Examples are numerous but not germane to this study. We do find a grudging defense of tragicomedy by George Colman as early as 1761: Shakespeare's plays are an "indigested jumble," but time and experience have proved they can be effective (*Critical Reflections*, 2 vols. [London, 1787], 2: 115). In 1763 John Brown is mildly sympathetic with Chinese "tragicomedy" (*Dissertation on the Rise . . . of Poetry and Music* [London, 1763], p. 169).

modified critical relativism he has been able to do justice to the English genre.[63]

We have seen that the opponents of tragicomedy, both French and English, often condemned the newer, domestic tragedy along with it. The two are not the same, however, and it remained for Diderot to draw the proper distinctions. He calls for a "tragédie domestique & bourgeoise" and cites *The London Merchant* as the finest example of this type, though he also appeals to Shakespeare. In every moral object there is a middle between two extremes, and in drama this middle is *le genre sérieux*. This genre embraces all the conditions of society, all the important actions of life, the imaginary and the real world. Both *le genre sérieux* and comedy can capture all the comic nuances; both it and tragedy can embody the pathetic nuances. Tragicomedy, however, Diderot roundly condemns. This genre rather *confounds* the two extremes, and, in its sharp contrasts, destroys unity. Repeating the opinion of critics three generations before, he sees nature as establishing an impenetrable barrier between the two extreme genres. In his censure of the grave senator playing *débauché* in *Venice Preserv'd*, or of similar disruptions of decorum in *Hamlet*, Diderot is thus the irreprehensible neoclassicist. But his new genre overcomes these objections; it has a *ton*, a sublimity even, all its own. It is closer to life; it is new.[64] As we have seen earlier, Diderot unreservedly rejected ideal character types; both in that discussion and here he is clearly arguing that drama ought to imitate sublunary nature. But at the same time he is as convinced as the most conservative critics that successful literature cannot dispense with a "continuity of tone." Thus he accuses tragicomedy, not of deviating from ideal nature, as La Place did, but of breaking this emotional continuity. His new genre, in imitating the variety and realism of "life," has all the virtues of tragicomedy and none of its defects. It can imitate the multiplicity of historical truth without sacrificing the unity of effect. In this way, an *order* is

63. P. A. de La Place, *Le théâtre anglois*, vol. 1 (London, 1746), pp. xvii-xxiii, xxvii and see pp. xlviii-lxxxii. See also Mercier, *Du théâtre*, pp. 94–108, who argues directly for the mingled drama and appeals to sublunary nature, and Le Tourneur, *Shakespeare traduit de l'anglois*, 1: lxxv (however, he distinguishes between the passions proper to each in 10: 236).

64. Diderot, *Oeuvres de théâtre*, 1: 212–56 and passim. In his *Essais sur la peinture*, Diderot extensively defends his *genre sérieux* because of its realism and the democratic sympathy which it arouses in us for the common people.

imposed on the "diary of fortune"—not an order which idealizes by selecting the noblest from the "gross and trumpery," but which casts upon *all* the objects a uniform light. In effect Diderot is saying that a drama may contain any number of elements, high and low, serious and comic, so long as they are all *treated* in a consistent manner to produce a unified effect. The relativity of the passions, a thought suggested but undeveloped by Fielding twenty years before, has provided the foundation for a new and most decidedly unclassical dramatic theory.

In the *Preface* Johnson freely admits that Shakespeare's plays

> are not in the rigorous or critical sense either tragedies or comedies, but compositions of a distinct kind; exhibiting the real state of sublunary nature, which partakes of good and evil, joy and sorrow, mingled with endless variety of proportion and innumerable modes of combination; and expressing the course of the world, in which the loss of one is the gain of another; in which, at the same time, the reveller is hasting to his wine, and the mourner burying his friend; in which the malignity of one is sometimes defeated by the frolick of another; and many mischiefs and many benefits are done and hindered without design.[65]

The ancients, Johnson continues, selected from this "chaos of mingled purposes and casualties" to create their comedies and tragedies, while Shakespeare has instead joined both laughter and sorrow. This practice is against the laws of criticism, but "there is always an appeal from criticism to nature." Tragicomedy instructs us by giving, more accurately than the other two forms, "the appearance of life, by shewing how great machinations and slender designs may promote or obviate one another, and the high and the low co-operate in the general system by unavoidable concatenation." Furthermore, its ability to please is not destroyed by the apparently incongruous passions which it evokes. Experience indicates that different emotions can succeed each other without difficulty: "Fiction cannot move so much, but that the attention may be easily transferred." The disruption of an emotion (e.g., melancholy) may in fact be a relief for many rather than a disturbance. And finally, he decides, "upon the whole, all pleasure consists in variety." In all his works, Shakespeare alternates seriousness with merriment and "never fails to attain his purpose." Once we understand this intent

65. *Works*, 7: 66; all further references will be from pp. 66–69.

and appreciate his success, we may neglect the objections of Rymer and Voltaire. We do not mind the low characters in *Hamlet* or the absurdities of Polonius; and even "the Gravediggers themselves may be heard with applause." Johnson's defense of tragicomedy, animated and lucid, far surpasses any of the earlier apologies. Only Dryden, ninety-seven years before, had argued with such spirit, and then it was marred by ineptitude and inconsistency. By contrast with this, Upton seems poorly cautious, and even Walpole, with his aristocratic condescension, fails to strike us with such force. But Johnson furnishes no new arguments; his contribution is in gathering together all the tentative defenses and articulating them more persuasively: that Shakespeare's plays are not to be judged by rigidly generic standards, that tragicomedy is closer than the other more selective genres to the complexity of real life, that the emotions it arouses are not necessarily discordant, and that it refreshes us by its pleasing variety.

Variety—this is the primary value of tragicomedy; it, more than any other genre, pleases us by variety; more than any other genre it imitates the "endless variety . . . and innumerable modes of combination" of real life. By this quality above all the "real state of sublunary nature" is known. Both Walpole and Mrs. Montagu are clearly appealing to this sort of nature; to do so becomes commonplace by the end of the century. But of the earlier critics only G. E. Lessing (1767) rivals Johnson in his enthusiasm for tragicomedy. Using the plays of Lope de Vega as his example, Lessing advocates a type of drama in which the farcical and the interesting are combined. Lope had himself apologized for the mixed form, laying the blame, as usual, upon the bad taste of the people, who demanded it. Lessing quotes Lope, but rebukes him for being so apologetic; after all (he says) Lope himself recognized that "die Natur selbst lehrt uns diese Mannigfaltigkeit, von der sie einen Theil ihrer Schönheit entlehnet." Lessing, in his own ensuing comments, defines *nature* in just this way, as a diversity, a tangled mixture of the trivial and the sublime.[66] Considering the paucity of interesting defenses before

---

66. Lessing, *Hamburgische Dramaturgie*, 2: 129–32 (st. 69, which was written December 1767). At about the same time, Johnson's friend Thomas Percy, in his "Origin of the English Stage," *Reliques of Ancient English Poetry*, 2d ed. (London, 1767), distinguishes Shakespeare's history plays from either tragedy or comedy and vindicates them "in defiance of Aristotle and all the critics of the classic school." However, Percy refrains from attacking the unities explicitly, and he condemns tragicomedy as "unnatural."

1765, it is rather remarkable that we should find, in the space of three years, three such comprehensive vindications as these of Walpole, Johnson, and Lessing. To defend tragicomedy, all three are appealing to that same nature which was used to justify the lowness and multiplicity of Shakespeare's characters: a sublunary nature marked by realism and variety. As we have seen, neoclassicists who opposed both indecorous characters and tragicomedy simply reaffirmed the pre-eminence of ideal or general nature in aesthetic matters. For example, Gravina had defended Ariosto's mingling of high and low scenes because it "resembles the productions of nature, which are never simple, but always compounded." But, counters Thomas Warton:

> Does not the nature of heroic poetry consist in a due selection of objects? . . . Is it not its immediate province to separate high from low, fair from deformed; to compound rather than to copy nature, and to present those exalted combinations, which never existed together, amid the general and necessary defects of real life?[67]

For years after 1765 critics would reason thus. William Richardson decides that Shakespeare followed nature "in a limited sense. He copied the reality of external things; but disregarded the idea of excellence which seems inherent in the human mind." And the author of the Cursory Remarks on Tragedy (1774), possibly also Richardson, gives Johnson just the answer he ought to have expected:

> Let it not be advanced as a merit, let it not be urged even as an excuse, that Shakespear followed nature in the busy walks of men; that he presented her, as he found her, naked and unadorned: for there are parts of nature that require concealment; there are others too that by the thin transparent veil, by the light, the careless drapery, are greatly heightened and improved. . . . The scene of the grave-diggers in Hamlet is certainly real life, or as it is vulgarly termed, highly natural, yet how misplaced, how unworthy the tragedian.[68]

67. Thomas Warton, Observations on the "Fairy Queen," 2d ed., 2 vols. (London, 1762), 1: 227–28.

68. Richardson, Essays on Dramatic Characters, p. 145; Cursory Remarks, pp. 39–40. His allusion to the "busy walks of men" suggests that he is replying to Mrs. Montagu, who, it will be remembered, had praised Shakespeare for drawing his characters from the "busy walks of human life."

That Johnson has abandoned all notions of general or ideal nature is indisputable. This is a clean break, not only with orthodox theory, but with his own earlier beliefs. As is well known, Johnson had criticized tragicomedy for the traditional reasons in *Rambler* no. 125; and though he favors it, for reasons similar to those exhibited in the *Preface,* in number 156, he emphasizes that one does not justify tragicomedy by appealing to the example of Shakespeare, but rather that Shakespeare himself must be praised all the more for his success, that he might have been greater had he "not counter-acted himself; and we might have been more interested in the distresses of his heroes had we not been so frequently diverted by the jokes of his buffoons." [69] In moving from the problem of dramatic character to that of the mingled drama, Johnson has summoned to his assistance that nature which is the diversity of real life; he has assumed a position which intelligent neoclassicists were then opposing and would oppose for years thereafter. Richardson, as we have just seen, criticized Shakespeare because he ignored the "idea of excellence" for the "reality of external things." This is Platonic aesthetics; and on precisely these grounds Johnson himself will deplore Shakespeare's violation of poetic justice. But as he was later to confess, even "uniformity of excellence" must tire at last; it is clearly with this mind that he defends tragicomedy. Sherbo is therefore quite correct: seen against the history of ideas, and his own individual history, Johnson's defense is bold and uncommon. We are justified, then, in asking two related questions: has Johnson compromised his critical principles to defend tragicomedy, and is his defense inconsistent with his understanding of dramatic characters as representing general nature? Without attempting to make Johnson what he is not, a thoroughly consistent theorist, we may make some jottings toward a resolution of these problems.

In interpreting a critic, one always runs the risk of reading him too stringently to do justice to his opinions, or so broadly that he

---

69. *Works,* 5: 69. Sherbo, *Samuel Johnson, Editor of Shakespeare,* p. 4, says of this *Rambler:* "The discussion of tragicomedy is contained, in little, in this essay." But Johnson is considerably more cautious in *Rambler* no. 156 than he is in the *Preface.* Cf. *Rambler* no. 107, where he comments that he tried to preserve consistency of tone in the *Rambler* "because it seems absurd for an author to counteract himself. . . . I have endeavoured sometimes to divert, and sometimes to elevate; but have imagined it an useless attempt to disturb merriment by solemnity, or interrupt seriousness by drollery" (*Works,* 4: 205).

seems to have no coherent or consistent principles whatever. In examining Johnson on dramatic character and tragicomedy, one sees his criticism at its most supple, and hence risks running into the latter extreme. If Johnson denies traditional notions of decorum and of generic distinctions when neoclassicists were supporting them, if he is found sometimes preferring men who "feel as we do" to heroes, or praising the realism of sublunary nature, is he not pre-Romantic in some sense at least, or at least radically inconsistent? But what Paul Ramsey has said about the importance of the general and particular in neoclassicism can be said of the other supposed "polarities" of Romanticism and classicism:

> The neo-classical insists on the universal, the romantic on the individual. So it is often said, and truly said, but I would insist on the "insists." Neo-classical theory insists on the one; it does not exclude the other; its theory provides a frame that can comprehend the real partial truth of the romantic ideal of the importance of the individual.[70]

So it is also of idealism vs. realism, uniformity vs. variety, and other trite if partly true distinctions.[71] Johnson praises both general and sublunary nature because both teach us about the world, a world which contains variety and complexity, but through which run the certitudes of human nature and morality, essentially immutable, though assuming many outward shapes. Tragicomedy instructs us by displaying the "innumerable modes of combination . . . of the world," just as the hermit may learn from Shakespeare's characters to estimate the "transactions of the world." The sentimentalists, whether they were theorizing about dramatic character or domestic tragedy, made much of sympathy and realism, values which tend to confuse art with life; whereas the dogmatic neoclassicists, with inflexible notions of decorum and genre, ran the danger

70. Ramsey, *The Lively and the Just*, p. 7.

71. With respect to "variety," for example, Dryden, *Essays*, 1: 249, defending the double plot of *The Spanish Friar*, appeals to the pleasure produced by alternating emotions. Both Gerard, *Essay on Taste*, pp. 10, 32 and passim, and Kames, *Elements of Criticism*, 1: 380–408, find genuine pleasure in variety and novelty, and this quality is often associated by Gerard with nature (since one of his examples of this variety is the uneven surface of the earth, there can be little question as to whether or not this nature is "sublunary"). Johnson approves of such alternating emotions in his "Notes to Shakespeare" (*Works*, 7: 489, 8: 602).

of severing art from life altogether. Johnson is too much an empiricist to scorn the "diary of fortune": poetry, after all, must teach us about the condition in which we find ourselves, and we happen to find ourselves in a fallen world. But he is not about to confuse fortune with Providence. Poetry must not only instruct us in the variety and vicissitudes of the real world; it must teach us to look beyond them by looking within; it must show the essential human nature as little disfigured as possible by the drapery of custom, the "gross and trumpery." Theories of decorum and genre, however, are worse than futile if they are superficially understood. If in Blake's scheme Johnson is on the side of the idiots, he will not be found standing next to Rymer or Voltaire.

But Johnson is to be distinguished as much from a Diderot as a Voltaire. In Diderot, whose theories of sympathy we shall consider shortly, we can see the implications which later critics were to unfold from the new values of realism and particularity. Both he and Johnson find appealing the realism and variety of the mingled drama and Shakespeare's characters; but for Johnson these things are valuable because they have increased our understanding, not because they have exercised our sensibility. He talks nowhere about sympathizing with the characters; he is not concerned with Diderot's continuity of emotional tone. Johnson's defense of tragicomedy, it is true, was adopted by later critics and used for sentimental purposes.[72] But for Johnson, to call Shakespeare's heroes men was not a cry for brotherhood; to defend tragicomedy not a plea to shed the social tear. Hasty critics may imagine similarities between Johnson's vindication of tragicomedy and Diderot's defense of bourgeois drama in his *Essais sur la peinture*. But Diderot, though he was in his grave in 1795 when this edition was published, would not, perhaps, have protested strenuously the form of the date on its title page: "L'An Quatrième de la République." What Johnson would have thought of it, however, is not beyond speculation. The apparent resemblances notwithstanding, they were men of different worlds.

---

72. William Kenrick, for example, uses Johnson's defense to invalidate Goldsmith's attack on sentimental comedy, even though this was an attack with which Johnson was probably in sympathy. He quotes copiously from the *Preface* and asserts: "When I add, that these are the sentiments of Dr. Samuel Johnson . . . I may safely leave the decision of this dispute to the reader" (quoted in Goldsmith, *Essays and Criticisms*, 3: 63 ff.).

Chapter III

Aut Prodesse aut Delectare

Johnson's criticism in the *Preface* is both theoretical and specific. Thus far we have explored the theoretical issues mainly: consensus, the characters and generic nature of Shakespeare's plays. When Johnson comes to consider Shakespeare's particular faults, and examines the extent of his learning and the quality of his genius, he becomes more specific and detailed. But several quite theoretical subjects taken up in the *Preface* have yet to be examined. It has seemed proper to discuss in one section the dramatic unities, dramatic illusion, and dramatic pleasure. For Johnson, as for most critics of the period, these three topics were strongly interrelated: the unities and dramatic illusion were alike defended or opposed because they were thought necessary, or unnecessary, to dramatic pleasure. And since for the neoclassicist instruction, as well as pleasure, is one of the ends of drama, many critics, having moved logically from the unities to dramatic illusion and pleasure—to an analysis, in other words, of dramatic effect—proceeded to consider the entire purpose of tragedy, in what ways it might instruct as well as please. In the second section I shall examine these theories. Johnson's discussion of the dramatic unities, illusion, and pleasure, running to seven pages in the Yale edition, touches only slightly on instruction. However, when later enumerating Shakespeare's faults, he writes at length of his gravest and most reprehensible deficiency, his want of a moral plan. Thus it has seemed convenient to consider at once the entire problem of dramatic effect.

THE UNITIES AND DRAMATIC ILLUSION: TO PLEASE

> *Bottom.* There are things in this Comedy of *Piramus* and Thisby, that will neuer please. First, *Piramus* must draw a sword to kill himselfe; which the Ladies cannot abide. How answere you that?

72

Snout. Berlaken, a parlous feare.
Starveling. I beleeue we must leaue the killing out, when all is done.
Bot. Not a whit. I haue a deuice to make all well. Write me a Prologue, and let the Prologue seeme to say, we will do no harme with our swords, and that *Pyramus* is not kill'd indeede: and for the more better assurance, tell them, that I *Piramus* am not *Piramus*, but *Bottome*, the Weauer; this will put them out of feare.

Midsummer Night's Dream

Bottom was neither the only nor the least ingenious theorist to try to solve the problem of dramatic illusion and dramatic pleasure. If, to be affected by a tragedy, we must believe in its reality, is it not then indecent (at the least) to take pleasure in those misfortunes of others that we regard as genuine? Now Bottom and Dr. Johnson are perhaps not so different, for if the weaver's solution was simply to break dramatic illusion, Johnson's was forthrightly to deny it. But although Johnson's denial is itself uncompromising enough, his entire discussion embraces contradictory features and produces some curious arguments. Despite his preliminary confessions of temerity, his assault on the unities is neither so original nor so audacious as his defense of tragicomedy; Sherbo is quite correct in evaluating the novelty of Johnson's sentiments here at a rather lower rate than earlier admirers were wont to do.[1] On the other hand, Johnson's treatment is again marked by individualism, if not idiosyncrasy; it reveals at once a familiarity with earlier criticism, and a disdain for mere consistency. I should like first to examine the arguments for and against the unities, and then discuss dramatic illusion and pleasure.

In general terms, the vicissitudes of the three unities have been adequately charted; another study would be unwelcome and indeed quite otiose.[2] But if the error at one time was to exag-

1. Arthur Sherbo, *Samuel Johnson, Editor of Shakespeare. With an Essay on The Adventurer, Illinois Studies in Language and Literature*, vol. 42 (Urbana: University of Illinois Press, 1956), p. 57.

2. See C. C. Green, *The Neo-Classic Theory of Tragedy in England during the Eighteenth Century* (Cambridge: Harvard University Press, 1934), pp. 194–218; Sherbo, *Samuel Johnson, Editor of Shakespeare*, pp. 57–59; R. W. Babcock, *The Genesis of Shakespeare Idolatry, 1766–1799* (Chapel Hill: University of North Carolina Press, 1931), pp. 45–56; T. M. Raysor, "The Downfall of the Three Unities," *Modern Language Notes* 42 (1927): 1–9.

gerate the originality of Johnson's position, it would be equally unwise to regard the issue as moribund by 1765.[3] From the beginning, the unities had been defended because they contributed, presumably, to verisimilitude. So it is argued in the *Defense of an Essay of Dramatic Poesy*: "The less change of place there is, the less time is taken up in transporting the persons of the drama, with analogy to reason; and in that analogy, or resemblance of fiction to truth, consists the excellency of the play." Dryden's view is adopted with remarkable unanimity.[4] Seventy years later, mid-century critics defend the unities with no less conviction. Warton praises *The Tempest* for observing them, and the anonymous author of the *Remarks on Mr. Mason's Elfrida* inquires in 1752:

> And now, after all, will any one say, that by preserving *all the Unities*, and subjecting himself to the most scrupulous and strict Observance of the dramatic Rules, as laid down by the best Critics of Antiquity, will any one say that the Genius of our Poet is at all strait'ned or cramp'd? Are those Rules to be look'd on as harsh and galling Chains, and not rather as *ipsis ex vincula sortis*?

Six years later Armstrong insists on them even more uncompromisingly: "they are established upon the firm foundation of good sense" and are as necessary to drama "as walls, doors, windows, a roof and chimneys are . . . to a convenient habitation." Without them, all is "irregular, slovenly, blundering, absurd, and improbable"; and although Shakespeare's example has encouraged us to be permissive, we must neither forget nor excuse his deficiencies. Finally, Paul Hiffernan provides in 1770 as resolute a defense of the unities as the most dogmatic neoclassicist could desire. As for unity of action and place, he says, "a sound and thinking mind is abhorrent from such a frequency of violent transitions, as must

3. T. R. Lounsbury, *Shakespeare and Voltaire* (New York: Scribner's Sons, 1902), p. 156, says that of mid-century defenders of Shakespeare none "had the audacity to deny the obligation of observing the unities. Disbelief in the Trinity would have incurred at the time less reprobation." As Raysor has demonstrated, this is undoubtedly false. On the other hand, aesthetic heresy had by no means certainly triumphed by 1765.

4. John Dryden, *Essays*, ed. W. P. Ker, 2 vols. (Oxford: Oxford University Press, 1926), 1: 128. See also: Thomas Rymer, *The Critical Works*, ed. C. A. Zimansky (New Haven: Yale University Press, 1956), p. 27; Charles Gildon, *Works of Shakespear*, vol. 7 (London, 1710), xxix; Joseph Trapp, *Praelectiones poeticae*, 3d ed., 2 vols. (London, 1736), 2: 154–55, 165–66.

destroy the first adopted illusion, and prevent its attention from fixing on a determined place." He is rather more lenient regarding time, but asserts, like Gildon sixty years before, that the real action of the drama ought ideally to be completed within the time of its representation.[5]

The periodicals contain many similar defenses. For example, the *Critical Review*, examining Richard Glover's *Medea* four years before the *Preface*, righteously vindicates the partisans of Greek drama:

> Some half-learned mongrel critics have lately taken it into their heads to bark loudly against the antient tragedy, which they don't understand, and been remarkably facetious on the chorus; but while the taste for antiquity is productive of such works as Medea, those who have any regard to their own pleasure will be careful how they condemn it.[6]

Those who were "facetious on the chorus" angered many conservative critics, who used the chorus as yet another justification for the unities. Mason, for example, believes that the "admission of a continued chorus" aids in dramatic illusion, and that the chorus itself would be absurd if the unities were not followed. The panegyrist responsible for the *Remarks on Elfrida*, seizing yet another opportunity to demonstrate his devotion, hails Mason's argument as convincing beyond conjecture. Francklyn in 1760 advocates following the unities, and regards the chorus as both necessary for the Greek theater and "useful and ornamental" for the English. If the public will not tolerate the chorus and its attendant simplicity of action, he says, we may at least enjoy such regular productions in the closet; thither we may carry *Elfrida* and *Caractacus* and con-

5. Warton's *Adventurer* no. 97, in A. Chalmers, ed., *The British Essayists*, vols. 23–25 (London, 1817), 25: 37; *Remarks on Mr. Mason's Elfrida* (London, 1752), p. 56; John Armstrong, *Miscellanies*, 2 vols. (London, 1770), 2: 241; Paul Hiffernan, *Dramatic Genius* (London, 1770), pp. 64–66. William Mason, *Elfrida, a Dramatic Poem* (London, 1752), pp. ii–ix, wishes Shakespeare had imitated the Greeks; William Guthrie, *An Essay upon English Tragedy* (London, [1747?]), p. 28, says the unities are essential; Melopoyn's tragedy is praised for following the unities in *Roderick Random*, chap. 62.

6. *Critical Review* 12 (October 1761): 303. Mason's *Elfrida*, Glover's *Boadicea*, and Home's *Douglas* are praised for their regularity: see *Monthly Review* 6 (May 1752): 387–90; Arthur Murphy, *The Gray's-Inn Journal*, 2 vols. (London, 1756), 2: 50; *Gentleman's Magazine* 23 (December 1753): 578; *London Chronicle*, no. 36 (22–24 March 1757).

trast them with Murphy's wretched if lucrative plays. In 1763 John
Brown agrees that the unities are merely the logical result of the
"choir." The chorus gives "so forcible a Conviction to the Senses,
of the *Sameness* of *Place*, and *Shortness* of *Time*, that any Deviation
from this apparent Unity must shock the Imagination with an
Improbability too gross to be endured." But he does not suggest that
the chorus be revived in modern dramas. As late as 1775 William
Cooke is saying much the same.[7]

The three unities elicited from French criticism a tiresome unanimity.[8] In Voltaire especially they discovered an articulate and
indefatigable champion. There are "laws of decency" (e.g., no
bloodshed on the stage) which are rather arbitrary and admit of
some exceptions; and then there are the "fundamental laws of
the theatre, which are the three unities." Because the mind is unable
to comprehend several things at once, there must be unity of
action; nature alone shows us this. And from this unity the other
two are deduced, all established on common sense and facilitating
noble simplicity. For more than forty years Voltaire defended the
unities against all those (chiefly the ghost of Shakespeare and his
living, unrepentant admirers) who presumed to doubt their necessity. And yet even before Voltaire had finished crusading for what
seemed a lost cause, Diderot, in an essay published in 1772, defends
the unities in a fresh way: our attention must be concentrated and
unperplexed in following dramatic works, which aim at producing

---

7. Mason, *Elfrida*, pp. iii–vii; *Remarks on Mr. Mason's Elfrida*, pp. 9, 15,
57–61; Thomas Francklyn, *A Dissertation on Antient Tragedy* (London, 1760),
pp. 23–24; John Brown, *A Dissertation on the Rise . . . of Poetry and Music*
(London, 1763), p. 42; William Cooke, *The Elements of Dramatic Criticism*
(London, 1775), p. 11.

8. See Corneille's *Third Discourse* and the examen of *La Suivante*; see also
his prefatory material before *Clitandre* and *La Veuve*, the examen of *Le Cid*.
Cf. Racine's preface to *Bérénice*. André Dacier, *Aristotle's Art of Poetry* (London,
1705), pp. 116–17, defends all the unities. For the eighteenth century see: Charles
Porée, *An Oration in Which an Enquiry Is Made Whether the Stage Is . . .
a School for . . . Virtue* (London, 1734), p. 68; Jean Baptiste Boyer, *Réflexions
historiques et critiques sur le goût* (Amsterdam, 1743), p. 92 and passim; P. A.
de La Place, *Le théâtre anglois*, vol. 1 (London, 1746), p. lxx; C. J. F. Hénault,
Nouveau théâtre françois (Paris, 1747), sig.. A2–A2ᵛ; L. J. L. de Pouilly, *Theory
of Agreeable Sensations* (London, 1749), p. 44, defends the unities, from newer,
psychological principles, against La Motte.

a consistent emotional effect.[9] The contrast between Voltaire and Diderot is instructive. As we have seen, Voltaire attacked tragicomedy on generic grounds, Diderot because it broke continuity of tone; so now Voltaire, the classicist, argues dogmatically for the unities, whereas the progressive Diderot reasons from psychological premises. If the claims of Aristotle and his commentators can no longer command an artist's obedience, those of the "sensibility" can.

Fundamentally, the three unities were defended because (it was thought) they were indispensable for credibility. It was also argued that they produced a desirable simplicity of plot; and finally, some contended that truly classical drama must have the chorus, and that the chorus—a group of characters continually present and vocal—is incredible if the unities are not preserved as well. Thus all the arguments, ultimately, turn on the presumed importance of credibility; for the century from Dryden until Diderot, apologies are as little various as they are inventive. Critics skeptical of the unities, however, argued from several possible positions, although the commonest attack was simply to assert that the requirements of credibility were not so rigorous as conservative critics believed, that once we know that a play is not reality (and we know so immediately), any rules may be broken with impunity. Others conceived a sort of balance sheet of beauties: it is well enough to preserve the unities, but often to do so results in the sacrifice of even greater beauties. Finally, some critics, while disinclined to obey the three unities in a dogmatic way, wished to preserve one, all-encompassing unity, which they called unity of action, unity of character, unity of tone, or the like. In examining these more liberal strains of criticism, it is important to remember two things: first, that the attack on the unities was not infrequently coupled with an attack on all the old rules, which were increasingly regarded by some as too abstract or mechanical; but, secondly, that critics attacking the unities often provided a "unity" of their own devising to satisfy the obvious requirements of order.

As is well known, Farquhar, in his *Discourse upon Comedy* (1702), conducts one of the earliest attacks on the unities. Even the most

---

9. Voltaire, *Critical Essays on Dramatic Poetry* (London, 1761), pp. 21, 44–46; Denis Diderot, *Oeuvres de théâtre* . . . , 2 vols. (Amsterdam, 1772), 1: 156–58. For a late, traditional defense, see Voltaire's impassioned *Letter to the French Academy* (1776) in *Oeuvres complètes*, 70 vols. (Paris, 1785–89), 49: 318 (and cf. his prefatory letter to *Irène* two years later, ibid., 6: 257).

particular critic, he observes, will permit a play, normally three hours in length, to cover a dramatic span of twelve hours, and some will even allow twenty-four. But if so much is allowed, why not much more? "For that a thousand years should come within the compass of three hours is no more an impossibility than that two minutes should be contained in one." Unity of place is no different: if the dramatist is able to make you think the stage is one other place, why not several places? Minimizing the demands of credibility, Farquhar simply suggests: "If you please to let your fancy take post, it will perform the journey in the same moment of time [as the playwright fashions it] without any disturbance in the world to your person." Since the mind of man is so malleable, why should the poet constrict his action unnecessarily? A few years later Gildon puts into the mouth of "Tyro" an adequate summary of Farquhar's reasoning. But he is no more persuaded by Farquhar's argument than he had been by Dryden's defense of tragicomedy; he merely retorts: "If you once pass the Bounds of *Truth* and *Probability*, I see not where you can stop, and why you should stop any where"— hence, there is all the more reason for not passing these bounds at all![10] Gildon's answer was accorded frequent, though by no means universal, approbation. The reaction, for example, of the author of the pamphlet *Some Remarks on the Tragedy of Hamlet* (1736) was rather: "If our Imagination will not bear a strong Imposition, surely no Play ought to be supposed to take more Time than is really employ'd in the Acting"—hence, the rules, especially the unity of time, are vain and arbitrary. Both this author and Gildon attempt to reduce the other side to absurdity. For Gildon, if we break the rules at all, we can do anything; hence, they must not be broken at all; whereas our pamphleteer, seeing that even the rules themselves fail to be sufficiently restricting, concludes that they may be utterly ignored. Such expenditures of ingenuity, while not unique to either side, are more often resorted to by Gildon's opponents.[11]

10. Farquhar, *Discourse*, in *Eighteenth-Century Critical Essays*, ed. Scott Elledge, 2 vols. (Ithaca: Cornell University Press, 1961), 1: 97–99; Charles Gildon, *The Complete Art of Poetry*, 2d ed., 2 vols. (London, 1724), 1: 228–29, 231.

11. *Some Remarks on the Tragedy of Hamlet* (London, 1736), p. 52. Fielding, *Tom Jones*, bk. 5, chap. 1, asks why the audience may not "be wafted fifty miles as well as five." And cf. William Chaignean's *History of Jack Connor* (1753): "If twenty-four hours business can be shown in so short a time [three hours], we may as well have twenty-four Years" (quoted in R. G. Noyes, *The Thespian Mirror* [Providence: Brown University Press, 1953], p. 216). Those

Thus at mid-century the earl of Orrery, admitting that we are "methodists in regard to Shakespear," urges that the dramatist would have sacrificed "certain strokes of nature" had he followed the unities. At about the same time Gerard confidently rejects the unities as *essential* to the drama: Shakespeare demonstrates that a dramatist may ignore them and yet have "other qualities productive of very high gratification," but he is perceptibly reticent to enumerate these other qualities.[12] Similar opinions are often found in the mid-century reviews, where such virtues as energy, nature (as variety), realism, sublimity, passion, etc., are opposed to the unities, and where, to vindicate these contentions, the example of Shakespeare is regularly invoked.[13] Although more infrequent, similar arguments are made in France.[14]

Finally, there were those critics who exalted one sort of unity over all the others. The unity of action, of course, had always been regarded as primary. John Upton's *Critical Observations on Shake-*

---

holding Farquhar's belief did not always reject the unities completely; they may be broken, some said, but not too violently. See: Pierre Corneille, *Oeuvres complètes*, 2 vols. (Paris, 1852), 2: 580–81; Chesterfield, *Letters to His Son*, ed. O. H. Leigh, 2 vols. (New York: n.p., [1937]), 2: 56.

12. Dryden, *Essays*, 1: 76; Orrery, Preface to *The Greek Theatre of Father Brumoy*, 3 vols. (London, 1759), 1: ix; Alexander Gerard, *An Essay on Taste*, ed. W. J. Hipple (Gainesville: Scholars' Facsimiles & Reprints, 1963), p. 258. See also: John Dennis, *Original Letters*, 2 vols. (London, 1721), 1: 73–74 (and also his *Critical Works*, ed. E. N. Hooker, 2 vols. [Baltimore: Johns Hopkins Press, 1939–43], 2: 68, and Hooker's note, 2: 453–56); *Some Remarks on Hamlet*, p. 53; Daniel Webb, *Remarks on the Beauties of Poetry* (London, 1762), pp. 103–6.

13. See: *Gentleman's Magazine* 24 (February 1754): 84; the variety of events in *Philoclea* are "an atonement and apology" for neglecting the rules (D. J. Greene thinks this review may be Johnson's; see chap. 2, note 24); *Monthly Review* 16 (May 1757): 427 (probably by Goldsmith); also in ibid.: 20 (June 1759): 507–8 (Kenrick), and 23 (December 1760): 461–62 (Ruffhead); *London Chronicle*, no. 22 (17–19 February 1757); and cf. no. 280.

14. The most vigorous opponent of the unities was L. Sébastien Mercier: see his *De la littérature et des littérateurs* (Yverdon, 1778), p. 123, for an example. But even René Rapin, *Reflections on Aristotle's Treatise of Poesie*, trans. Thomas Rymer (London, 1694), p. 84, concedes that unity of action should not be allowed to counteract those other delights springing from variety; however, there must be a pervading order: "as one Palace may contain the various Ornaments of Architecture . . . provided it is built in the same *Order*."

speare (1746) is sufficiently representative. Although Shakespeare, he agrees, did not write tragedies in the strict sense, his plays at least have one action "serious, entire, and of a just length"; since plot is the soul of tragedy, it is imperative that it be *whole*. But by the middle of the century, a certain "unity of character" had often come to be preferred to the other three. In a remarkable essay "Of Correctness" in the *Museum* for 1746, one of the two disputants contends: "To oppose the irregular Starts and Sallies of the *English* Drama to the Unity, Truth, and just Œconomy of the *French*, is to prefer the vast Heaps of Rock in a Quarry, or craggy Shore, to the Proportions of a beautiful Temple or Theatre." But for all of his metaphorical ingenuity, he cannot convince his opponent, who believes that unity of character is more important than unity of action, and that in this the English, especially Shakespeare, excel the French. His adversary proceeds to defend English drama at length, insisting on its realistic and consistent portrayal of character: this is the "true correctness." Just one year later Samuel Foote, in his essay on comedy, adds to the three unities, which he neither contemns nor extols, that of character. Shakespeare, by adhering only to this unity and ignoring the rest, has produced "more Matter for Delight and Instruction, than can be collected from all the starv'd, strait-lac'd Brats, that every other Bard has produc'd." In 1750 the anonymous author of *An Examen of . . . Edward the Black Prince* pronounces: "It is very certain that *Shakespear* never observ'd any Rule, but that essential one of *Character*, and it is as certain perhaps that *Shakespear* was the best Dramatick Writer the World ever produced." George Colman in 1761 praises Shakespeare's consistency of character "amidst the most open violation of the lesser critical Unities." And John Gregory, in a discourse published the same year as Johnson's *Preface*, asserts confidently: "Shakespear, by his lively creative Imagination, his strokes of Nature and Passion, and preserving the consistency of his characters, amply compensates for his transgressions against the rules of time and place, which the Imagination can easily dispense with." Gregory's statement, it is worth noting, combines very conveniently the three customary arguments against the unities: that there is a higher unity which takes precedence (consistency of character), that certain excellencies (strokes of nature and passion) compensate for not following the unities, and that the imagination is not really so dependent upon that supposed credibility provided by the unities.[15]

French criticism was no less emphatic about unity of action.[16] But a "unity of interest" soon challenged its importance. The liberal Houdart de La Motte seems to have introduced the controversy, though probably not the notion, in an essay published in 1730. Having discussed a number of points to be considered when writing a drama, he comes to the unities, and with an apparent hesitation anticipating Johnson's, he says cautiously: "Je hazarderai ici un Paradoxe; c'est qu'entre les premières règles du Théâtre on a presque oublié la plus importante." In fact, he continues, the three unities are useless without the truly important one: "L'unité d'intérêt qui est la vraie source de l'émotion continue." He objects to unity of place on the grounds that the dramatist often *breaks* probability to follow it, and that experience shows that the audience *will* tolerate changes of place if these are achieved between the acts. Unity of time rests on the same assumption, and La Motte objects on the same grounds: it leads to improbabilities and can be broken successfully. Unity of action, he continues, is the most fundamental, but it is to be distinguished absolutely from unity of interest. For example, several characters may be involved differently in a single event, and one may be interested in them all in different ways, now losing sight of one, now of another: here, then, is unity of action, but not of interest. To preserve unity of interest, the dramatist must indicate, from the beginning of the play, "à l'esprit & au cœur, l'objet principal dont on veut occuper l'un & émouvoir l'autre." [17] La Motte's distinction between unity of action

15. John Upton, *Critical Observations on Shakespeare*, 2d ed. (London, 1748), pp. 26, 61; *Museum* 1 (1746): 85–89; Samuel Foote, *The Roman and English Comedy Consider'd and Compar'd* (London, 1747), pp. 20–21; *Examen of . . . Edward the Black Prince* (London, 1750), pp. 6–7; George Colman, *Prose on Several Occasions*, 3 vols. (London, 1787), 2: 114; John Gregory, *A Comparative View of the State and Faculties of Man* (London, 1765), p. 134. Some critics subordinated the unities to other considerations; see: *Gentleman's Magazine* 18 (November 1748): 502, and 22 (April 1752): 163.

16. See Vinaver's discussion in Jean Racine's *Principes de la tragédie*, ed. E. Vinaver (Manchester: Manchester University Press, 1944), pp. 39–40, and also Jean-François Marmontel, *Poétique françoise*, 2 vols. (Paris, 1763), 2: 141–42; Charles Batteux, *Les beaux arts réduits à un même principe* (Paris, 1747), p. 167.

17. Houdart de La Motte, *Oeuvres de théâtre*, 2 vols. (Paris, 1730), 1: 38–41, 44–45.

and unity of interest is possibly obscure. Voltaire, at least, finds it so, arguing that the two, as fundamental ordering principles, are the same, but that in the best French tragedies there may be several minor interests, but only one principal action. In the same year (1730) La Motte replied to Voltaire in his *Suites réflexions sur la tragédie.* He reiterates that unity of action is fundamental, but that it and unity of interest are not synonymous. For example, the action is single in Corneille's *Oedipus,* but the interest double: first in Theseus accused of murdering Laïus, then secondly in Oedipus himself.[18] It is apparent that for La Motte unity of action has strictly to do with structure, plot manipulation, and so forth; whereas unity of interest means continuity of emotional tone, unity of sentiment or effect, just that quality so much esteemed by Diderot a generation later. La Motte anticipates a movement away from older conceptions of unity to newer ones defined more by emotional than mechanical criteria; we are in fact seeing the groundwork laid for theories of "organic unity" and other such Romantic sophistications. In England, "unity of character" tended to perform the same function: the pervasive "personalities" of Shakespeare's characters compensate for his structural ineptitudes.[19]

Finally, since the chorus was believed to necessitate the unities, one manner of attack was to deny the chorus altogether. Reviewers frequently resort to this tactic, often provoked by Mason's factitious productions. The *Gentleman's Magazine,* in a review pos-

18. Voltaire, *Works,* 38 vols. (London, 1778–81), 25: 15 (Voltaire attacks La Motte on the unities directly here, and also in a note in his *Théâtre de Corneille,* 12 vols. [(Geneva), 1764], 2: 547); La Motte, *Oeuvres de théâtre,* 1: 25.

19. Unity of interest, though it is not always so called, became especially popular in France. See: Diderot, *Oeuvres de théâtre,* 1: 158 ff., 230, 241; L. Sébastien Mercier, *Du théâtre* (Amsterdam, 1773), pp. 145–47; P. F. Le Tourneur, *Shakespeare traduit de l'angois,* vol. 6 (Paris, 1782), 287. In the preface in Guizot's revised edition (1821) of Le Tourneur it is explicitly maintained that if a "unity of impression" is preserved, the other unities may be disregarded (see F. W. M. Draper, *The Rise and Fall of the French Romantic Drama* [London: Constable and Co., 1923], pp. 84–85). Unity of impression is surely a Romantic development of La Motte's unity of interest ninety years before. Lessing in his early *Beyträge* (1749) defends Plautus's structure by appealing to La Motte (see J. G. Robertson, *Lessing's Dramatic Theory* [Cambridge: Cambridge University Press, 1939], p. 101). In the *Hamburgische Dramaturgie,* 2 vols. (Hamburg, 1769), st. xliv–xlvi, he discusses the unities generally and finds unity of action primary. On English unity of character, see P. H. Frye, cited chap. 2, note 21.

sibly by Johnson, utterly rejects Mason's argument for a revival of classicism: the old fondness for antiquity is now ridiculous, "nor is it more absurd to prefer the philosophy of *Aristotle* to that of *Newton*, than to prefer his rudiments to the more perfect plan of the modern drama." The chorus, the reviewer continues, does not conduce to credibility, but, quite the contrary, it is plainly absurd to have a company of women present at every incident: their presence renders the drama "totally different from life." [20] Mason is also rebuked, and Shakespeare defended, by the *Covent-Garden Journal*, no. 62. Like the *Gentleman's Magazine*, the earl of Orrery urges seven years later that the chorus makes the drama more improbable: "Delusion may compel us to imagine ourselves at Athens," but not that fifteen people are "of the same mind, thought, voice, and expression." And finally, Lord Kames in 1762 agrees that the continued representation of Greek drama required the unities and hence perhaps the chorus, but that the modern practice of allowing time to elapse between the acts is preferable.[21] Thus, by one of those paradoxes frequent in literary criticism, the chorus, even as it was defended for contributing to dramatic credibility, was attacked for obstructing that most desirable quality. Similarly, both the unities of time and place had been criticized for destroying probability and defended for preserving it. Behind this apparent paradox is a disagreement over the nature of con-

---

20. *Gentleman's Magazine* 22 (May 1752): 224–25 (Greene, in the article cited chap. 2, note 24, suggests that this also may be Johnson's).

21. *The Covent-Garden Journal*, ed. G. E. Jensen, 2 vols. (New Haven: Yale University Press, 1915), 2: 93–95; Orrery's preface in *Greek Theatre of Brumoy*, 1: xi; Kames, *Elements of Criticism*, 3 vols. (Edinburgh, 1762), 3: 272–77. In fairness to the French it must be remembered that Corneille, *Oeuvres complètes*, 2: 579, had long before expressed a similar preference for the modern division into acts. Even Voltaire, recollecting that Dacier had urged him to put a chorus into every scene, remarks that "he might as well have advised me to walk about the streets of Paris with Plato's gown on" (*Works*, 25: 4). Marmontel, *Poétique françoise*, 2: 204–6, recognizes the merits of the chorus, but considers them overbalanced by its disadvantages. For other attacks on the rules, see: *Critical Review* 13 (May 1762): 404, and 3 (March 1757): 259; *London Chronicle*, no. 12 (25–27 January 1757); *Monthly Review* 25 (December 1761): 461–65; Elizabeth Montagu, *An Essay on the Writings and Genius of Shakespeare* (London, 1769), pp. 6–7; John Brown, *Essays on the Characteristicks*, 5th ed. (London, 1764), p. 34; Laurence Sterne, *Tristram Shandy*, vol. 3, chap. 12; George Colman, Prefatory Discourse to the *Works of Massinger*, reprinted in *Companion to the Play-House*, 2 vols. (London, 1764), 1: xxx.

ventions: the more classical critics believed that once the audience has accepted certain conventions (e.g., the unities, the chorus), it will forget them; and the conventions themselves once "got over," they will actually facilitate credibility by unifying the plot. But the newer critics found the conventions too immediately unrealistic and absurd: if in fact they cannot be "got over," they will seriously hinder dramatic illusion. The mistake of the conservative critics lay, not in defending convention, but in defending conventions that had always been alien to the English theater; thus, while they were misled in apologizing for the unities and the chorus, their understanding of the place of convention in art was considerably more sophisticated than that of their successors. Attacks on the unities multiplied rapidly in the fifties and sixties, both in books and periodicals, and are sufficiently numerous to deprive Johnson of originality; but as we have seen, they were often enough countered by defenses to indicate that the issue, like that of taste and ideal nature, was very much unsettled at mid-century.

The dispute over dramatic illusion and pleasure is even more tangled. The arguments of both defenders and critics of the unities, we have seen, centered around credibility: just how credible must a play be to engage our affections? And this question having been asked (if not answered), there is this further one: does our pleasure arise from dramatic credibility (from taking for fact what is illusion), or, just the reverse, from our knowledge that the play is fiction rather than fact? It is especially difficult to reduce to coherence the multiplicity of theories by which late seventeenth- and eighteenth-century aestheticians attempted to penetrate the mysteries of theatrical delusion and delight.[22] While recognizing that these theories are far too diversified to yield to a simple scheme, we may distinguish provisionally between the *reflective* and the *sentimental*. The former tend to minimize the importance—sometimes the very

22. The following articles are helpful in sketching general trends and tendencies: Baxter Hathaway, "The Lucretian 'Return upon Ourselves,'" *PMLA* 62 (1947): 672–89; E. R. Wasserman, "The Pleasures of Tragedy," *ELH* 14 (1947): 283–307; A. O. Aldridge, "The Pleasures of Pity," *ELH* 16 (1949): 76–87; Ralph Cohen, "The Transformation of Passion: A Study of Hume's Theories of Tragedy," *Philological Quarterly* 41 (1962): 450–64. See also W. J. Bate, "The Sympathetic Imagination in Eighteenth-Century English Criticism," *ELH* 12 (1945): 144–64. On Johnson and dramatic illusion, see J. H. Adler, *Shakespeare Quarterly* 11 (1960): 225–28, and B. K. Kaul, *Notes and Queries*, n.s. 207 (1962): 261–64.

existence—of illusion and to emphasize certain mental acts of reflection; the latter, on the contrary, lay much stress on illusion, and, by the end of the century, have united in sympathy both the highest pleasure and the final value of tragedy. Although there are dissimilarities in emphasis and mode of argument, the sentimental theories, which I shall consider first, share three assumptions: that we must believe in what we see to be affected by a play; hence, that the play must be "realistic" (in some sense or another); and that the imagination willingly favors dramatic delusion—we *permit* ourselves to be deceived.

The earl of Shaftesbury, in his *Letter concerning Enthusiasm* (1708), makes all three points. He argues that *"Truth is the most powerful thing the the World"* (his italics) and that thus even fiction can please only by its resemblance to the real: "The Appearance of Reality is necessary to make any Passion agreeably represented." Yet he adds also that men "are wonderfully happy in a Faculty of deceiving themselves, whenever they set heartily about it." Sixty years later Mrs. Montagu not only expresses these three considerations, but indicates the use which later critics would make of them. Tragedy imposes a delusion; it "is addressed to the imagination, through which it opens to itself a communication to the heart, where it is to excite certain passions and affections: each character being personated, and each event exhibited, the attention of the audience is greatly captivated, and the imagination so far aids in the delusion, as to sympathize in the representation." She follows this with an analysis of *Oedipus, King Lear, King John,* and *Macbeth,* in each instance emphasizing that the realism of the play, and the illusion it evokes, arouse in the audience a sympathetic response. Thus by 1769 we have already intimations of those theories of sympathy which later critics were to deduce from sentimental premises. Finally, William Cooke in 1775 makes precisely the points that Shaftesbury had made sixty-seven years before. Attacking the use of rhyme in drama, he rejects the defense that we know the play to be a play, the words those of the poet, "for though we know we are to be deceived, and we desire to be so, no reasonable man was ever yet deceived, but with a probability of truth." [23]

23. Shaftesbury, *Characteristicks*, 5th ed., 3 vols. (London, 1732), 1: 4–5; Montagu, *Essay on Shakespeare*, pp. 30–33; Cooke, *Elements of Dramatic Criticism*, p. 81. Similar arguments are in *Some Remarks on Hamlet*, pp. 52–54; Upton, *Critical Observations on Shakespeare*, p. 61; *Greek Theatre of Brumoy*, 1: li.

The realism and heightened credibility of the stage made it for many sentimental critics the highest form of art. Dryden had been traditionally neoclassical in preferring the epic to tragedy in dignity. But the epic is too merely descriptive, and by 1754 a critic like Arthur Murphy is prepared to place dramatic above epic poetry, indeed above all other kinds:

> The Drama may be full as sentimental as any other Kind of Writings; nay, its Excellence frequently consists in being so, and with Regard to the Passions, the Mode of Imitation, renders its Influence more forcible, and when we are deceived into a Notion, that the Personages are actually before our Eyes, the Performance assumes a Kind of Reality, and more keen and intenser Sensations agitate our Breasts, than in Pieces where the Description is left to operate upon us without any other Aid than that of lively and impassioned Expressions.

The essential superiority of drama, then, is its illusion. And if Murphy opposes this illusion to descriptive poetry, John Gregory, seven years later, opposes it to any kind of reflection whatever. At a well-performed tragedy our emotions are too aroused

> to allow Reason to reflect that we are agitated with the feigned distress of people entirely at their ease. We suffer ourselves to be transported from place to place, and believe we are hearing the private soliloquy of a person in his chamber, while he is talking on a stage so as to be heard by a thousand people.[24]

Gregory, who is usually a very sensible critic, shows how extravagantly the belief in dramatic illusion might be entertained; we must remember such expressions as this, published the same year as the *Preface*, to understand the vehemence with which Johnson contradicts such beliefs. We must realize, too, that the amount of interest in theatrical delusion from the late forties onward cannot be exaggerated. The belief in this "deception" was held enthusiastically and promulgated with conviction; and it was finally to supplant the traditional understanding of dramatic effect, both with respect to how the drama pleased and how it taught.[25]

24. Murphy, in *The Gray's-Inn Journal*, 2: 265–66; Gregory, *Comparative View*, p. 137.

25. See: *Gentleman's Magazine* 5 (February 1735): 87–88; James Ralph, *The Touch-Stone* (London, 1728), p. 42; Thomas Wilkes, *A General View of the*

But it must again be observed that although the sentimental theories, broadly considered, are characterized by these three assumptions, all of them dependent on dramatic illusion, the critical contexts are often quite different. It cannot securely be predicted, for example, whether two different critics, sharing these values, will regard the unities as indispensable or not. Both Upton and Gregory seem to hold sentimental beliefs; yet Upton argues for the unities, while Gregory denies their necessity. Thus two critics may share a belief in dramatic illusion but quarrel over the nature and degree of its requirements. As a result, when sentimental critics set about to discuss dramatic *pleasure*, they may take several lines of approach. Two are of the most importance, however, and cannot absolutely be distinguished. In the moving of the passions alone, some argued, inheres dramatic pleasure; while other later critics found pleasure in the exercise of our sympathy and benevolence. Of the first theory, the most famous advocate is the Abbé Dubos, who defines pleasure as simply the exercise of passion: it is always better to be excited than inactive. Dubos's sentimentalism is evidenced by his refusal to distinguish between the impressions of real life and those produced by artistic imitation: a play may affect us less profoundly than a real scene, but this is only a difference in degree. But in England John Dennis, many years before Dubos, had arrived at essentially the same definition. Pleasure is derived from passion, but passion moderated by reason; thus in a tragedy the passions are pleasantly aroused, but so controlled as to be harmless.[26] Although some scholars have voiced doubts,[27] the kinship

---

Stage (London, 1759), p. 234; Joseph Warton, *An Essay on the Genius and Writings of Pope*, 4th ed., 2 vols. (London, 1782), 1: 262 (on *The Unfortunate Lady*); *Monthly Review* 34 (March 1766): 219; Morgann on Falstaff (in *Eighteenth-Century Essays on Shakespeare*, ed. D. N. Smith [Oxford: Oxford University Press, 1963], p. 235); Chesterfield, *Letters to His Son*, 2: 56. In French criticism see: Corneille, *Oeuvres complètes*, 1: 395; Rapin, *Aristotle's Treatise of Poesie*, pp. 111–12; Batteux, *Les beaux arts*, pp. 222–23 de Pouilly, *Theory of Agreeable Sensations*, p. 46; Diderot, *Oeuvres de théâtre*, 2: 309, 342; and especially Marmontel, *Poétique françoise*, 1: 391. See also Robertson, *Lessing's Dramatic Theory*, chap. 15 passim.

26. Jean Baptiste Dubos, *Réflexions critiques sur la poésie et sur la peinture*, 2 vols. (Paris, 1719), 1: 5–23 and passim; Dennis, *Critical Works*, 1: 148–50 (see Hooker's note, 1: 488). Cf. de Pouilly, *Theory of Agreeable Sensations*, pp. vii–viii, 25 (he was probably influenced by Dubos).

27. See Hathaway's article, cited above, note 22, for the finer discriminations among these theories.

of such "emotional" theories with the later, sentimental ones should be apparent. Such aestheticians as Kames and Smith stress the delight we derive from the exercise of our compassion or our sympathy with the distressed. For Young, our pleasure in tragedy proceeds from our "depth of concern." The movement even of our melancholy feelings can be pleasant, and Young makes a great point of explaining that this pleasure is "to show us the divine goodness"—that "none of our passions were designed to give us pain, except when being pain'd is for our advantage on the whole." Aikin regards the sympathy we have with misery as itself painful, but, when combined with love, complacency, etc., the "spring of tears," it can produce pleasure. The difference between a Dubos and a Young is not great; they both find dramatic pleasure in emotional excitation, and they would agree that only the healthy emotions ought to be aroused. But in the later critics the *delectare* and the *prodesse* of the drama are more consciously and carefully combined: we enjoy having our benevolent feelings excited and their very arousal makes us better moral beings. This, however, introduces the general problem of instruction, which must yet be deferred awhile. For our present purposes we must bear in mind that the sentimental theories of pleasure placed much stress on the emotions immediately to be aroused and very little on subsequent reflection; they emphasized the operation of the drama upon the mind rather than the operation of the mind upon the drama.[28]

But if a critic denies dramatic illusion, or even minimizes its power, he is going to be hard pressed to justify any theories of sympathy or direct emotional excitation. Thoroughgoing rejections of dramatic illusion such as that, ostensibly, by Dr. Johnson, are very infrequent. Some are patently facetious and are often provoked by a desire to run down Garrick's skill. Considering the purpose of such denials, it might well be argued that dramatic illusion is in fact assumed, while at the same time being denied to the contemptible abilities of a Garrick.[29] Of some interest, however,

28. Kames, *Elements of Criticism*, 1: 72–73; Adam Smith, *The Theory of Moral Sentiments* (London, 1774), p. 4 and passim; Edward Young, *Conjectures on Original Composition*, ed. E. J. Morley (Manchester: Manchester University Press, 1918), p. 41; J. Aikin and A. L. Aikin, *Miscellaneous Pieces* (London, 1773), p. 194 (cf. p. 120, where the pleasure arising from a scene of misery derives from the "reflex act of self-approbation attending virtuous sympathy").

29. See: *The Gray's-Inn Journal*, 1: 103; *Garrick's Looking-Glass* (London, 1776), p. 44.

is the following argument against the unities in John Langhorne's *Effusions of Friendship and Fancy* (1763): "We must be sensible, if we are awake at all, that the whole representation is a fiction. And why cannot we as well follow the imagination of the poet from region to region? It is still but a fiction, and, if it be *spirited* fiction, I am sure it will not be without its effect." The absence of other attacks on dramatic illusion makes Langhorne's, two years before the *Preface*, conceivably an influence on Johnson, although whether he was a diligent reader of the *Effusions* may be doubted.[30] On the other hand, subsequent denials are certainly influenced by Johnson's own firm stand.[31]

Much more significant are those theories I have termed reflective. These may permit a certain amount of illusion, but argue that our pleasure as such springs, not from our being deluded into emotions of sympathy, but from our recognition of the unreality of the drama. These theories are often coupled with the notion, found in Hobbes and many later critics, that the pleasure arises as well from the reflection that we are secure from the dangers we see. The opening lines of *De rerum natura* 2 were frequently cited to show how one may have a secret sense of pleasure and complacency at being able to view, securely and from a distance, storms, catastrophes, and the like.[32] But for most critics, beginning perhaps with Fontenelle, this *complacency* theory was rather too severe an indictment of human nature. Addison's remarks are typical:

30. The passage is quoted in Noyes, *Thespian Mirror*, p. 20; Noyes proposes the influence on Johnson, although there is nothing but internal evidence to suggest it.

31. Both Le Tourneur, *Shakespeare traduit de l'anglois*, 1: cv, and Joseph Baretti, *Discours sur Shakespeare et sur Monsieur de Voltaire* (London and Paris, 1777), pp. 54–56, paraphrase Johnson's *Preface* very closely on this point. Joshua Reynolds, *Discourses on Art*, ed. S. O. Mitchell (New York: Bobbs-Merrill, 1965), pp. 203–4, rejects as implausible Fielding's account of Partridge seeing Garrick's *Hamlet* (*Tom Jones*, bk. 16, chap. 5). Reynolds treats the episode too solemnly, but he is perceptive in remarking that no one is really deceived, and that the low and illiterate are even less apt to be so, unused as they are to stage conventions: they will feel, even more strongly than the veteran playgoer, the difference between drama and life.

32. "Suave, mari magno turbantibus aequora ventis/ E terra magnum alterius spectare laborem;/ Non quia vexari quenquam est jucunda voluptas,/ Sed quibus ipse malis careas quia cernere suave est."

When we read of Torments, Wounds, Deaths, and the like dismal Accidents, our Pleasure does not flow so properly from the Grief which
such melancholly Descriptions give us, as from the secret Comparison
which we make between our selves and the Person who suffers. Such
Representations teach us to set a just Value upon our own Condition,
and make us prize our good Fortune which exempts us from the like
Calamities.

But Addison is careful to add that we must know the representation to be fiction, that we would not feel this pleasure if the scenes
were real. Joseph Trapp speaks to the same purpose: the pleasure
involved in tragic terror derives from the delightful reflection that
"omnia esse ficta, & nos esse incolumes." This softening effect may
be achieved by *distance* as well. The two are so linked in Gerard's
account of how our "*uneasy* impressions" are converted into delight.
Suspense, anger, and similar emotions agitate the mind pleasantly,
"while at the same time, our implicit knowledge that the occasion
is *remote or fictional*, enables the pleasure of imitation to relieve
the pure torment which would attend their primary operation."
This distancing effect is most important for Hume, who in the
third book of his *Treatise of Human Nature* (1739–40) approves of
Lucretius's psychology, but comments that if we should see a floun-
dering ship so closely as to detect the passengers' cries, "no man has
so savage a heart as to reap any pleasure from such a spectacle."
The compassion aroused would inhibit Lucretian "complacency."
And in the same passage Hume points up the fundamental difference between the reflective and the sentimental explanation of
tragic pleasure: the "principles of sympathy, and a comparison
with ourselves," he decides, "are directly contrary." [33] Critics like
Gregory and Hume, then, could agree that sympathy and reflection
are persistently at odds, though they would draw from this supposition very different conclusions about tragic pleasure.

Our pleasure comes from our reflection that the play is "remote
or fictional." There is a third source as well: we may reflect upon

33. Addison and Steele, *The Spectator*, ed. Donald F. Bond, 5 vols. (Oxford:
Oxford University Press, 1965), 3: 568–9 (no. 418); Trapp, *Praelectiones poeticae*,
2: 275; Gerard, *Essay on Taste*, pp. 51–52 (italics mine); Hume, *Treatise of
Human Nature*, ed. L. A. Selby-Bigge (Oxford: Oxford University Press, 1967),
p. 594 (cf. his picture of the Stoic in *Essays and Treatises on Several Subjects*,
2 vols. [London, 1768], 1: 167). The core of Addison's argument remains
unchanged in *Greek Theatre of Brumoy*, 1: xxxvi–xxxviii, and Hiffernan,
Dramatic Genius, pp. 49 ff.

the *artistry* with which terrible events are portrayed. This had been suggested by Aristotle, and by Boileau's time had become commonplace:

> There's not a Monster bred beneath the Sky,
> But, well dispos'd by Art, may please the Eye:
> A curious Workman, by his Skill Divine,
> From an ill Object makes a good Design.

That this should be offered as a primary source of pleasure is not remarkable; traditional neoclassicism explained the enjoyment we find in any art as the result of that natural delight which we take, from infancy onward, in all forms of imitation.[34] But critics were seldom more specific than this. In Aristotle and Boileau it is presumably the design which delights, but little more of an explanation is offered. Of mid-century critics, only Hume, in his essay "Of Tragedy" (1757, but written 1749–51) develops this theory further. He finds Dubos's explanation of the pleasures of tragedy "in part, satisfactory." Yet he thinks it is not entirely so, for it "is certain, that the same object of distress, which pleases in a tragedy, were it really set before us, would give the most unfeigned uneasiness." He quotes Fontenelle, who locates the pleasure in our sneaking knowledge that a play is fiction, a knowledge which sufficiently weakens the affliction to make it pleasant. But to this "just and convincing" explanation Hume adds that the genius required and the art employed in a work not only overpower, but *convert* the melancholy passions into pleasure: "The soul, being, at the same time, rouzed by passion, and charmed by eloquence, feels on the whole a strong movement, which is altogether delightful." This occurs at a tragic performance, "with this addition, that tragedy is an imitation, and imitation is always of itself agreeable." Hume rightly regards this theory as an improvement on Fontenelle's, because the "fiction of tragedy softens the passion, by an infusion of new feeling, not merely by weakening or diminishing the sorrow." Reflective theories are at best negative; they would explain the pleasure

34. Boileau-Despréaux, *Art of Poetry*, 3, lines 429–32 (trans. Dryden in *Poems of John Dryden*, ed. James Kinsley, 4 vols. [Oxford: Oxford University Press, 1958], 1: 343). On the ability of imitation to make the unpleasant agreeable, see: Dacier, *Aristotle's Art of Poetry*, pp. 36–37 n.; Dubos, *Réflexions critiques*, 1: 63; *Greek Theatre of Brumoy*, 1: xxxvii; de Pouilly, *Theory of Agreeable Sensations*, pp. 56–57; Trapp, *Praelectiones poeticae*, 2: 271.

we take in tragedy by lessening the pain. Of the three sources of
pleasure, only the artistry could contribute a positive delight, and
even it was usually viewed as merely softening an otherwise dis-
tressing or disagreeable experience. Hume is the first intelligent
critic to try to solve this difficulty, intrinsic to all reflective accounts,
and it is impossible here to explore the complexities of his "con-
version" theory. Nevertheless, some scholars have made Hume's
conceptions rather more complex than they are. The conclusion of
his essay places it quite securely in the "fiction-artistry" tradition.
Summing up, he says that the pleasure which poets give us by
exciting grief "is not so extraordinary nor paradoxical, as it may
at first sight appear." A passion may be painful when aroused by
a real object, but "is so smoothed, and softened, and mollified,
when raised by the finer arts, that it affords the highest entertain-
ment." The "charms of imitation" are naturally delightful, and
this delight comes to predominate over our distress. For all of his
subtleties, Hume is a reflective theorist. In his discussion ten years
before in the *Treatise of Human Nature* he availed himself of the
"distance" metaphor to explain pleasure. Now he develops the
other two possibilities: that we know a play to be fictional, and
(going all the way back to Boileau) that we have a natural delight in
artistic imitation.[35] And, what is most significant, for Hume, as
for all the reflective theorists, sympathy and pleasure are at odds.
If we should believe the events genuine, we would be obliged to
pity and even to attempt to help; and although these obligations
are justly felt by moral beings, they are not necessarily pleasant—
at least not for Hume, who was something of an old-fashioned
moralist in spite of his agnosticism. No, if we can sympathize
only with what we believe to be real, we can take no such pleasure
in the mere imitation of distress; hence, our delight must be the
result of reflecting on the unreality or artistry of a dramatic production.

To recapitulate, two lines of thought (they are far too diverse
internally to be called schools) aspired to explain theatrical pleasure.
The sentimentalists placed much emphasis on the power of dramatic
illusion and the facility with which the imagination allows itself to

35. Hume, *Essays and Treatises*, 1: 246–49, 251. Wilkes, *General View of the
Stage*, pp. 34–36, praises Hume's explanation, but he attempts to paraphrase
it by giving the usual, reflective account; thus, he is quite oblivious to the
subtler implications of Hume's theory.

be deceived; they regarded the mind as rather passive, worked on by the performance to excite those emotions which were pleasant in themselves, or morally satisfying. This belief triumphed in the nineteenth century with Shelley's notions of the sympathetic imagination and Coleridge's theory of dramatic delusion. The reflective critics, on the other hand, denied or minimized dramatic illusion; the pleasure, they said, derives from a positive operation of the mind itself, reflecting on such facts as: the play is fictional; *we* are secure from the evils represented before us; the play is an imitation and may pleasantly be compared with reality. The vitality of such thought evanesces quite rapidly after the eighteenth century, although it may survive in the dramatic theories of Brecht. We are witnessing another manifestation of the shift from imitative to affective conceptions of art: the reflective understanding of artistic effect, though variously named, had been fundamental to the classical and medieval world, as well as to the Renaissance. Thus with respect to dramatic theory especially, the Romantic movement was indeed revolutionary.[36]

But at mid-century both views of dramatic pleasure, for all that can be determined in retrospect, were equally fashionable. Richard Hurd, whose criticism so often and so instructively bridges the classical and the modern age, provides a particularly interesting example of the extent to which these theories could be combined, and even confused, without apparent sense of contradiction. Glossing Horace's *Tunc tua me infortunia laedent,* Hurd wonders why, the more we are *hurt,* the more we are *pleased* by dramatic representations. He begins by discounting Hume's solution. Hurd shrewdly objects "that it supposes the impression of grief or terror, excited by a well-written tragedy, to be weaker than that which arises from our observation of the faculties of the writer, the power of numbers, and imitation." This not only runs against common sense, but would deny to the tragedian any ability to engender pity and terror. In the discussion which follows, he seems to assume a sentimentalist position: the powers of the artist actually *heighten*

36. I know of no more incisive analysis of the transition from what I have termed *reflective* to *sentimental* theories than that by D. W. Robertson, Jr., in his introduction to *A Preface to Chaucer* (Princeton: Princeton University Press, 1963), especially pp. 38–46. His recent study of *Abelard and Heloise* (New York: Dial Press, 1972), which in part is an examination of the treatment of that story from the seventeenth to the twentieth century, well illustrates the influence which such a shift has exerted on literature and the visual arts.

the effects of grief, except when we stop to reflect on them. But the spectator does not stop to reflect, nor should he be encouraged to do so, since this would counteract any dramatic effect. Hurd thus repudiates Hume as too ingenious and unrealistic, and proceeds to offer five "hints" as to the proper solution. They are summarized here:

1. Pleasure arises from the very raising of our attention and gratifying our curiosity (this is generally Dubos's position, cited directly by Hurd).
2. "The representation, however distressful, is still seen to be a representation." We are first pained, but then recollect that all is fictitious; our concern is thus abated and we have a "secret joy" that the occasion of our uneasiness is not real (Fontenelle is cited).
3. At the same time we are pained we feel a "secret complacency."
4. At a tragedy, we are indignant at "prosperous vice" and we pity "suffering virtue." These emotions are "accompanied with a certain delight which was, no doubt, intended to quicken us in the exercise of those social offices." This obtains in real life as well as on the stage.
5. "To the pleasure directly *springing* from these passions we may add another, which naturally . . . steals in upon us from *reflexion*." We are conscious of our humanity, of the rightness in feeling as we do, and hence our "pain is softened by a secret exultation in the rectitude of these sympathies."

He closes by asserting that we are not so much delighted *by* as *through* the passions. "The art of the poet indeed consists in giving *pain*. But nature and reflexion fly to our relief." [37]

Hurd's rejection of Hume, and his hints numbers one and four, align him with the sentimentalists: our attention is not drawn away by the artistry; our pleasure instead comes from attending to the play itself (as Dubos said) and also from feeling such moral emotions as righteous indignation and pity (so Young, for example, had argued). Numbers two and three, and his conclusion (though that is equivocal) resemble reflective theories: we are pleasantly relieved by recollecting that the play is a fiction and that we are not ourselves exposed to danger (Fontenelle, Addison, etc.). The fifth hint would seem to partake of both: we have pleasure in feeling moral

37. Richard Hurd, ed., *Q. Horatii Flacci epistolae ad Pisones, et Augustum,* 4th ed., 3 vols. (London, 1766), 1: 97–102.

feelings, and also in reflecting that they are moral. Now Hurd's attempt to explain tragic pleasure is one of the most interesting and comprehensive in the eighteenth century. Although he may not grasp entirely Hume's theory, his objection to it is thoughtful: it *does* seem too ingenious to be true. But Hurd's collection of hints, thrown together with so little regard for consistency or system, indicates the confusion which attended any discussion of the subject. In the 1750s, to be comprehensive meant, almost necessarily, to be contradictory. If the reflective critics minimized too much the powers of the imagination, the sentimentalists ignored far too easily the operations of our intellect. To some critics it seemed evident that both forms of mental activity were present, and they were determined to preserve truth even at the cost of consistency. Dr. Johnson was one of this number.

Johnson devotes nineteen paragraphs to the unities, dramatic illusion, and pleasure, and they are in their way among the most fascinating and least satisfying parts of the *Preface*. The section begins and concludes with expressions of extremely uncharacteristic caution and modesty, but contains between these an uncompromising rejection of the unities and an injudicious denial of dramatic illusion. The trepidation detected in La Motte's "Je hazarderai ici un Paradoxe," as he began his attack on the unities in 1730, was, perhaps, not mere rhetoric, but such timidity, thirty-five years later, is surely immoderate. One is therefore encouraged to seek irony in these initial paragraphs. On the other hand, the unities were not a completely settled issue by 1765; and his concluding remarks, equally apologetic, seem to contain little Johnsonian irony. At any rate, after deciding to attack the unities "with due reverence" for his opponents, Johnson proceeds to exempt the history plays from the charge: they do not pretend to be either comedies or tragedies. He then claims unity of action for Shakespeare's other plays. It is not, to be sure, a regular action, but it has a beginning, middle, and end, "one event is concatenated with another, and the conclusion follows by easy consequence."[38] For Johnson, unity of action is primary. And it is apparent from the sentence just quoted, as from his general discussion, that Johnson means structure, organization, the relating of one part to another. This is of course what La Motte had meant by it, and why he was so distressed that Voltaire should confuse it with unity of interest. By the latter La Motte signified

38. *Works*, 7: 75; all further references will be from pp. 75–81.

a consistency of impression or feeling, and the unity of character favored by some English critics is similar in that it prefers a less mechanical or strictly rational unity to the others. No such unity is preferred in the *Preface*. When defending tragicomedy, Johnson was indifferent to Diderot's continuity of tone, and he is no more attracted by La Motte's unity of interest now.

The unities of time and place next receive Johnson's attention; he states the problem immediately and precisely: "The necessity of observing the unities of time and place arises from the supposed necessity of making the drama credible." In two paragraphs he then summarizes quite adequately the essential arguments for the unities: that the "mind revolts from evident falsehood" and hence, to render a play realistic and acceptable, both these unities are required. "Such," says Johnson, "is the triumphant language with which a critick exults over the misery of an irregular poet, and exults commonly without resistance or reply." Replies were produced more often than Johnson suggests. But his own reply *was* uncommon. He simply asserts: "It is false, that any representation is mistaken for reality; that any dramatick fable in its materiality was ever credible, or, for a single moment, was ever credited." Such an emphatic denial is extraordinary. He immediately proceeds, however, to give what could justifiably be called the *common* reply:

> Delusion, if delusion be admitted, has no certain limitation; if the spectator can be once persuaded, that his old acquaintance are Alexander and Caesar, that a room illuminated with candles is the plain of Pharsalia, or the bank of Granicus, he is in a state of elevation above the reach of reason, or of truth, and from the heights of empyrean poetry, may despise the circumscriptions of terrestrial nature.

To this grandiloquent expression the pens of Dryden, Farquhar, Fielding, Kames may well have contributed, all of whom argued in this way that the unities were not essential to dramatic illusion.[39] But in point of fact—though it may pain a modern and enlightened critic to recognize it—this marvelous paragraph is an additional and indeed an irrelevant stricture against the unities. As Johnson immediately observes, this is not "the truth"; and it is therefore

39. The passage from Kames is quoted, together with Johnson's, in Sherbo, *Samuel Johnson, Editor of Shakespeare*, pp. 57–58; the language and the examples are sufficiently similar, Sherbo believes, to suggest "conscious or unconscious borrowings" from Kames.

curious that such scholars as Irving Babbitt, George Sherburn, and W. J. Bate should discover here an appeal "to the imaginative basis of literature."[40] The truth, says Johnson in the next paragraph, "is, that the spectators are always in their senses, and know, from the first act to the last, that the stage is only a stage, and that the players are only players. They come to hear a certain number of lines recited with just gesture and elegant modulation." Thus, Johnson returns to his original argument and denies dramatic illusion. Many things indeed may happen "if delusion be admitted," but the rational playgoer will not admit it in the first place. However, in the paragraph following *this* one, some acceptance of illusion lies necessarily behind Johnson's discussion of the unity of time. Like Kames and other supporters of at least partial delusion, Johnson argues that so long as extensive flights of time are caused to elapse between the acts, we shall not be disturbed: "Time is, of all modes of existence, most obsequious to the imagination; a lapse of years is as easily conceived as a passage of hours. In contemplation we easily contract the time of real actions, and therefore willingly permit it to be contracted when we only see their imitation."

Johnson, then, attacks the unities first because the drama is not credited at all, and then because if it *is* credited, the unities will still not be essential. Now I shall not presume to say that these two theories are intrinsically inconsistent; but after all, they are two theories, and by treating them here as though they were one, Johnson has introduced an element of confusion. An examination of Johnson's other remarks on the unities and illusion will do little to clear up the matter. In his practical criticism Johnson inclines to prefer that liberal interpretation of the unities which allowed time to pass between the acts.[41] Liberal or not, this shows some concern

40. *A Literary History of England*, ed. A. C. Baugh (New York: Appleton-Century-Crofts, 1948), p. 993. See: W. J. Bate, *The Achievement of Samuel Johnson* (New York: Oxford University Press, 1955), p. 202; Irving Babbitt, *Rousseau and Romanticism* (New York: World Publishing Co., 1955), p. 30 (implicitly); Babcock, *Genesis of Shakespeare Idolatry*, p. 49, also seems to miss the implications of Johnson's statement, as does David Daiches, *Critical Approaches to Literature* (Englewood Cliffs, N.J.: Prentice-Hall, 1956), p. 191. But Green, *Neo-Classic Theory of Tragedy*, pp. 209–10, had years before understood the matter correctly, and Adler, in the article cited above, note 22, sets it all straight.

41. In his "Notes to Shakespeare" see: *Works*, 8: 625, 747, and cf. 7: 216; 8: 1048; see also: *Lives*, 2: 76; *Oxford Works*, 2: 148 and 3: 240–41.

for the unities; and in the preface which he wrote for Thomas Maurice's translation of *Oedipus Tyrannus* he praises the "scrupulous exactness" with which "the three grand unities of time, place, and action" are observed—and this in 1780! At about the same time, however, his discussion of *Samson Agonistes* in the *Life of Milton* shows him to be very far from William Mason and the other advocates of reviving classical drama. He is especially severe on the chorus, which he dismisses as an "encumbrance." How shall we account for such inconsistency? Furthermore, the evidence is persuasive that Johnson believed in some sort of dramatic illusion. In *Rambler* no. 156 he permits a certain disruption of unity of time, explaining: "Since it will frequently happen that some delusion must be admitted, I know not where the limits of imagination can be fixed"—Farquhar's view, and that expressed in the *Preface*, although there to be denied immediately. In his "General Observation on *Lear*" he objects to "the extrusion of Gloucester's eyes, which seems an act too horrid to be endured in dramatick exhibition, and such as must always compel the mind to relieve its distress by incredulity." Elsewhere he recognizes the powers of sympathy:

> All joy or sorrow for the happiness or calamities of others is produced by an act of the imagination, that realises the event . . . by placing us, for a time, in the condition of him whose fortune we contemplate; so that we feel, while the deception lasts, whatever motions would be excited by the same good or evil happening to ourselves.[42]

In the light of these remarks, it is reasonable to think that Johnson did believe in the kind of illusion to which any introspective playgoer will testify: a voluntary focusing of one's attention on the activities of the stage, while always being conscious, to varying degrees, of the distinction between real and simulated life. As we have seen, the question of theatrical delusion could be handled in a most unsophisticated way, so handled, in fact, as to suggest, sometimes quite intentionally, that theatrical delusion was like *real*

42. *Samuel Johnson's Prefaces & Dedications*, ed. Allen T. Hazen (New Haven: Yale University Press, 1937), p. 140; *Lives*, 1: 188–89; *Works*, 5: 68; 8: 703; 3: 318–19. Sherbo, *Samuel Johnson, Editor of Shakespeare*, pp. 3-4, sees *Rambler* no. 156 as containing "the germ of the more elaborate attack on the unities in the Preface." In fact, this *Rambler* paper is a more consistent and thorough, if less elegant, demolition. What was clear in Johnson's mind in 1751 seems to have become confused with another, more dubious mode of attack in 1765.

delusion. There is no reason to suspect that Johnson had read John Gregory's account of it, quoted above, although it was also published in 1765. But Gregory is merely representative; and it is hardly surprising that Johnson, with his great fear of *real* delusion, should have opposed so dogmatically such dramatic theories. That he overstated the matter cannot be denied; but it is an understandable reaction to the equally extravagant beliefs of critics like Gregory, who seemed to delight too much in the powers of the imagination. "All power of fancy over reason," Johnson had written six years earlier, "is a degree of insanity."[43]

But regardless of Johnson's final opinion about delusion, it is clear that in the *Preface* he intends to minimize, if not really to deny, its importance. Having done so, he is immediately aware of the next question to be answered: how then does the drama affect us if it is not believed? "It is," he says, "credited with all the credit due to a drama." His following remarks place him among the reflective critics. He gives, first, a variation on the complacency theory:

> The reflection that strikes the heart is not, that the evils before us are real evils, but that they are evils to which we ourselves may be exposed. If there be any fallacy, it is not that we fancy the players, but that we fancy ourselves unhappy for a moment; but we rather lament the possibility than suppose the presence of misery, as a mother weeps over her babe, when she remembers that death may take it from her.

And, like Addison and others, he adds immediately: "The delight of tragedy proceeds from our consciousness of fiction; if we thought murders and treasons real, they would please no more." Having made two observations often found in reflective critics, Johnson proceeds directly to the third: that we are pleased by imitations of reality.

> Imitations produce pain or pleasure, not because they are mistaken for realities, but because they bring realities to mind. When the imagination is recreated by a painted landscape, the trees are not supposed capable to give us shade, or the fountains coolness; but we consider, how we should be pleased with such fountains playing beside us, and such woods waving over us.

43. *Oxford Works*, 1: 293 (*Rasselas*, chap. 44). For the more philosophical implications of Johnson's rejection of illusion, see Jean H. Hagstrum, *Samuel Johnson's Literary Criticism* (Chicago: University of Chicago Press, 1967), pp. 165–66.

C. C. Green, in his *Neo-Classical Theory of Tragedy in England during the Eighteenth Century*, calls Johnson's use of this theory "a substitute for the theory of real delusion" and dubs it "sacrilegious." He regards it as somehow a *rationalization* of the effects of a drama, to which Johnson, having been so imprudent as to deny dramatic illusion, has had to resort; and he further observes: "The neo-classic system had had many ironic jokes played on it, but none more ironic than this."[44] But if there is any rationalization or irony here, Johnson is not alone guilty of it. If we assume that he merely intends to reduce greatly the power of illusion, then all of the explanations he offers, including that of delighting in imitation, are precisely those relied on by Hume and other reflective critics. To be sure, he has neither the complexity of Hume nor such comprehensiveness as Hurd. His illustrations are admittedly curious. The mother weeping over her child and reflecting on infant mortality is a singular example of the complacency theory. For Johnson, the relief arises, not simply from our sense of being uninvolved in the events, but from our recognition that we are not *now* involved in them; the possibility remains. Although this is merely a variation on the standard theory, Johnson's emphasis is appreciably more somber. Likewise, his account of the pleasure of imitation makes very little of our delight in comparing it with the original or admiring its artistry: though we do not take the trees or fountains for real, we enjoy imagining how we *should* be pleased if they *were* real. Throughout, then, Johnson departs from the usual examples in his elucidation of dramatic effect. In the first instance he may depart from it to add a new subtlety to the complacency theory; it is at least arguable. It is far more doubtful whether his explanation of our pleasure in imitation is very satisfactory: the difference between delighting in a real tree, and delighting in a tree as if it were real, is not obvious.

It is nevertheless clear from his denial of dramatic illusion that Johnson belongs in the reflective tradition. What has confused or puzzled scholars is his rather idiosyncratic expression—the absolute denial of dramatic delusion, the somewhat odd and indirect manner of explaining dramatic effect. But Johnson is very far from being

44. Green, *Neo-Classic Theory of Tragedy*, pp. 210–11. Although Johnson's phraseology is a bit eccentric, it does not account for Green's difficulty with this passage.

through with his subject, and the paragraphs which ensue serve only to make his argument more tortuous.

A dramatick exhibition [he says, returning to the problem of illusion] is a book recited with concomitants that increase or diminish its effect. Familiar comedy is often more powerful on the theatre, than in the page; imperial tragedy is always less. The humour of Petruchio may be heightened by grimace; but what voice or what gesture can hope to add dignity or force to the soliloquy of *Cato*.

A play read, affects the mind like a play acted. It is therefore evident, that the action is not supposed to be real, and it follows that between the acts a longer or shorter time may be allowed to pass, and that no more account of space or duration is to be taken by the auditor of a drama, than by the reader of a narrative, before whom may pass in an hour the life of a hero, or the revolutions of an empire.

Johnson's refusal to distinguish between a reading and a live performance is consistent with his earlier denial of illusion and equally provocative; no other critics had gone so far as to characterize a staged production as a "book recited." Such belligerent opacity as to the nature of the dramatic experience evokes immediate dissent, and yet what Johnson *means* is reasonable enough: that a reader is no more bothered by conflict between real and literary time than a spectator at a play. Both accept certain artistic conventions. As with his discussion of delusion, Johnson's explanation is comprehensible, even though one may deplore both the rhetoric and the conduct of his argument.[45]

Johnson's position is made even more complicated by the next several paragraphs, where he turns more directly to the three unities. He first approves of Shakespeare's not observing them, whether he did so by design or "happy ignorance." He repeats that the unities of time and place "arise evidently from false assumptions," that only unity of action is important; and he decides, with many a progressive critic, that such "violations of rules merely positive, become the comprehensive genius of Shakespeare, and such censures are suitable to the minute and slender criticism of Voltaire." Yet in the following paragraph he recognizes how many arguments may be brought against his own position, and, almost as an after-

45. This problem of why Johnson gives such short shrift to the effect of a staged representation deserves more of an explanation than I can properly give it here. See Appendix C.

thought, he makes the old point that the unities "are always to be sacrificed to the nobler beauties of variety and instruction."' Johnson has now made all three of the standard objections to the unities: they are unnecessary for making the drama credible, they are subordinate to one more general unity, and they must not be observed at the cost of other, greater beauties. Developing this last point, Johnson writes:

> He that, without diminution of any other excellence, shall preserve all the unities unbroken, deserves the like applause with the architect, who shall display all the orders of architecture in a citadel, without any deduction from its strength; but the principal beauty of a citadel is to exclude the enemy; and the greatest graces of a play, are to copy nature and instruct life.

It will be remembered that Armstrong, eight years before, had identified the unities with the "walls, doors, windows, a roof and chimneys" of a comfortable home, thus employing an architectural metaphor to just the opposite purpose. Three years before the *Preface*, however, the *Critical Review* very closely anticipates Johnson's own use of the metaphor:

> Modern tragedy seems greatly to resemble modern architecture. . . . Our houses are extremely neat and elegant, rules and proportions are strictly observed, and every thing so constructed as to catch the eye, but at the same time of the slightest materials, and totally void of that noble simplicity and magnificence which appears in our ancient structures; and it is just the same with our tragedies, where every thing is measured out by rule and line, the unities strictly and religiously observed, and all the little substitutes which art hath invented, to supply the place of genius industriously sought after, and constantly employed.[46]

For the reviewer, as for Johnson, following the unities is like preserving the niceties of architecture; this is all very well, but nothing can compensate for *nature* and *genius*. Here, one feels, Johnson is warming to his subject.

The final two paragraphs, however, fall sadly off. Johnson is "almost frighted" at his own temerity and is ready "to sink down in reverential silence" before those who oppose him. He then con-

---

46. *Critical Review* 13 (January 1762): 54.

cludes with the weakest defense of Shakespeare which even the most callow critic could make: that the readers "will easily, if they consider the condition of his life, make some allowance for his ignorance." Now to be sure, there are sights more easily conceived than Johnson sinking down in reverential silence. But either these paragraphs are not ironical, and Johnson has debilitated still further a discussion characterized throughout by hesitation and inconsistency, or they are ironical without success. Thus Johnson's discussion ends.

What, then, are we to make of these nineteen paragraphs which occupy such a central section of the *Preface*? Are they, as the *Critical Review* proclaims, "worthy Mr. Johnson's pen"? We cannot confidently affirm it. Johnson attacks the unities—but Farquhar had done that, and with more consistency, sixty-three years before. He analyzes dramatic pleasure, but both Hurd and Hume had done so a decade or more previous; and while Johnson is not obviously less successful or consistent than they, his argument is developed awkwardly and his illustrations are strained. Indeed, his discussion of the entire matter is curiously vacillating. Its opening and conclusion (especially the conclusion) might almost be called contemptibly cautious, while at the same time his denial of theatrical delusion appears far too intemperate. But all this must not be allowed to obscure the fact that Johnson remains a reflective critic; poetry is an imitative, not an affective art, and our pleasure proceeds from our rational consideration of the beauty and justness of its representations. Nor must his contributions be disregarded: his attack on the unities—still an open issue—doubtless hastened their downfall; and his denial of illusion, while energetically expressed, may well have delayed the triumph of those theories which too confidently identified drama with life.

MORALITY AND THE DRAMA: TO INSTRUCT

> The norms in his plays are indeed compatible with more philosophies than are comprehended in most of our dogmas; it is precisely this centrality, this lack of bias, this capacity to cut to the heart of problems which all philosophies attempt to deal with in conceptual terms, that makes his plays what we call universal.
>
> Wayne C. Booth, *The Rhetoric of Fiction*

Publicly and—judging from the best-selling collections of sermons—seriously, the eighteenth century was an ethical age; it was not so enlightened as to question whether poetry had moral obligations. These questions, however, it did ask: *Was* the stage in fact moral? Was "poetic justice" indispensable for moral drama? Were Shakespeare's plays moral? And underlying all of these was a much more significant question: How was the drama most effectively to instruct? The decision preferred by this century was to exercise a permanent influence on later poetry, both its theory and practice.

It would be an error to suppose that the descendants of Jeremy Collier had been silenced by the acclaim which attended Garrick's triumph. Harry W. Pedicord finds no fewer than fifty diatribes against playhouses published between Collier's attack in 1698 and 1800, and more than twenty of these appeared after 1747.[47] The majority of such productions have encountered the oblivion they deserve, although there are a few intelligent attacks.[48] Even contemporary reviewers derided them openly. Typical is the attitude taken by the *Gentleman's Magazine*, two years after Johnson's *Preface*, toward *The Stage the High Road to Hell*, where that zealous work is dismissed as an inferior Collier. The reviewer agrees that plays are not truly schools of virtue, but accuses the author of pushing his case too far, and concludes: "Though the entertainments of our stage are still liable to objections, it is not probable that the time allotted to them would be more innocently or less dangerously spent elsewhere, by the far greater part of those that frequent them."[49] The state of affairs at mid-century is well illustrated by the reception in England of Rousseau's diatribe against the stage, the famous *Lettre à d'Alembert sur les spectacles* (1758).[50]

47. Harry W. Pedicord, *The Theatrical Public in the Time of Garrick* (New York: King's Crown Press, 1954), p. 40.

48. William Law furnished one, and Hartley, *Observations on Man*, 2: 254, assumed a stern position: "Upon the whole, it will follow, that the polite arts are scarce to be allowed, except when consecrated to religious purposes."

49. *Gentleman's Magazine* 37 (March 1767): 122–24.

50. This letter was provoked by d'Alembert's "Short Account of the Government of Geneva," in which he deplored the prohibition of stageplays and argued that dramatic works "form the taste of the citizens, and give them a delicacy of feeling, and an elegance of sentiment, which are very difficult to be acquired without this resource" (*Miscellaneous Pieces* [London, 1764], p. 66). For the heart of Rousseau's argument, see *Oeuvres*, 15 vols. (Geneva, 1782), 11: 215–90.

Rousseau's puritanical side is nowhere more exposed than in this long and occasionally perceptive attack; English reviewers accorded him respectful disagreement. William Kenrick in the *Monthly Review* concedes a number of points, and admits that Rousseau "plainly shews that the stage, in its present state, is far from being the best school of morals." However, he remains much more optimistic than Rousseau as to the possibility of reform. The *Critical Review* quotes extensively from the letter but decides: "We are convinced the sphere of our happiness and misery, of our pains and our pleasures, is enlarged by a due use and direction of the theatre, since upon it depends, in a great measure, a national taste, and a just sense of the beauty, decorum, and propriety of manners." The reviewer points out, too, that Rousseau's arguments, pushed to the extreme, would deny the moral validity of all the arts.[51]

Among educated people the opinion was prevalent that the theater, though possibly corrupt, *can* be reformed, and that the stage is, ideally, a school of virtue. Gildon, for example, devotes several pages of his *Complete Art of Poetry* (1718) to a reasoned argument against Collier: the stage ought to be reformed and cleansed of its abuses rather than destroyed. And in 1735 Aaron Hill's *Prompter* paints with italic exultation the power and influence of the reformed stage:

> There, That *Reason*, which was *read* but with a cold *Consent, wounds, animates,* and *compells* us. There we *stamp*, not on our *Memory* only, but on our *Heart*, Ideas which make their Way with the *Passions.* . . . We are taught, without *Learning*; become polish'd, without *Travel*; find ourselves humaniz'd, without *Sufferings*: and rise, insensibly, by one and the same Progress, into *Life*, and its *Refinements*.

James "Hermes" Harris's *Three Treatises* (1744) protracts the argument; what improvement can be greater than "that which is derived from a just and decent Representation of Human Manners, and Sentiments?" he asks, adding in a footnote that "moral science" is the end common to tragedy, epic, and comedy. One year before the *Preface* the *Companion to the Play-House* says of the theater: "In this humanizing and instructing Academy, the young Spectator may learn the Manners of the World, without running through the

51. *Monthly Review* 20 (February 1759): 115–34; *Critical Review* 7 (January 1759): 48–49.

Perils of it." And in 1767 the *London Magazine,* in the introductory installment of its series "The British Theatre," is quite satisfied with the moral condition of the stage. It is

> growing every day more able to assist the great purposes of genius and virtue . . . no performances are tolerated whose ends are not evidently moral, and the whole public find infinitely more delight now, in shedding a benevolent tear of sensibility, in their very comedies, than in the unmeaning roar of laughter, which was formerly calculated to the prejudice of their principles, and the disgrace of their understanding.

Thus, although diatribes against the stage are frequent, they are commonly the productions rather of zeal than of reason. The more polite critics, on both sides of the Channel, both in books and periodicals, believed that the stage not only should, but could be moral.[52] In what *way* it could be moral, and whether or not Shakespeare himself was—these were questions less easily answered.

Convinced of the evil potentialities of drama, Plato fastened on the obvious way to render its effect beneficial, a way which Rymer was perhaps the first to dignify by the term *poetical justice.* Aristotle was often cited as a promoter of this doctrine, and he does, certainly, postulate an ethical purpose for tragedy. But poetic justice can be traced to Plato alone, and, assumed or explicit, it is in English criticism from the beginning. As M. A. Quinlan says: "The doctrine of poetic justice was traditional in English literary criticism more than a century in advance of the time when Addison rebelled against it." Despite Addison's rebellion, it continued to be maintained for almost another century. That Macheath, in the revival

52. Gildon, *Complete Art of Poetry,* 1: 39–42; *Prompter* 30 (1735); James Harris, *Three Treatises* (London, 1744), p. 86; *Companion to the Play-House,* 1: v; *London Magazine* 36 (June 1767): 268. See also: Leonard Welsted, *Works* (London, 1787), p. 146; W. R. Chetwood, *A General History of the Stage* (London, 1749), p. 28; T. Cibber, *Dissertations on Theatrical Subjects* (London, 1756), p. 2; Wilkes, *General View of the Stage,* pp. 2–3; *London Chronicle,* no. 278 (7–10 October 1758) (on *The Beggar's Opera,* but see this magazine passim, especially nos. 10, 12, 21, 28, 283). But as late as the 1760s and 1770s the old arguments of Collier were resurrected by the admirers of Whitefield to attack Foote's anti-Methodist *The Minor.* In French criticism see: Rapin, *Aristotle's Treatise of Poesie,* pp. 12–13; Jean Terrasson, *La philosophie applicable à tous les objets de l'esprit et de la raison* (Paris, 1754), p. 176; Voltaire, *Works,* 26: 38; La Motte, *Oeuvres de théâtre,* 1: 17–18; G. Alexandre de Méhégan, *Considérations sur les révolutions des arts* (Paris, 1755), p. 224; Porée, *An Oration,* passim.

of *The Beggar's Opera* at Covent Garden, 1777, should have been sent to the hulks for three years, is a remarkable testimony to the tenacity with which the doctrine was held and the rigor with which it was applied.[53]

Restoration criticism, then, inherited a doctrine already prevalent. Poetic justice, like decorum, was intimately allied with idealistic conceptions of poetry; and, like decorum, one way of demonstrating its necessity was to distinguish between poetry and history. Rymer comments that history was found by the Greek tragedians "neither proper to *instruct*, nor apt to *please.*" Its *"yesterday-truths"* were ill suited "to illustrate the *universal* and *eternal truths*," and its *"unequal* distribution of rewards and punishments . . . by the *Atheist* was made a scandal to the *Divine Providence.*"[54] As Dennis says: "The great Design of Arts is to restore the Decays that happen'd to human Nature by the Fall, by restoring Order." Poetry is more than a diary of fortune; it is an imitation of the providential ordering of the universe. As moral beings, we are obliged to try to comprehend this order through the mass of daily events, but a poet is particularly expected to display it. For a critic like Dennis, poetic justice is a logical consequence of this view, and he makes all of the important arguments which were to be devised in its behalf. His fundamental contention is developed as early as 1698 in his reply to Collier, *The Usefulness of the Stage*: "Poetick Justice would be a Jest if it were not an Image of the Divine, and if it did not consequently suppose the Being of a God and Providence." He repeats this opinion in his *Essay on the Genius and Writings of Shakespeare* (1712): "The Good must never fail to prosper, and the Bad must always be punish'd: Otherwise the Incidents, and particularly the Catastrophe which is the grand Incident, are liable to be imputed rather to Chance than to Almighty Conduct and to Sovereign Justice." Although Dennis has other arguments—an ill-advised appeal to Aristotle among them—this is his essential point. In a letter to Sir Richard Blackmore (1716) he maintains that good actions must always be rewarded, for to do otherwise would remove

---

53. M. A. Quinlan, *Poetic Justice in the Drama* (Notre Dame: Indiana University Press, 1912), p. 107 (on this subject see ibid., passim; Green, *Neo-Classic Theory of Tragedy*, pp. 139–49; Hooker's note in Dennis, *Critical Works*, 2: 435–38); for the account of *The Beggar's Opera*, see A. S. Turberville, ed., *Johnson's England*, 2 vols. (Oxford: Oxford University Press, 1933), 2: 174.

54. Rymer, *Critical Works*, pp. 22–23. See also Dryden, *Essays*, 1: 142.

instruction, "resolving Providence into Chance or Fate." And in his letter to Addison, who had argued against the doctrine, he makes a further point. He agrees that "good and evil happen alike to all Men on this Side the Grave." Nevertheless: "the Creatures of a poetical Creator are imaginary and transitory; they have no longer Duration than the Representation of their respective Fables; and consequently, if they offend, they must be punish'd during that Representation." This, he concedes, is but an imperfect type of almighty justice, but poetic justice is "forc'd by temporal to represent eternal Punishments." A play, then, reflects the ideal, and as its characters have no afterlife, they must be shown receiving their reward in this one; otherwise it has not rightly imitated divine Providence. In an age when rationalism was threatening faith in Providence, Dennis embraced poetic justice in order to fortify the conviction that God operates among the affairs of men; plays are not to be realistic in a sublunary sense merely, but ought to imitate the dispensations of eternal Providence.[55]

It required no courage to take up the banner of poetic justice, and hence it was taken up many times in the ensuing years. Gildon quotes Dennis's rebuttal of Addison with approval; and Trapp, while admitting that good and evil are impartially distributed in this life, believes that tragedy, like theology, must remind spectators of the future rewards of virtue and the punishments of vice. Thomas Wilkes in 1759 defines tragedy as that art which reconciles one to "the dispensations of that wonderful Providence which has permitted such vicissitudes." And nine years after Johnson's *Preface* William Richardson upholds poetic justice vigorously and praises Nahum Tate's *Lear*, from which the audience retire "exulting in the mutual happiness of paternal affection and filial piety." [56] The

55. Dennis, *Critical Works*, 1: 336, 183; 2: 6; *Original Letters*, 1: 8, 414. Thus H. S. Robinson, *English Shakesperian Criticism in the Eighteenth Century* (New York: H. W. Wilson, 1932), p. 52, is radically wrong when he says, apropos of Dennis's letters on Shakespeare: "In citing disregard of poetic justice as a defect, Dennis must have done violence to his private feelings, for nothing is more evident than his intense admiration for the writer who discarded all the rules which he advocated." Dennis was no simple-minded dogmatist, but then poetic justice was for him no simple-minded rule.

56. Gildon, *Complete Art of Poetry*, 1: 189; Trapp, *Praelectiones poeticae*, 2: 260–61; Wilkes, *General View of the Stage*, p. 22; William Richardson, *Cursory Remarks on Tragedy* (London, 1774), pp. 45–46. See also Thomas Davies, *Dramatic Miscellanies*, 3 vols. (Dublin, 1784), 2: 264–66, who prefers Tate's *Lear*, and John Hippisley, *A Dissertation on Comedy* (London, 1750), p. 11.

periodicals in the fifties and sixties are equally partial to the doctrine.[57]

Attacks on poetic justice, in the first two-thirds of the century, are even more infrequent than defenses of tragicomedy. Addison is the first, foremost, almost only adversary. Although he furnishes several arguments, not the least destructive being that there is no authority in Aristotle for the doctrine, he conducts his primary assault by simply denying Dennis's aesthetic Platonism:

> We find that Good and Evil happen alike to all Men on this Side the Grave; and as the principal Design of Tragedy is to raise Commiseration and Terrour in the Minds of the Audience, we shall defeat this great End, if we always make Virtue and Innocence happy and successful.

Addison here advances two propositions subsequently to become extremely fashionable: that the drama should imitate sublunary nature and leave Providence to fend for itself, and that, by implication, its purpose is less to teach didactically than to arouse sympathy. With respect to dramatic illusion, Addison espoused reflective theories; but on this point he anticipates two qualities with which the sentimentalists were to be very much concerned: realism and sympathy. He brings other arguments to bear against poetic justice, but these two are certainly the most fundamental. Addison's opinion was ultimately to win the day; but during the first sixty years further attacks are infrequent and unskillful. Samuel Richardson, however, must be excepted from this generalization; who in his expanded postscript (1751) to *Clarissa* defends his failure to observe poetic justice. Richardson opens his defense with a proper and persuasive reply:

> And after all, what is the *poetical justice* so much contended for by some . . . but another sort of dispensation than that which God, by Revelation, teaches us, He has thought fit to exercise mankind; whom placing here only in a state of probation, he hath so intermingled good and evil, as to necessitate us to look forward for a more equal dispensation of both.

57. See: *Critical Review* 1 (March 1756): 161; and especially *Gentleman's Magazine* 22 (June 1752): 254 (preferring Tate's *Lear*); *Gentleman's Magazine* 39 (January 1769): 43; *Universal Magazine* 12 (1753): 88.

The author of the History (or rather Dramatic Narrative) of Clarissa, is therefore well justified by the *Christian System,* in deferring to extricate suffering Virtue to the time in which it will meet with the *Completion* of its Reward.

To Addison's arguments Richardson has added another, turning the religious point against Dennis's well-intentioned if imprudent defense of Providence. If we are confident Christians, we shall not insist upon so superficial a doctrine as poetic justice. The relinquishing of ideal theories which Addison had instigated forty years before is now complete: it is *this* life which poetry is to imitate; for Richardson, one notices, the distinction between a *history* and a *dramatic narrative* is not significant. But though Richardson quotes at length from Addison, he weakens his whole case in the end by affirming that *Clarissa,* in point of fact, *does* observe poetic justice. After all, Lovelace and the rest are punished, and

> who that are in earnest in their profession of Christianity, but will rather envy than regret the triumphant death of CLARISSA; whose piety . . . whose diffusive charity; whose steady virtue; whose christian humility; whose forgiving spirit; whose meekness, and resignation, HEAVEN *only* could reward?

Richardson's inconsistent defense stands virtually alone in mid-century criticism.[58]

But even for Dennis, poetic justice was but one of the more expedient ways by which the drama might instruct. The most effective instrument for achieving its moral end was not so much Plato's poetic justice as Aristotle's catharsis. This mysterious phenomenon taxed the ingenuity of many neoclassical theorists, but their several interpretations, and the distinctions which prevail among them, need not be examined here.[59] As with theories of dramatic pleasure, a useful if inexact division may be made between reflective and

---

58. Addison, *Spectator,* 1: 169 (no. 40—cf. *Tatler* no. 82); Richardson, *Clarissa: Preface, Hints of Prefaces, and Postscript* (Los Angeles: Augustan Reprint Society, 1964), pp. 350–51, 360 (see Ira Konigsberg, "The Tragedy of Clarissa," *Modern Language Quarterly* 27 [1966]: 285–98, who disagrees with my interpretation). Frances Sheridan's *Memoirs of Miss Sidney Bidulph* (1761) takes Addison's line and appeals to "real life" (quoted in R. G. Noyes, *The Neglected Muse* [Providence: Brown University Press, 1958], p. 171).

59. See the articles by Wasserman and Bate, cited above, note 22. Few critics then employed the now familiar term *catharsis.*

sentimental critics. As we have seen, some found dramatic pleasure to derive finally from our self-consciousness (we are safe, we know the play is fiction); likewise, they saw the instruction to consist in a conscious reflecting upon our own condition. But others, more interested in exciting the emotions, developed a theory which Shelley was to bring to completion and which aimed at exercising, and thereby refining, the imagination or the sensibility. To these critics, the doctrine of poetic justice was repugnant; it not only was "unrealistic," but, because it satisfied our intellect, was ill suited to arouse our pity.

Reflective critics developed several different interpretations of catharsis, but they share similar assumptions. A spectator, by seeing the misfortunes which befall even the great, and by reflecting on his own situation, learns better to bear his lot; this is fundamentally how the drama improves. Then, too, by seeing immoderate passions at loose on the stage, he appreciates the value of controlling his own. Dacier's commentary on Aristotle, and kindred works, define the ethical effect of tragedy in this way. Tragedy excites feelings of terror and compassion to refine them; but this refinement is of the most obviously didactic sort. We witness the misfortunes of "those who are like our selves, have fallen by involuntary Faults," and, having been familiarized with these misfortunes, bear our own with greater fortitude. Tragedy also instructs the miserable to be happier by enabling them to contrast their situation with that of those on the stage. And finally: "Tragedy is a true Medicine, which Purges the Passions. Since it teaches, the Ambitious to Moderate his Ambition; the Wicked, to Fear God; the Passionate, to restrain his Anger, &c. but 'tis a very agreeable Medicine, and works only by Pleasure." For Dryden, catharsis operates in a similarly didactic way: tragedy arouses fear because we see that "no condition is privileged from the turns of fortune" and pity because we see that even the virtuous are not exempt from misfortune. Even the earl of Shaftesbury, whom we might expect to anticipate the sentimentalists, so defines the purpose of tragedy: it is to give "lively Representations of the Disorders and Misery of *the Great*" to make the people more content with their lower and securer state. Gildon and others repeat such explanations *ad nauseam*. For a reflective critic, the effect of catharsis must almost necessarily be that of destroying, or at least reducing, the emotions. Dennis, as usual, gives the most common of ideas its most colorful expression:

. . . as the Humors in some distemper'd Body are rais'd, in order to the evacuating that which is redundant or peccant in them; so Tragedy excites Compassion and Terrour to the same end: For the Play being over, an Audience becomes serene again, and is less apt to be mov'd at the common Accidents of Life, after it has seen the deplorable Calamities of Hero's and Sovereign Princes.

Two years before the *Preface* John Brown says that tragedy eliminates pity and fear by making the people "familiar with distressful and terrible Representations." Thus this understanding of catharsis was still current in Johnson's time. Although these critics may differ considerably in their actual definitions, they generally agree on at least two important points: that much of the instruction of drama consists in reflecting on one's own situation, and that this instruction is accompanied by the eradication or diminution of the passions. Moral instruction, then, tends to become outright didacticism; and thus Dacier advocates reviving the chorus primarily on ethical grounds: it provides the dramatist with a ready-made vehicle for moral commentary.[60]

To illustrate the difference between reflective and sentimental theories, nothing can be more instructive than to compare Dennis's account of catharsis with that of Lord Kames nearly two generations later. The commentators on Aristotle, Kames says, have been most perplexed by what he means.

But no one who has a clear conception of the end and effects of a good tragedy, can have any difficulty about Aristotle's meaning. Our pity is engaged for the persons represented, and our terror is upon our own account. Pity indeed is here made to stand for all the sympathetic emotions, because of these it is the capital. There can be no doubt, that our sympathetic emotions are refined or improved by daily exercise. . . . One thing is certain, that no other meaning can justly be given to the foregoing doctrine than that now mentioned.

The "other meaning" of Dennis—that a dramatic performance wears our emotions out of us—is not even given the benefit of a

---

60. Dacier, *Aristotle's Art of Poetry*, pp. 78–80; Dryden, *Essays*, 1: 210; Shaftesbury, *Characteristicks*, 1: 218–19; Dennis, *Critical Works*, 1: 33 ("The Impartial Critick"); Brown, *Dissertation*, p. 118; Dacier, *Aristotle's Art of Poetry*, sig. B1ᵛ (on the chorus). See also: Gildon, *Works of Shakespear*, 7: xxx; William Egerton, *Faithful Memoirs of . . . Mrs. Anne Oldfield* (London, 1731), p. 100.

repudiation. Kames wrote in 1762. In 1765, at almost the very moment that the *Preface* appeared, a letter was published in the *Gentleman's Magazine* which exhibited more explicitly the implications of Kames's "meaning." Aristotle's explanation is obscure, the correspondent complains:

> It looks as if it meant that the spectators, by accustoming themselves to calamitous objects on the stage, should learn not to be moved by them in real life. If this was his intention, it is, by no means, a good moral effect, and does not at all seem to recommend tragedy. . . . It appears much more natural that the effect of tragedy should be by raising Pity and Terror, to purge the contrary passions, that is, to subdue that confidence in prosperity to which all men are liable; to melt away hardness of heart, and, by giving us a quick sense of the calamities incident to our common nature, to chastise the vain, to soften the cruel, and, in a word, to humanize the whole man, and make him, by this means, a wiser and a better creature.

We have seen that Brown, a year before, had expressed the reflective view; but many began to believe that if catharsis in fact wears out the passions, this is "by no means, a good moral effect."[61]

Once the older understanding of Aristotle had been questioned, it was only a matter of time before other related doctrines were challenged. But although Addison had recognized years earlier that commiseration and poetic justice were incompatible, it was rather the chorus which sentimental theorists first attacked. Possibly Johnson himself wrote a review of *Elfrida* for the *Gentleman's Magazine* in 1752 (see note 20) which repudiates the moral function of the chorus and recommends a more indirect manner of instruction: "incident and event become the vehicles of instruction, not by giving occasion to a *Chorus* to repeat moral sentences, but by the series in which they happen, and the causes by which they are produced." What the reviewer means is that moral instruction ought to be related more intrinsically (we must not yet say *organically*) to the characters and plot. The *Monthly Review* in 1759 is rather more lenient toward Mason's other production, *Caractacus*, but is similarly unable to approve the chorus:

61. Kames, *Elements of Criticism*, 3: 229; *Gentleman's Magazine* 35 (October 1765): 462. The theory of sympathy is set forth quite explicitly, though with no specific reference to the drama, in Hartley, *Observations on Man*, 2: 291–92, and of course in Smith, *Theory of Moral Sentiments*, passim, ten years later.

It is the more peculiar province of dramatic poetry, to instruct rather by example than precept; to animate to virtue, rather by exciting the passions than informing the judgment. So that we might as well find fault with a play, because it is not a sermon, as to censure the omission of the chorus, in modern tragedies, merely on this account.

The reviewer has drawn his distinctions well: implicit in the senti- mental understanding of catharsis is the belief that tragedy works its moral effect "rather by exciting the passions than informing the judgment." If so, what is more ponderous and less effective than a sermonizing chorus? What more tedious than set moral maxims and insipid didacticism? But in English criticism, these are as yet mere tentatives, premonitions of a new understanding of Horace's *prodesse*. Poetic justice has so far preserved her authority.[62]

French critics first developed the implications of sentimentalism. We have noticed that Hurd, when he was discussing tragic pleas- ure, combined or confounded reflective and sentimental explana- tions. Marmontel, an equally transitional figure writing just two years before Johnson, succeeds also in fusing the two. He presents first the older explanation that tragedy *accustoms* us to horrible events. But, Marmontel argues, this tragic fear would seem to be deleterious rather than salutary: it discourages us, since we see man a helpless toy of the fates. Despite Aristotle's apology, Oedipus has really committed no crime, and any lesson he may convey must tend to impiety. As for pity, Marmontel cannot see why this sweetest of passions should be purged. Tragedy, he decides, offers two benefits: it prepares us for the evils which are reserved for us, by showing the misfortunes of others and accustoming us to them; and by exercising our pity it actually *increases* our sensibility, "la tendre humanité." The first advantage we have noted in such critics as Dacier, but the second—the engendering of pity—involves a direct denial of reflective theories of purgation.[63]

By the time Diderot is writing, a decade later, pity has assumed all of the moral functions of tragedy. Some plays, he concedes, may be didactic effectively; but on the whole a play is sufficiently moral if it is noble, honest, and touching. With this argument he rebuts

62. *Gentleman's Magazine* 22 (May 1752): 224–25; *Monthly Review* 20 (June 1759): 508. See also Hurd, *Horatii epistolae*, 1: 142–43, 260, who accepts a less rigorous definition of dramatic instruction.

63. Marmontel, *Poetique françoise*, 2: 103–17.

Rousseau's attack. A year later (1773) L. Sébastien Mercier is even more explicit. Drama has a moral end, but it must achieve this end through moving the passions. Dramatic art exercises our entire sensibility, awakens and strengthens our pity and other virtuous feelings. Mercier pours contempt on the *froid moraliste* and inveighs against legislators, who have treated man as though he were a ferocious animal to be yoked by laws; they need only have appealed to his sympathy. He objects to poetic justice because it is unrealistic and fails to arouse pity; "la condition humaine" (the phrase is his) must be duly imitated, else tragedy will fall short of its goal. Providence has hidden the purpose of evil beneath an impenetrable veil, and the poet will only make himself ridiculous if he attempts to impose a poetic justice. Seeing virtue struggling in adversity will be sufficient, and its own justification; for if the poet sincerely detest crime, he may depict its seeming triumph without reproach. Clearly, a moralizing chorus would be abhorrent to such a philosopher as this. Mercier, the exuberant liberal, boldly bids the moralist take away his dry maxims; it is rather by "ces larmes délicieuses" that the poet imperceptibly develops our intrinsically benevolent moral sense.[64] It is remarkable, however, that criticism specifically of Shakespeare, up to 1765, is quite uninfluenced by sentimental tendencies. To be sure, the poet was both praised and censured for his morality throughout the eighteenth century, but before the *Preface* both positions were argued, by and large, from reflective premises. Thus for Shaftesbury Shakespeare is rude and ungraceful, but pleases "by the Justness of his MORAL." He praises *Hamlet* primarily for being "almost one continu'd *Moral*; a Series of deep Reflections." In short, even for Shaftesbury, who did his part to drive morality from the cerebrum into the viscera, the moral value resides in set speeches, moralizing soliloquies, instructive *passages*. For the same characteristic Shakespeare is praised in *Tatler* no. 111, written jointly by Addison and Steele:

> This admirable author, as well as the best and greatest men of all ages, and of all nations, seems to have had his mind thoroughly seasoned with religion, as is evident by many passages in his plays.

64. Diderot, *Oeuvres de théâtre*, 1: 345–46; Mercier, *Du théâtre*, pp. 1–12, 135, 247–51. Diderot, *Oeuvres de théâtre*, 2: 277–78, attacks plays which have excellent but detached *pensées*: it is not the words, but the impressions which are important. For earlier suggestions of this sort, see La Motte, *Oeuvres de théâtre*, 1: 117–18, 172–73.

Sentimental critics were to develop the notion suggested by the phrase "his mind thoroughly seasoned with religion" into a less didactic theory of moral instruction—a mind so thoroughly seasoned need not condescend to provide set pieces of moralizing; but the older attitude only is revealed here: we are to single out moral passages and reflect upon them with pleasure. Shakespeare's characters, as well as his passages, were praised as moral.[65] Through the 1770s, then, a number of critics leapt to Shakespeare's defense on the moral matter, but almost all argued from reflective premises: Shakespeare includes moral passages in his plays, and his characters are fine moral examples.

From the same premise Shakespeare was attacked for being insufficiently moral. Mrs. Lennox's *Shakespear Illustrated* (1753–54), for which Johnson provided a dedication, serves only to illustrate the futility of applying strict moral standards to Shakespeare. *Measure for Measure* is "absolutely defective in a due Distribution of Rewards and Punishments," and hence is erroneously titled. Of *All's Well*: the poet certainly "has violated all the Rules of poetical Justice in conducting . . . the two principal Persons of the Play to Happiness; when they both . . . merited nothing but Punishment." Shakespeare is to be censured for the catastrophe of *Hamlet*, where "one Fate overwhelms alike the innocent and guilty." In 1770 Francis Gentleman essays the same task, with much the same result: of *Hamlet* "all the moral we can deduce is, that murder cannot lie hid, and that conscience ever makes a coward of guilt." And five years later William Cooke praises the moral of *Lear*, but only as "altered from *Shakespeare* by *Tate*; because almost every Character in that Play is an Instance of Virtue being rewarded and Vice punished." Thus improved, the moral of the play is that of so many of Archbishop Tillotson's excellent sermons, that even "if we extend our Happyness no farther than the Grave, the Interest of all Mankind is to pursue Virtue and fly from Vice."[66] It is

65. Shaftesbury, *Characteristicks*, 1: 275–76; *The Tatler*, in Chalmers, *British Essayists*, 3: 152. On Shakespeare's characters, see: Egerton, *Faithful Memoirs*, p. ii; *Some Remarks on Hamlet*, p. 60. See also: *Gentleman's Magazine* 18 (November 1748): 503: Shakespeare is unequalled for providing "some *prudential maxim*, or *moral precept*." This review, and its continuation in December (p. 553) praise Shakespeare highly for his moral passages and characters. *The Gray's-Inn Journal* for 24 March 1753 praises *Hamlet* for its moral lessons.

66. Charlotte Lennox, *Shakespear Illustrated*, 3 vols. (London, 1753–54), 1: 36–37, 195; Francis Gentleman, *The Dramatic Censor*, 2 vols. (London, 1770),

therefore safe to say that both the defenses and attacks, prior to 1770, are in the main conducted on reflective principles. The defenders are inclined to dwell on particular passages or characters which seem moral, while the attackers are most distressed by the immoral implications of a plot or a catastrophe. As the century progressed, the number of attacks decreased, but the idolators do not gain the upper hand until considerably after 1765.

Even well into mid-century, then, few if any praised Shakespeare for being moral in the sense of refining or strengthening our sensibilities; sentimental theories, although they contributed to Kames's definition of catharsis and to the downfall of the chorus, had not yet been applied to particular dramatists. Mrs. Montagu, in a really exceptional passage, was perhaps the first to do so.

> We are apt to consider Shakespear only as a poet; but he is certainly one of the greatest Moral Philosophers that ever lived.
>
> Euripides was highly esteemed for the moral sentences, with which he has interspersed the speeches in his tragedies; and certainly many general truths are expressed in them with a sententious brevity. But he rather collects general opinions into maxims, and gives them a form, which is easily retained by memory, than extracts any new observations from the characters in action, which every reader of penetration will find the invariable practice of our author; and when he [sc. Shakespeare] introduces a general maxim, it seems forced from him by the occasion. As it arises out of the action, it loses itself again in it, and remains not, as in other writers, an ambitious ornament glittering alone, but is so connected as to be an useful passage very naturally united with the story.

Admittedly, this is very far from Mercier's confidence in the ethical sufficiency of delicious tears; yet she clearly looks forward to him in her depreciation of maxims and her insistence that the instruction be a part of the action itself, arising naturally from it. For the first time, Shakespeare is being praised, rather than blamed, for failing to include didactic passages; his maxims are not imposed

---

1: 59; W. Cooke, *Elements of Dramatic Criticism*, pp. 51–52. Elizabeth Griffith's *The Morality of Shakespeare's Drama* (London, 1775) carries on the tradition of Mrs. Lennox and Gentleman. See also: Egerton, *Faithful Memoirs*, p. 105; T. Cooke, *An Ode on the Power of Poetry* (London, 1751), p. 5. There is, however, an interesting attack on Tate's *Lear* in *An Examen of . . . The Suspicious Husband* (London, 1747), p. 35.

gratuitously on the dramatic fabric like some gaudy and ill-suited jewel; they are *forced* from him by the events themselves and hence are intimately related to them. Kenrick in 1774, certainly influenced by Mrs. Montagu, considers Shakespeare even greater as a moral philosopher than as a poet: his works contain "a practical system of ethics, the more instructive and useful as the precept is almost every where joined to example." His precepts and reflections are not, as with many dramatists, an "adventitious appendage." They "rise naturally from the situation and circumstance of the speaker, and flow spontaneously from his lips, as the genuine effusions of his heart." For this reason, they are more effective, "and have perhaps contributed more to form our national character, for humanity, justice, and benevolence, than all the theoretical books of morality, which have appeared in our language."[67] Kenrick adds a new element: the greater subtlety of Shakespeare's instruction not only renders it more effective, but more apparently sincere and spontaneous (the two being equated by sentimentalists) than that of the obviously didactic author. These opinions swiftly descend into mere popularity until reinvigorated by such critics as Coleridge and Shelley; but it is surely clear how little a Montagu or a Kenrick would relish the factitiousness of Dacier's moralizing chorus.

Johnson's first and most serious objection to Shakespeare is that he is not sufficiently moral:

His first defect is that to which may be imputed most of the evil in books or in men. He sacrifices virtue to convenience, and is so much more careful to please than to instruct, that he seems to write without any moral purpose. From his writings indeed a system of social duty may be selected, for he that thinks reasonably must think morally; but his precepts and axioms drop casually from him; he makes no just distribution of good or evil, nor is always careful to shew in the virtuous a disapprobation of the wicked; he carries his persons indifferently through right and wrong, and at the close dismisses them without further care, and leaves their examples to operate by chance. This fault the barbarity of his age cannot extenuate; for it is always a writer's duty to make the world better, and justice is a virtue independent on time or place.[68]

67. Montagu, *An Essay on Shakespeare*, pp. 59–60; William Kenrick, *Introduction to the School of Shakespeare* (London, 1774), p. 15.
68. *Works*, 7: 71.

Johnson criticizes Shakespeare for precisely those two qualities esteemed by the sentimentalists: the casualness of his precepts and his violation of poetic justice (surely the remark "he makes no just distribution of good or evil" admits of no other interpretation). Having already described Shakespeare as giving a just picture of life, Johnson can hardly avoid admitting that he is moral in a sense; he has, after all, copied nature well, and, moreover, "he that thinks reasonably must think morally." Johnson attributes to Shakespeare a connatural understanding of the moral law; as a thoughtful and reasonable man, the dramatist has perceived, perhaps without much conscious reflection, those moral and universal truths underlying the crude and undigested material of primary experience. Few would deny that there is a morality—a world of values—which informs the sentiments and imparts meaning to the action of his plays. Wayne C. Booth, in the passage serving as an epigraph for this section, plainly promotes the understanding we have inherited from Mrs. Montagu: Shakespeare is undeniably moral, but moral in a comprehensive, rather than dogmatic, sense. He shows us good and evil as they are at war in the world, not as they are anatomized on the theologian's page. But this sort of morality, although good so far as it goes, does not go far enough for Johnson. Unlike Diderot and Mercier, he is not inclined to put away the demands which reason makes upon morality merely because the emotions aroused by a play may be "healthy." Furthermore, he resolutely refuses to excuse this deficiency because of Shakespeare's society and age; barbarity or ignorance cannot invalidate the claims of morality.[69]

Throughout his life Johnson seems never to have decided finally whether art should copy life realistically, or improve it at the expense of verisimilitude. There is something of this indecision in the audacity with which Johnson, as we have noted, defends sublunary nature in the language of generality. No one is more aware than he of the importance of man's ability to generalize his experience; it is this above all that distinguishes us from other

69. Wayne C. Booth, *The Rhetoric of Fiction* (Chicago: University of Chicago Press, 1961), p. 141. Cf. Montagu, *An Essay on Shakespeare*, pp. 123–24: Decorum may change from age to age, but "whatever is immoral is especially blamable in all ages, and every approach to obscenity is an offence for which wit cannot atone, nor the barbarity or the corruption of the times excuse." John Brown, however, *Dissertation*, pp. 79–80, finds Homer immoral, but is disposed, because of his society, to pardon him. So Lessing excuses Plautus for his immorality (J. G. Robertson, *Lessing's Dramatic Theory*, p. 100).

creatures. Yet few preserve a more uncompromising candor in the
face of the real world. As a moralist, he is not prepared to release
the poet from his "duty to make the world better." Thus he says in
Rambler no. 4: "If the world be promiscuously described, I cannot see of what use it can be to read the account; or why it may
not be as safe to turn the eye immediately upon mankind, as upon
a mirror which shows all that presents itself without discrimination." This he says in order to deny that a character or story can
be justified because it is like life: in fiction a realistic and attain-
able virtue should be shown, and vice should always disgust. In
the dedication which Johnson assisted Thomas Maurice in writing
for his *Poems* (1780), the exemplary function of drama is stressed:

> To animate mankind to the practice of virtue, and the conquest of
> those passions which are most detrimental to society, by holding forth
> examples taken from real life, either of vice degraded or triumphant
> virtue, hath ever been the chief aim of those who duly considered the
> nature and origin of theatrical composition.

The examples are to be drawn from "real life," yes—but *selected*
from real life; the artist is to *shape* his work to moral ends. In his
preface for Maurice's translation of *Œdipus Tyrannus* in the same
volume, Johnson is diligent to identify poetic justice in the play.
Oedipus's fate, he says, is not so unjustified as some would suggest:
although he is a good king, Oedipus in private life displays a
number of faults: haughtiness, obstinacy, impatience, etc. "By
making him criminal in a small degree, and miserable in a very
great one, by investing him with some excellent qualities, and
some imperfections, he at once inclines us to pity and to condemn."
Johnson is no less emphatic in his "Notes to Shakespeare" than in
his *Preface*, where he rebukes the poet for failing to instruct, censure, and observe poetic justice.[70]

70. *Works*, 3: 22; Hazen, ed., *Johnson's Prefaces*, pp. 138–39, 141. For the
"Notes to Shakespeare," see *Works*, 7: 135, 213, 265, 326, 512. Oedipus could be
a problem for defenders of poetic justice. La Motte, *Oeuvres de théâtre*, 1:
188–89, regards Oedipus as in reality innocent, and regrets that Sophocles condemned to such horrors a man who was not at all at fault. And in the *Anecdotes
by Joseph Cradock* Johnson himself is recorded as saying: "Oedipus was a poor
miserable man, subjected to the greatest distress, without any degree of culp-
ability of his own" (*Johnsonian Miscellanies*, ed. G. B. Hill, 2 vols. [Oxford,
1897], 2: 62).

But if the artist's duty is to make the world better, it is also to guide us in the one where we find ourselves. Writing to Bennet Langton in 1758 Johnson reflects: "Whether to see life as it is will give us much consolation I know not, but the consolation which is drawn from truth, if any there be, is solid and durable, that which may be derived from errour must be like its original fallacious and fugitive." In his *Life of Addison* he quotes generously from Dennis's attack on *Cato* for its want of poetic justice, but decides:

Whatever pleasure there may be in seeing crimes punished and virtue rewarded, yet, since wickedness often prospers in real life, the poet is certainly at liberty to give it prosperity on the stage. For if poetry has an imitation of reality, how are its laws broken by exhibiting the world in its true form? The stage may sometimes gratify our wishes; but, if it be truly the *mirror of life*, it ought to shew us sometimes what we are to expect.

He is elsewhere quite indifferent to the frequent charge that *The Beggar's Opera* was written "without any moral purpose." And he comments of Milton's Adam: "There is no reason why the hero should not be unfortunate except established practice, since success and virtue do not go necessarily together." But he adds, like Richardson of *Clarissa*, "However, if success be necessary, Adam's deceiver was at last crushed; Adam was restored to his Maker's favour, and therefore may securely resume his human rank."[71] Most revealing of all is his "General Observation on *Lear*." There he agrees that the moral of the play—that villainy leads to villainy— is well enforced; but "Shakespeare has suffered the virtue of Cordelia to perish in a just cause, contrary to the natural ideas of justice, to the hope of the reader, and, what is yet more strange, to the faith of the chronicles." Even the chronicles—history—have in this rare instance reflected providential justice—what could be a more felicitous subject for a moral poet? Yet Shakespeare, perversely it seems, has ignored the instructive ending which even history has supplied. Johnson then refers to the Addison-Dennis controversy, and concludes:

A play in which the wicked prosper, and the virtuous miscarry, may doubtless be good, because it is a just representation of the common

71. Johnson, *The Letters*, ed. R. W. Chapman, 3 vols. (Oxford: Oxford University Press, 1952), 1: 111; *Lives*, 2: 135, 278–79; 1: 176.

events of human life: but since all reasonable beings naturally love justice, I cannot easily be persuaded, that the observation of justice makes a play worse; or, that if other excellencies are equal, the audience will not always rise better pleased from the final triumph of persecuted virtue.[72]

Perhaps no eighteenth-century critic has stated the problem more delicately in one sentence; art should indeed imitate life, but at the same time reasonable beings not only "think morally" but "naturally love justice." The Addisons and Merciers have their way until the colon: it is true that ours is a fallen world, and we cannot fairly deny the artist his right to copy it. But the rest of Johnson's remark vindicates Dennis, who after all was neither a stupid nor a naïve man: we are reasonable and moral beings; our sense of justice is superior to the real justice which prevails in the world, but is not this sense, too, a part of our experience, and fittingly to be imitated by the poet? If Dennis's poetic justice is not subtle, Addison's appeal to sublunary nature is not profound, nor is it sensitive. A play *may* be good if it copies mere reality, but as reasonable beings we are justified in demanding more of art. Johnson is not criticizing Shakespeare for his failure to include a moralizing chorus or to devise some pollyanna ending which would outrage our sense of truth. A skillful dramatist need not resort to these. But Johnson is, undeniably, asking from Shakespeare a more conscientious *structuring* of life than he provides. The ethical suppositions of his plays have perplexed even the sophistication of modern critics; and if today we still cannot agree on whether Shakespeare was an orthodox Christian or a humanist, we must not pretend to wonder at Johnson's dissatisfaction with the ambiguity of his "moral purpose."[73]

The reflective and sentimental theories have been called by Yvor Winters didactic and Romantic. The one, he says, "offers us

---

72. *Works*, 8: 705.

73. Hagstrum, in my opinion, plays down Johnson's didacticism too much. Because Shakespeare imitated both general and sublunary nature, Hagstrum says, "By Johnsonian standards [he] must be, in spite of occasional and incidental lapses from the strictest morality, the most moral of poets precisely because he is the most natural" (*Johnson's Literary Criticism*, p. 72). By Wayne C. Booth's standards, perhaps, but patently not by Johnson's, else what are we to make of this, Johnson's criticism of Shakespeare's "first defect," one "to which may be imputed most of the evil in books or in men"? Johnson, after all, *is* severe on Shakespeare.

useful precepts and explicit moral instruction"; while the other theory "assumes that literature is mainly or even purely an emotional experience, that man is naturally good, that man's impulses are trustworthy, that the rational faculty is unreliable to the point of being dangerous or possibly evil."[74] It is easy enough to situate Johnson within such a framework. The sentimental critics held consistently to two related principles: the drama must be like real life, and it must evoke pity or sympathy for the protagonists; having established this much, they went on to formulate theories of catharsis which emphasized the strengthening or refining of our emotions: if our moral impulses are located in our sensibility, then a drama, to fulfill its instructive purposes, must exercise and develop that sensibility. The reflective theorists were thus apt to apply idealistic, rather than realistic, criteria to drama: if poetic justice reflects providential will, it has imitated the ultimate Form of things even while being unfaithful to life "this side the grave." They believed that instruction ought to be directed at the reason through explicit passages of moralizing, rather than at the sensibility; accordingly, their theories of catharsis involve exhausting or reducing the emotions. Now Johnson, evidently, was of two minds regarding poetic justice specifically and, in general, the amount of idealizing appropriate to dramatic works; in the *Preface*, however, he takes the conservative view on both matters. His judgments might have been regarded by Mrs. Montagu or Lord Kames as somewhat antiquated, but not really reactionary. He is silent on the question of catharsis, and this in itself is possibly revealing. Johnson was quite aware of the emotional power of tragedy, but there is reason to think that he more feared than admired this power. His account of Aristotelian purgation, recorded in Boswell's *Life* for 1776, strongly resembles Dacier's of nearly ninety years before. Finally, considering his often declared and vehement contempt for *feelers*, one can easily guess what he would have thought of Mercier's belittling the rules, whether those of society or of art. For Johnson, man *was* a "ferocious animal" one of whose few claims to decency was that he could sometimes restrain his passions by reason. Mercier's assurance that a dramatist, if he raises the "proper" emotions, might safely dispense with poetic justice is as well founded as his

74. Yvor Winters, *In Defense of Reason* (Denver: Alan Swallow, 1947), pp. 3, 8.

faith in progress and human perfectibility. At least, Johnson would very likely have found them equally fanciful and dangerous.

But the didactic theory was imperfect and by Johnson's time had exhausted much of its vitality. As Winters and others have noted, this theory failed to account for how art *differed* from moral instruction: Was it an adequate explanation to say that art merely *dressed up* truth? The artist is not necessarily *better* than a preacher, but he is at least different, and if he is moral in a different way, he must be moral in a less didactic, more emotive way. Romantic theories sought to strike a more equitable balance between the purely didactic and the imaginative modes of instruction. Thus Mrs. Montagu tried to find a subtler, less explicit way. The moral passages which Johnson desired she regarded as extrinsic, preferring instruction which arises naturally from the complications of the fable, and the actions (rather than the *words*) of the characters. She was truly addressing herself to the aesthetic problems of the immediate future, while Johnson cared little for such problems. As a result, his didacticism, epitomized by his preference for Tate's *Lear*, seems unimaginative when compared with the best Romantic criticism, although it may well have been for Johnson an unavoidable preference. A modern critic might find Yvor Winters's own "moralistic" or "absolutist" position tenable, for it enables him at once to reject Romantic theories as false and dangerous in their subjectivism, and yet to account coherently for the aesthetic *and* moral superiority of the original *Lear* over Tate's; but this is a uniquely twentieth-century solution, and not itself perfectly satisfactory.[75] For an eighteenth-century critic who was so obstinate as to prefer a moral *reason* to a moral *sense*, there can have been no alternative to the didactic theory. That Johnson held the theory reasonably and with sophistication is his great virtue; and the modesty and deliberation with which he recommends the Tate version, in his "General Observation on *Lear*," must surely exempt him from the rage of modern Shakespeare idolators.

And lest we too hastily proclaim the present consensus all adverse

---

75. This theory is developed in the foreword to *In Defense of Reason*, especially pp. 11–14. It is possible that Johnson would have discerned an element of cant in Winters's logic. For an energetic defense of poetic instruction and its relationship to delight, see Paul Ramsey, *The Lively and the Just* (Tuscaloosa: University of Alabama Press, 1962), pp. 11–16, where he also provides a constructive criticism of Winters's theory.

to Johnson, we might at least contemplate the adjudications of the precise and plausible Prosser Hall Frye, of modern critics the most Johnsonian in principle, who similarly reproaches Shakespeare for those frequent and inadequate moral resolutions which, supplying no true restoration of the ethical order, he declares at best "sentimental and lenitive"; and who has indeed the temerity to censure, on aesthetic but even on moral grounds, the "blundered" fifth act of *Lear* with the "extrinsic and superfluous" fatalities of Cordelia and her father. But Frye, though no reactionary disciple of poetic justice, is a classicist whose taste favors Sophocles over Shakespeare. So it is Booth's more modern emphasis, not his, that enjoys the preponderance of academic conviction.[76]

The sentimentalists' redefinition of *instruction*, residing as it does upon a redefinition of morality itself, was their greatest intrusion on Johnson's world. They, finally, would prevent man from rising above his primary and peculiar experiences. By reducing criticism to taste, they imprison each of us within our own feelings, and by directing the artist's attention exclusively to the individual and domestic, they confine him within the merely particular. By equating our pleasure in the things and people around us in life with those in art, they have confounded the two. But if criticism is more than feeling, it must enunciate principles; if art is different

76. See Prosser Hall Frye, *Romance and Tragedy* (Lincoln: University of Nebraska Press, 1961), pp. 106, 245, 290 (cf. p. 285: "Shakespeare was . . . concerned rather to reflect life than to interpret it"). Even more fundamental to Frye's criticism than to Johnson's is the distinction between literature and naturalistic writing (or as he sometimes calls it, journalism), the former dealing with the moral order perceived through or imposed upon the natural phenomena. With this, at least, the classical literature is concerned, while the Romantic is interested in the natural, the scientific, the physical law. See ibid., pp. 51, 163–64, 173–74, 296–98, 350–52; *Literary Reviews and Criticisms* (New York and London: G. P. Putnam's Sons, 1908), pp. 185–89; *Visions & Chimeras* (Boston: Marshall Jones, 1929), pp. 274–77. His friend and fellow-critic Paul Elmer More, throughout his voluminous and trenchant essays, protests continually the sequestration of ethics from literature. See, for example, *New Shelburne Essays*, vol. 3 (Princeton: Princeton University Press, 1936): pp. 194–95. And John Crowe Ransom, *The World's Body* (Baton Rouge: Louisiana State University Press, 1968), pp. 55–75, rather pensively analyses the effects of this separation on modern poetry. In view of these and similar critics, Johnson's judgments here may seem less eccentric. In any event, it is fatuous to dismiss them as merely the prejudices of an "eighteenth-century mind." The problem of morality is fundamental to aesthetics, and no respectable critic, disdaining the vacuous rigmarole of *ars gratia artis*, can capably skirt it.

from life, it must comment upon life. This ability to generalize Johnson instinctively defends. Morality, however, is' man's most indispensable form of generalization; it is his most extensive and serious attempt to categorize and impose order on the discrete particles of existence. By identifying morality with sentiment or feeling, the Merciers and Diderots would again confine us within our personal sensibilities, but it is unlikely that Johnson would have found this a satisfactory substitute for didacticism, a didacticism which for the most part is sophisticated, sensitive, and principled. Such doctrines as poetic justice are not essential to it, but—disagreeable as they may be—they are perhaps preferable to Mercier's exuberant confidence in our natural rectitude; and they are certainly preferable to that criticism which has descended to us from Mercier and which would actually esteem art for its imagined independence of ethical values.

Chapter IV

Faults Sufficient

Even in an age when judicial criticism was the rule, few critics practiced it more assiduously than Johnson. No poet is so miserable as to be utterly without merit, or so skillful as to be faultless; a critic, then, is to be above the easy temptations of a eulogy or an assault, since he is required by his office to examine both the beauties and the failures. "Shakespeare is the poet of nature"—Johnson's favorable criticism radiates outward from this central contention. His characters are just representations of general nature, and his plays depict the real state of sublunary nature; he disregards the unities because they are unnecessary to an effective portrayal of nature. Shakespeare's first and most serious defect—the obscurity of his moral purpose—is a failure to perceive the moral order underlying sublunary nature; so, too, is his second fault: the defective structure of his plots. An artist is expected to impart order to experience, and Shakespeare, in ethical or purely structural matters, is inadequate to Johnson's expectations. Next, Shakespeare fails to preserve verisimilitude—he is not *true* to nature. And finally, his language sometimes deviates *from* nature. Shakespeare's imperfect structure, his lack of verisimilitude, and his faulty language— these imperfections, together with his want of a moral plan, are the objects of Johnson's criticism, and they are all in some degree unnatural. However individualistic or idiosyncratic Johnson may be in other portions of the *Preface,* here he is conventional, though his use of *nature* in several different senses is confusing. And yet, although a thorough examination of the background of his remarks would be gratuitous, we must explore a little both his ideas and those of his contemporaries. Even in his own day, and often since, Johnson has been accused of unreasonable severity. We must consider this charge, for no one can deny that Johnson chooses emphatic language with which to open his attack: "Shakespeare with all his excellencies has likewise faults, and faults sufficient to ob-

127

scure and overwhelm any other merit." By "any other merit" Johnson probably means any merits less estimable than those he has just imputed to Shakespeare; but even tempered so, his animadversions have been a source of discomfiture for his admirers and of vituperation for his enemies.

Although they might easily have been improved, Shakespeare's plots, Johnson believes, are too loosely formed and "carelessly pursued." He might have included many instructive or affecting scenes, but has let the opportunities slip by, and he seems to become even more negligent toward the end of his plays, falling back on improbable or imperfect catastrophes.[1] Perhaps the twentieth century is better able to understand Johnson's objections than the nineteenth, when unities of character or organicism had so far prevailed as almost to eradicate the values traditionally attached to plot. To be sure, when a play contains such a person as Manfred or Prometheus, one readily forgives its paucity of interesting or reasonable events; an association of ideas or a continuity of character replaces a "chain of events, logically concatenated." But neoclassicists accepted Aristotle's belief, reiterated by Rymer, that fable is the soul of tragedy and that it is primarily through the plot, rather than the characters, that instruction is communicated:

> And besides the *purging* of the *passions* [says Rymer]; something must stick by observing that constant order, that harmony and beauty of Providence, that necessary relation and chain, whereby the causes and the effects, the vertues and rewards, the vices and their punishments are proportion'd and link'd together; how dark soever are laid the Springs, and however intricate and involv'd are their operations.

Gildon, following Aristotle, defines tragedy as the imitation, not of a man, but of an action, and hence the fable is the most important part; it is in the forming of plot that "the Poet's principal Care ought to be employ'd." Nor did neoclassicists underestimate the difficulty of devising a good plot. Brumoy decides that it is a more exacting task to write tragedy than comedy, because it requires more ingenuity to form a proper plan. In comedy "the characters come upon the stage with very little artifice or plot" and thus the "disposition of parts" is only a minor aspect in the

---

1. *Works,* 7: 71–72. All subsequent quotations will be from pp. 72–74.

excellence of a comedy. But in tragedy a good plot is the supreme accomplishment of a genius. Brumoy also compares a well-contrived plot

> to a large and beautiful temple, which the skill of the architect hath so contrived as to make it appear at first view of much less extent than it really is, wherein the farther you advance, the more you are surprised at the vast intervening space, which the extraordinary symmetry and proportion of it's parts had conceal'd from the eye.

Joseph Warton unreservedly pronounces: "To produce, and carry on with probability and decorum, a series of events, is the most difficult work of invention."[2]

Early critics agree that Shakespeare has failed in this "most difficult work." At the same time, they are willing to praise his characters. Thus Dryden, Rowe, and Gildon censure his plots but find some atonement in his delineation of character. More than two generations after Dryden, the argument is much the same. Mrs. Lennox, who was the first to undertake any study of Shakespeare's sources after Gerard Langbaine (1691), usually discovers that his plots are *less* well constructed than those of the originals; and even the partisan Mrs. Montagu finds she must deplore them.[3] Thus critics in the first half of the century unite in condemning Shakespeare's plots, and while some suggest that he partly compensates for this by the excellence of his characters, this is *only* a compensation.

Defenders of Shakespeare multiplied in the fifties and sixties, and they might argue either that his plots were not so defective as his

2. Thomas Rymer, *The Critical Works*, ed. C. A. Zimansky (New Haven: Yale University Press, 1956), p. 75; Charles Gildon, *Works of Shakespear*, vol. 7 (London, 1710), p. xxvii; *The Greek Theatre of Father Brumoy*, 3 vols. (London, 1759), 3: 160 (the second passage, containing the *temple* metaphor, is picked up by Thomas Francklyn, *A Dissertation on Antient Tragedy* [London, 1760], p. 15); Joseph Warton, *An Essay on the Genius and Writings of Pope*, 4th ed., 2 vols. (London, 1782), 2: 2.

3. Charlotte Lennox, *Shakespear Illustrated*, 3 vols. (London, 1753–54), passim (see 2: 238 for one example); Elizabeth Montagu, *An Essay on the Writings and Genius of Shakespeare* (London, 1769), p. 71. See also: John Dryden, *Essays*, ed. W. P. Ker, 2 vols. (Oxford: Oxford University Press, 1926), 1: 211, 165; Rowe in *Eighteenth-Century Essays on Shakespeare*, ed. D. N. Smith (Oxford: Oxford University Press, 1963), pp. 15–16; Gildon, *Works of Shakespear*, 7: xlv; John Upton, *Critical Observations on Shakespeare*, 2d ed. (London, 1748), p. 25.

critics supposed, or that plot itself was not so important. Lord Kames stands virtually alone in taking the first position.[4] The more popular because safer approach is cautiously adopted as early as 1748, when Peter Whalley, having complained conventionally about the plots, adds that Shakespeare is unrivalled in his expression of characters and manners, and that these are more "useful, and perhaps more conducive to the End of Tragedy, than the Design and Conduct of the Plot." Five years later Arthur Murphy throws Whalley's caution to the winds. Defending Shakespeare against Voltaire, he calls plot a "secondary Beauty; the Exhibition of Character, and the Excitement of the Passions, justly claiming the Precedence in dramatic Poetry":

> It is in Writing as in Gardening; where Natures [sic!] does not afford spontaneous Beauties, recourse must be had to the Embellishments of slow endeavouring Art, to the Regularity of uniform Vistas, the Intricacy of elaborated Mazes, and a studied Insertion of Evergreens; but when the Course of the Country of itself presents attractive Scenes on every Side, when the Trees branch out with a free Expansion, and the bold Prospect surprizes with the Heath, the Lawn, the Hill, and Valley, in wild Variety, the Littleness of tedious Culture is unnecessary, and trifling Ornaments are unlooked for.

We have come very far, and in only a few years, from Brumoy, for whom a well-ordered plot was as a "large and beautiful temple." Murphy prefers the irregular countryside of character and passion; far from being the "most difficult work of invention," for Murphy plot is a "trifling ornament." Indeed, the older scale of priorities is now reversed: a mediocre talent, by devising a careful plot, can compensate, somewhat, for his inability to draw living characters or to describe the passions! That this was something of a critical revolution Murphy was quite aware; he speaks even more plainly a year later: "*Aristotle* was certainly mistaken when he called the Fable the Life and Soul of Tragedy; the Art of constructing the dramatic Story should always be subservient to the Exhibition

4. Kames, *Elements of Criticism,* 3 vols. (Edinburgh, 1762), 3: 266–67: "A play analyzed, is a chain of connected facts, of which each scene makes a link. Each scene, accordingly, ought to produce some incident relative to the catastrophe or ultimate event. . . . A barren scene can never be intitled to a place, because the chain is complete without it. . . . How successfully is this done by Shakespear! in whose works there is not to be found a single barren scene."

of Character; our great *Shakespear* has breathed another Soul into Tragedy, which has found the Way of striking the Audience with Sentiment and Passion at the same Time." Finally, ten years after the *Preface,* the anonymous author of *The Correspondents* praises Shakespeare and remarks: "I have no time to consider how he strains probability in his *events,* my attention is wholly engaged by the innumerable strokes of truth and nature in his *characters."* Shakespeare's characters, no longer a mere compensation for his faulty plots, are now his primary excellence; and even a good plot cannot compensate for their absence. Already by the fifties, then, character had been exalted over plot and the older notions of unity associated with it; Murphy's agricultural metaphors are prophetic of the kind of unity that was to take their place.[5]

Predictably, Johnson expresses the older view. In his dedication for Mrs. Lennox he states that the first and most valuable power of a poet is invention, that the highest degree of invention is the ability to produce a series of events—a story—and that to determine Shakespeare's quality of invention precisely, one must examine his sources. In his *Proposals* (1756) he promises that for his edition he will read the originals and compare them with Shakespeare's versions; and yet, as Karl Young has demonstrated, Johnson did little or nothing in this way. Considering how highly he valued plot, this failure is a little surprising and certainly regrettable. As it stands, his criticism of Shakespeare's plots is reasonable and judicious, quite uninfluenced by newer theories. He objects to them on grounds which are moral ("omits opportunities of instructing"), psychological ("rejects those exhibitions which would be more affecting, for . . . those which are more easy"), and logical (implausible catastrophes), all of which had long been traditional reasons for censure.[6]

Johnson's next criticism is that Shakespeare "had no regard to distinction of time or place, but gives to one age or nation, without

5. Peter Whalley, *An Enquiry into the Learning of Shakespeare* (London, 1748), pp. 16–17; Arthur Murphy, *The Gray's-Inn Journal,* 2 vols. (London, 1756) 1: 263–64; 2: 267 (but cf. 2: 222, where he wishes that the "noble Wildness" of Shakespeare's genius had not produced such irregular plots); *The Correspondents,* quoted in R. G. Noyes, *The Thespian Mirror* (Providence: Brown University Press, 1953), p. 66.

6. Lennox, *Shakespear Illustrated,* 1: iv–vii; see Karl Young, "Samuel Johnson on Shakespeare: One Aspect," *University of Wisconsin Studies in Language and Literature,* Vol. 18 (Madison: University of Wisconsin Press, 1923), pp. 146–226.

scruple, the customs, institutions, and opinions of another, at the expense not only of likelihood, but of possibility." He objects to the mingling of classical with gothic mythology, and arraigns Sidney as another offender. Again, there is little remarkable here: Johnson is with the vast majority of neoclassical critics who condemned such violations of verisimilitude.[7] Horace had long ago enjoined the poet to preserve the characteristics of an age or time—propriety—and his injunction was not forgotten by mid-century critics. For Wilkes in 1759 it is an essential duty of the author that he know the age, nation, and manners of his characters; Shakespeare, he continues, did not always excel in this, although in one thing he *is* exact: he always makes his Romans speak like Romans, his Englishmen like Englishmen. Even Mrs. Montagu, a decade later, is no less insistent than the most adamant neoclassicist: "It is strange that Painters, who are to give the mute inanimate figure, are required to be rigid observers of the Costumi, and the dramatic Poet, who is to imitate sentiment, discourse, and action, should be allowed to neglect them." But both Wilkes and Montagu present us with a possible contradiction. They, like Johnson, argue for verisimilitude, but Wilkes praises Shakespeare's Romans for being like Romans, while Mrs. Montagu urges poets not to neglect the costumes. Has not Johnson earlier said that the poet *should* in fact "neglect the drapery," and has he not congratulated the dramatist for refusing to make his Romans especially Roman? We must be careful not to push Johnson's drapery metaphor to an unseemly literalness. By drapery, Johnson understands a too minute and insignificant particularity. But what both he and Mrs. Montagu are interested in here is that element of verisimilitude necessary to make a drama probable and plausible. Admittedly, this may very well be inconsistent with his denial of dramatic illusion—if we take *that* literally; but not necessarily with the value which he placed on generality. Doubtless a Mrs.

7. There are a few exceptions. William Collins's *Verses . . . to Sir Thomas Hanmer* (1743) praises Shakespeare for his historical verisimilitude. Theobald partly defends Shakespeare by attributing his anachronisms to "the Effect of Poetic License, rather than Ignorance" (*Eighteenth-Century Essays on Shakespeare*, p. 81); and Thomas Davies, *Dramatic Miscellanies*, 3 vols. (Dublin, 1784), 2: 208–10, justifies his "giving the manners of London to the inhabitants of any other part of the globe." Thomas Warton, *Observations on the "Fairy Queen,"* 2d ed., 2 vols. (London, 1762) 1: 66 ff., praises Spenser's deviations from history and mythology.

Montagu would insist on *more* particularities than Johnson, but this is a matter of degree. In his "Notes to Shakespeare" he shows a similar concern for accuracy, which in these matters was not drapery, but a realism which he apparently regarded as much more necessary than, say, the unities to sustain credibility. One might observe, too, that historical perspective was largely a product of the eighteenth century, and this very probably reinforced the old doctrine of propriety.[8]

The inappropriateness, extravagance, or deficiencies of Shakespeare's language excite the rest of Johnson's unfavorable criticism. With regard to inappropriateness, he complains of the gross jests which often occur in the comic scenes, and also that people of quality, as well as clowns, indulge in them. While Johnson admits that he does not know whether or not this reflects the actual conversation of the time, he is certain that a less offensive banter must have been available, and that a poet ought to choose the best. Eighteenth-century critics, of course, always censured licentious language, and often charged Shakespeare with being its chief practitioner.[9] No genre was regarded as so common that genuinely offensive language was suitable for it. Batteux, for example, distinguishes between high and low comedy, but in even the low, although the dialogue ought to be naïve and simple, no grossness must be permitted. Dennis defends the inclusion of "realistic" language in comedy, even to the point of using dialect, but generally he recommends a polite style.[10] Johnson's criticism, then,

---

8. Thomas Wilkes, *A General View of the Stage* (London, 1759), p. 30; Montagu, *An Essay on Shakespeare*, p. 51; in Johnson's notes, see: *Works*, 7: 173, 374, 433, 445; 8: 724, 884. Cf. Upton, *Critical Observations on Shakespeare*, p. 127. In French criticism see: Pierre Corneille, *Oeuvres complètes*, 2 vols. (Paris, 1852), 2: 554–55; Jean Baptiste Dubos, *Réflexions critiques sur la poésie et sur la peinture*, 2 vols. (Paris, 1719), 1: 232; Voltaire, *Works*, 38 vols. (London, 1778–81), 19: 315–16; Denis Diderot, *Oeuvres de théâtre*, 2 vols. (Amsterdam, 1772), 2: 396.

9. See: *The Works of Beaumont and Fletcher*, ed. Lewis Theobald, Thomas Seward, et al., vol. 1 (London, 1750), p. liii; Rymer, *Critical Works*, pp. 96–97; *Some Remarks on the Tragedy of Hamlet* (London, 1736), p. 39 and passim; Zachary Grey, *Critical, Historical, and Explanatory Notes on Shakespeare*, 2 vols. (London, 1754), 1: vi.

10. Charles Batteux, *Les beaux arts réduits à un même principe* (Paris, 1747), pp. 136 ff.; John Dennis, *Critical Works*, ed. E. N. Hooker, 2 vols. (Baltimore: Johns Hopkins Press, 1939–43), 1: 224–25 (see Hooker's notes, 1: 486–87 and 493–94).

is quite traditional; he objects on moral grounds, and on grounds of decorum (gentlemen should not speak as rudely as rustics).

Shakespeare's "false sublimity" and conceited language are the final subjects which arouse his displeasure. In spontaneous expressions, Johnson believes, he excels, but when he "solicits his invention, or strains his faculties, the offspring of his throes is tumour, meanness, tediousness, and obscurity." Much earlier, Dennis among others had remarked:

> There are Lines that are utterly void of that celestial Fire, of which *Shakespear* is sometimes Master in so great a Degree. And consequently there are Lines that are stiff and forc'd, and harsh and unmusical, tho' *Shakespear* had naturally an admirable Ear for the Numbers. But no Man ever was very musical who did not write with Fire, and no Man can always write with Fire, unless he is so far Master of his Time, as to expect those Hours when his Spirits are warm and volatile.

We think of neoclassicism—and properly—as disdaining emotional or inspirational theories of composition. Nevertheless, even the most rigorously rationalistic critic agreed that when language comes easily to a poet, it is likely to be less "stiff and forc'd" than when it comes with difficulty. This is only common sense, not pre-Romanticism. Thus, almost half a century after Dennis, Robert Lloyd criticizes the turgidity of Richard Cumberland's *Banishment of Cicero*. Nature, he says, disdains all "labour'd artifice of speech." We admire Shakespeare's descriptions, he continues, because these spring from "luxuriance of fancy"; but we must needs think, in seeing writers hunt after description, *In tenui labor et tenuis gloria*. Johnson is, however, a more unrelenting critic than either Dennis or Lloyd; as a man who had himself often written when his spirits were not "warm and volatile," he would have had little sympathy with Dennis's apology. If even Shakespeare labors at times, then even Shakespeare must be censured. But if Johnson still seems too severe, this may be as much the result of his sensitivity as of his rigorism. He appears to have been especially affected by pathetic scenes, and especially disgusted when such scenes were too strongly laced with inflated, bombastic, or hyperbolical language. He is a little stern with Shakespeare, then, but not remarkably so.[11]

11. Dennis, *Critical Works*, 2: 16; Lloyd in *Monthly Review* 24 (June 1761): 395–96. Johnson comments with approval on the absence of bombast in *Henry VIII*, act 4, scene ii, a "tender and pathetick" scene (*Works*, 8: 653). On Johnson

Shakespeare can be labored, too, in his narrative passages. He may relate an incident in too many words and in a tedious and unanimated manner. Such narration should be rapid and interrupted, but Shakespeare, "instead of lightening it by brevity, endeavoured to recommend it by dignity and splendour." Just as he tried to compensate, when language failed to come, by inflating it, so he tried to counteract the slowness of his narration, not by tightening it up, as he ought to have done, but by relying on turgidity, the false sublime. Johnson's criticism reflects the growing preference for action and celerity to description and narration. Trapp may be taken to represent the older and classical view: many things are shown on the stage which, if narrated, would have been less offensive and horrible. But although all critics would have agreed to proscribe many incidents, some began to expand the range of permissible subjects and to place more emphasis on vigor, variety, and activity. Twenty years after Trapp the *Prompter* inquires: "Who is so ignorant of the Rules of Dramatic Poetry, as not to know, that *these clashing* Opinions, these *opposite* Passions and Interests, these *Reasons which destroy one another* . . . are the *Life* and *Support* of the Theatre; which is *cold* and *unanimating,* where-ever such *Agitation* is wanting." The French are the worst offenders here; they follow the unities, "but the best of their tragedies [says Warton] . . . have defects of another kind, and are what may be justly called, *descriptive* and *declamatory* dramas; and contain the sentiments and feelings of the *author* or the *spectator,* rather than of the *person* introduced as speaking." So important had this distinction become, that John Brown in 1763 regards it as one of the most significant transitions in the development of sophisticated from primitive poetry; the primitive was eventually improved "into a more perfect Form," with representation taking the place of relation. In 1774 William Richardson attacks the French, but praises Shakespeare:

---

and the pathetic, see Jean H. Hagstrum, *Samuel Johnson's Literary Criticism* (Chicago: University of Chicago Press, 1967), pp. 137–44. And see also: Dryden, *Essays,* 1: 203, 224; *Some Remarks on Hamlet,* p. 51; *Adventurer* no. 93; *Spectator* nos. 39, 285 (on Milton); Kames, *Elements of Criticism,* 1: 419, 513. But cf. Dodd's preface to his *Beauties of Shakespeare* (1752) where he defends what other critics have falsely called his bombast.

We often confound the writer who imitates the passions with him who only describes them. Shakespeare imitates, Corneille describes. . . . But perfect imitation can never be effectuated, unless the poet in some measure becomes the person he represents, clothes himself with his character, assumes his manners, and transposeth himself into his situation.[12]

In favoring action and vigorous, reciprocal dialogue, Johnson is perceptive but not surprising.[13]

Johnson's next objection is that Shakespeare's "declamations or set speeches are commonly cold and weak, for his power was the power of nature." The object of frequent complaint, this, too, is a failing peculiar to "poets of nature": the turgidity of artificial and labored language, the unanimated narration, the set declamations—all are in one way or another deviations from natural expression. Johnson then remarks that the sentiments are often confusedly expressed, the language is too intricate, and that Shakespeare was unwilling to take the time to clarify either. Again, Johnson is simply repeating the convictions of five earlier editors and numerous commentators. Upton, perhaps, comes closest to Johnson's phraseology: "Shakespeare labouring with a multiplicity of sublime ideas often gives himself not time to be delivered of them by the rules of *slow-endeavouring art.*" He provides examples from *Hamlet* and *Macbeth* of the poet's crowding metaphors on metaphors, losing himself in the syntax, and the like. Other critics, while recognizing

12. Joseph Trapp, *Praelectiones poeticae*, 3d ed., 2 vols. (London, 1736), 2: 174; *Prompter* no. 148 (1736); Warton, *Genius and Writings of Pope*, 2: 350; John Brown, *A Dissertation on the Rise . . . of Poetry and Music* (London, 1763), p. 42; William Richardson, *A Philosophical Analysis and Illustration of Some of Shakespeare's Remarkable Characters*, 2d ed. (London, 1774), p. 26. Richardson anticipates the direction in which the Romantics would take this extreme understanding of imitation: the author is believed to dissipate his personality among his characters; Shakespeare is the "Proteus of the drama; he changes himself into every character, and enters easily into every condition of human nature" (ibid., p. 38). I shall consider this notion in chap. 5, section 2. Kames, *Elements of Criticism*, 2: 155, 220, and Montagu, *An Essay on Shakespeare*, pp. 30–31, attack pure narration or description, Montagu criticizing the French particularly.

13. Johnson even recommends a certain amount of dialogue in the epic (*Lives*, 1: 188). See also James Ralph, *The Touch-Stone* (London, 1728), p. 63; Daniel Webb, *Observations on the Correspondence between Poetry and Music* (London, 1769), p. 138. In French criticism, see: Corneille, *Oeuvres complètes*, 2: 558; Houdart de La Motte, *Oeuvres de théâtre*, 2 vols. (Paris, 1730), 1: 119–20; Dubos, *Réflexions critiques*, 1: 95–96; *Greek Theatre of Brumoy*, 1: cviii; L. Sébastien Mercier, *Du théâtre* (Amsterdam, 1773), p. 144.

this defect, were rather more lenient. Kames, for example, asserts that Shakespeare is "superior to all other writers in delineating passion," praises his sentiments and avoidance of declamation, but confesses: "By endeavouring . . . to raise his dialogue above the style of ordinary conversation, he sometimes deviates into intricate thought and obscure expression." Hippisley in 1750 is even more sympathetic. He makes precisely Johnson's objection, but tries to divert the blame from Shakespeare to the English language: "As to his Style and Diction . . . Our Language sunk under him, and was unequal to that Greatness of Soul which furnished him with such glorious Conceptions." In France by 1763 the Academician Marmontel can approve Shakespeare's sublime style almost without qualification.[14] Johnson's criticism, then, is quite conventional, although perhaps rather more severe than that of a number of his fellow critics. That an epic might avail itself of a great many images and figures was allowed; but a tragedy, it was thought, which must affect us more immediately, should avoid such complexities;[15] it may be that Johnson had this distinction in mind. In any event, if a sentiment cannot be rendered clearly, he believes it ought not to be rendered at all; he also suggests that Shakespeare might have spent more time trying to *make* his thoughts clear. Johnson, despite his praise of Shakespeare's spontaneous and natural expressions, was far from loving spontaneity for its own sake. Those who did were willing to tolerate that obscurity which it commonly produces, and thus they commended, while Johnson condemned, Gray's odes. For Johnson a poet, even if he be a genius, is expected to *work* at his craft. And he would certainly have dismissed Hippisley's suggestion that language "sunk under" Shakespeare as a paltry excuse for slovenly writing. He had had often enough to set himself *doggedly* to write—and to write well; there was no reason why "the Bard" should not have done the same.

The sentiment, as we have seen, may be too complex or obscure

---

14. Upton, *Critical Observations on Shakespeare*, pp. 128 ff.; Kames, *Elements of Criticism*, 2: 213; John Hippisley, *A Dissertation on Comedy* (London, 1750), p. 37; Jean-François Marmontel, *Poétique françoise*, 2 vols. (Paris, 1763), 1: 129–30. Cf. Richard Hurd, ed., *Q. Horatii Flacci epistolae ad Pisones et Augustum*, 4th ed., 3 vols. (London, 1766), 1: 61.

15. See John Brown, *Essays on the Characteristicks*, 5th ed. (London, 1764), pp. 23–24.

for the language. The reverse of this fault may occur, Johnson continues: the language may sometimes be too great for the sentiment; "the equality of words to things is often neglected." A common criticism of Shakespeare, this was viewed as false wit, the false sublime, or bombast, all of which violate the neoclassical regulation that *"there must be . . . a Proportion betwixt the Words and things."* [16] This tenet was held ardently throughout the century and is well articulated by Kames: "One species of false sublime, known by the name of *bombast,* is common among writers of a mean genius. It is a serious endeavour, by strained description, to raise a low or familiar subject above its rank; which instead of being sublime, never fails to be ridiculous." As he later says: "Words have an intimate connection with the ideas they represent; and the representation must be imperfect, if the words correspond not precisely to the ideas." [17] For Johnson, the capital artistic fault, as he says in *Rambler* no. 3, is a "secret inequality . . . between the words and sentiments, or some dissimilitude of the ideas and the original objects." He concedes in *Rambler* no. 168 that no words are *intrinsically* lower than others, but some are certainly lower or higher through association. In the *Life of Cowley* he says that language is the dress of thought, and that though truth and reason have an unalterable value and are indestructible gold, yet "gold may be so concealed in baser matter that only a chymist can recover it; sense may be so hidden in unrefined and plebeian words that none but philosophers can distinguish it." This inequality, regardless of whether the words be greater than the subject, or the reverse, is hence a very serious imperfection and admissible only in such inferior forms as the burlesque or the mock epic, whose very effects depend on it. It has been said that the aesthetics of an age share fundamental principles with its philosophy; nothing enforces more convincingly the truth of this observation than the neoclassical tenet now being considered. Johnson himself makes the connection in the *Life of Butler:*

16. René Rapin, *Reflections on Aristotle's Treatise of Poesie,* trans. Thomas Rymer (London, 1694), p. 51. See also: Dryden, *Essays,* 1: 224; *Spectator* no. 285; *Remarks on Mr. Mason's Elfrida* (London, 1750), p. 29.

17. Kames, *Elements of Criticism,* 1: 303; 2: 207. See 2: 259: "Language may indeed be considered as the dress of thought; and where the one is not suited to the other, we are sensible of incongruity, in the same manner as where a judge is dressed like a fop, or a peasant like a man of quality."

Burlesque consists in a disproportion between the style and the sentiments, or between the adventitious sentiments and the fundamental subject. It therefore, like all bodies compounded of heterogeneous parts, contains in it the principle of corruption. All disproportion is unnatural; and from what is unnatural we can derive only the pleasure which novelty produces.[18]

Johnson concludes his criticism with two paragraphs on conceits and quibbles. The first paragraph again indicates Johnson's especial concern for pathetic passages: one of Shakespeare's worst offenses is that he "is not long soft and pathetick without some idle conceit or contemptible equivocation. He no sooner begins to move, than he counteracts himself; and terrour and pity, as they are rising in the mind, are checked and blasted by sudden frigidity." Neoclassicists repeatedly affirmed the incompatibility of wit and figures of speech with scenes of powerful or pathetic emotion. "In the extremities of passion," Daniel Webb declares in 1762, "all studied and ambitious ornaments are to be avoided . . . true passion is impatient of studied embellishments." [19] Shakespeare's offenses against this tenet were notorious. Not only were quibbles and puns wit, but they were, as Shaftesbury says, a "false sort of Wit, which so much delighted our Ancestors" in poems, plays, and sermons; Shakespeare is thus to be reproved for speaking "in wretched Pun and Quibble." Thomas Warton complains of Shakespeare that in the same scene "he descends from the meridian of the noblest tragic sublimity, to puns and quibbles, to the meanest merriments of a plebeian farce." Mrs. Montagu decides that because Falstaff is not made to quibble so much as his other comic characters, Shakespeare was probably aware that it was "a false kind of wit, which he practised from the hard necessity of the times." One must surely forgive the dramatist, she says, since in that age the professor and the judge, the prelate and the statesman, and even majesty itself, quibbled. The use of quibble or pun, too, neglects the equality of word and subject. Pathetic passages possess a unity of tone which is as easily disrupted by a low figure of speech as by a low word;

18. *Works,* 3: 17 (*Rambler* no. 3); *Lives,* 1: 58–59, 218 (he makes similar remarks about Philips's *Splendid Shilling* in 1: 317).

19. Daniel Webb, *Remarks on the Beauties of Poetry* (London, 1762), pp. 107, 109. See also Kames, *Elements of Criticism,* 2: 29. Quite representative is Voltaire's *Essay on Wit,* the purpose of which is to demonstrate the incompatibility of wit with genuine passion (*Works,* 17: 199).

puns and quibbles, then, like Shakespeare's other faults, are "unnatural."[20] The second paragraph embellishes, but does not develop, Johnson's objections. A quibble becomes an *ignis fatuus,* a
malignant power, a golden apple, and that paragon of fatal beauty,
Cleopatra herself, for whom the poet was willing to sacrifice "reason, propriety, and truth." It is at once one of the most extravagant paragraphs in the *Preface*—its "purple patch," to use
Wilde's phrase—and a tour de force, devoid of much significant
meaning, exuberant in connotation, and with its very metaphors
challenging the equality of words to things. Certainly, it testifies
to Johnson's exceptional interest in this problem, although it is a
little extraordinary that Johnson should have provided the "contemptible quibble" with the robes of such an irresistible temptress.

Johnson's criticisms of Shakespeare, then, are neither uncommon
nor remarkably penetrating. They are the traditional strictures
of orthodoxy; and although Sherbo has argued that Johnson's
notes are more influenced by Romantic tendencies than the *Preface,*
Johnson on the whole criticizes specifically there what he pillories
generally here.[21] Indeed, his opinions, when set next to the undis-
criminating and passionate adulation vented by certain nineteenth-
century critics, seem rather close to those of our own age. His criticism of Shakespeare's plots shows no influence of new conceptions
of unity or the importance of character. Similarly, his remarks on
the language are immune from the Longinians and the school of
the sublime. As early as Dennis and Welsted, critics on occasion
had either *excused* Shakespeare's stylistic lapses because they aimed
at the sublime (even though they failed) or *defended* them as in
fact being, by their very obscurity, sublime.[22] But Johnson's impatience with the opacity of Gray's odes was not to be sus-
pended for Shakespeare, nor the cant of sublimity allowed to
excuse syntactical confusion or verbal impropriety. Throughout

20. Shaftesbury, *Characteristicks,* 5th ed. 3 vols. (London, 1732), 1: 64, 217;
Thomas Warton, *History of English Poetry,* 3 vols. (London, 1840), 3: 401–2;
Montagu, *An Essay on Shakespeare,* p. 108.

21. See *Works,* 8: 862, 905, 1045, and Arthur M. Eastman, *A Short History
of Shakespearean Criticism* (New York: Random House, 1968), pp. 24–28, for
other examples.

22. Welsted's *Remarks on Longinus* (1712) so defends a number of passages
from Shakespeare and Milton. Dennis at times, and Dr. Dodd (see note 11 above),
preserve this minor rhapsodic strain until the Romantic dispensation turns it
into a major key.

his discussion, Johnson plainly assumes the traditional prescriptions of neoclassicism: language is the dress of thought, and,
to preserve beauty, propriety, and sense, the two must be suited
to each other. It is this insistence, together with his apparent
obliviousness to Shakespeare's "wild, imaginative flights," that
doubtless provoked some critics to accuse Johnson of undue severity;
it is this, certainly, that led Mrs. Thrale to remark upon his "extreme distance from those notions which the world has agreed . . . .
to call romantic." But Johnson's censures are judicious and accurate. There are difficulties with Shakespeare's plots which a
ritualistic appeal to some ineffable "organic" unity cannot exorcise;
and while we are more sympathetic with puns than eighteenth-
century critics, it is arguable that we have not a more sensitive,
but a less scrupulous, ear. Moreover, in his assault upon tedious
narration and cold declamation, Johnson displays a real sense of
dramatic requirements. In both instances, he emphasizes the need
for action and variety; and in both he freely praises Shakespeare's
"unlabored" attempts. These criticisms, then, complete his delineation of Shakespeare as poet of nature; whether in pompous nar-
rations or set speeches, Shakespeare never falls into the false sublime but when he injudiciously deviates from natural and easy
expressions. Johnson has furnished a catalogue of defects which
is conventional, reasonable, and quite consistent with his earlier
praise of Shakespeare; as such, it need occasion Johnson or his
partisans no embarrassment, though at the same time it affords
the historian of ideas with little that is exceptional or new.

Chapter V

Shakespeare and His Age

Johnson has about completed his work as a judicial critic. He has examined Shakespeare's merits and his deficiencies: he has defended him against the "minute and slender criticism" of the Voltaires on such larger and more theoretical issues as decorum, tragicomedy, and the unities; and he has joined the attack on more specific points—language, plot structure, poetic justice. But before he can make the final assessment, he must consider Shakespeare's *milieu*. Johnson had opened the *Preface* with an affirmation of those gradual and comparative principles by which true criticism conducts its investigations. He has not forgotten those principles: "Every man's performances, to be rightly estimated, must be compared with the state of the age in which he lived, and with his own particular opportunities."[1] So Johnson begins his discussion, and it would be difficult to state the problem more concisely. A *milieu* comprises both the general and peculiar circumstances which contribute to the production of a work of art. By the "state of his age" is meant, then, all those pervasive and external conditions which necessarily exercise a real if indeterminate influence on any literary performance. But Shakespeare's "particular opportunities" must be known as well, and by this Johnson understands, not merely the extent of his learning and originality, but the very quality of his genius itself. First to be examined in this chapter are Johnson's credentials as an historical critic, then his attitude, and that of his contemporaries, toward the Elizabethan Age: the state of its culture and the effect which it was presumed to have had on Shakespeare's plays. The second section will be concerned with Shakespeare's learning and originality.

1. *Works*, 7: 81. All subsequent quotations from the *Preface* will be from pp. 81–92.

THE INFANCY OF NATIONS

The *workmanship* is the primary consideration of both a critic and a reader, but one is naturally curious as to the *instruments* as well: "to know how much is to be ascribed to original powers, and how much to casual and adventitious help." At the beginning of the *Preface* Johnson had used the spaciousness and loftiness of a building to represent qualities determined by comparison; now he again resorts to an architectural metaphor: "The palaces of Peru or Mexico were certainly mean and incommodious habitations, if compared to the houses of European monarchs; yet who could forbear to view them with astonishment, who remembered that they were built without the use of iron?" Having examined the workmanship of Shakespeare's plays, Johnson now investigates the "casual and adventitious help."

He practices an historical, not a relativistic, criticism. Mexican palaces, he says, are "certainly" uncomfortable; but if we know that they were constructed without iron, we cease to despise them and instead admire the proficiency of their architect. As he has observed a few lines before, "there is always a silent reference of human works to human abilities." But our final *judgment* is not necessarily altered: "mean and incommodious," like "spacious and lofty," are not *relative* (a word Johnson avoids) but qualities which are determined upon principles "gradual and comparative." This is to say, they *are* determined: our final judgment concludes that Peruvian palaces *are* in fact mean, even though the Peruvian monarch was happily unaware of the fact. But although we judge them to be so, we admire the ingenuity of their builder. Our judgment is but a part of our whole response, and a part which may be very difficult to separate from the rest. I call Johnson historical, then, because he employs his history more in elucidation than in evaluation: he would perhaps be a relativist if he esteemed the Mexican palaces as significant monuments of ironless art. Nevertheless, it is awkward to keep "admiration" (even of savages ignorant of iron) from intruding into evaluation. The distinction, therefore, between historical and relativist criticism is itself relativistic: it has more to do with a matter of emphasis than a mode of judgment.[2] Johnson's principles are not relative, but he is very much

2. Emerson R. Marks, *Relativist and Absolutist: The Early Neoclassical Debate in England* (New Brunswick: Rutgers University Press, 1955) distinguishes too

aware of the importance of understanding the society and circumstances of an author. He is at once confident of his own standards and conscious of the inequalities of different ages; it is this consciousness which makes Johnson a more liberal critic than Rymer, for example, but it is his confidence that prompts G. M. Miller to decide, perhaps too positively, that he "failed to respond to the new critical influences set in motion by the Wartons, Hurd, and others." [3] Johnson was modern enough to sense the fluctuations of history, and conservative enough to know the enduring values behind them.

Historical criticism of Johnson's sort had been often practiced by 1765. Gildon objects to Rymer's severity in judging Shakespeare, and enumerates three aspects of the Elizabethan Age to account for the imperfections of *Othello:* the taste for tragicomedy, the lack of financial support for the stage, and the need to conciliate the talent of the actors. Thus Gildon *explains* faults by referring to the age. The *Remarks on Mr. Mason's Elfrida* (1752) *excuses* Shakespeare for "writing to the Populace, and directing his Endeavours solely to hit the Taste and Humour of his Age, in which it was his Misfortune to live: He was to write for his livelihood; and as for Rules of Composition, they were hardly so much as heard of then." Two years later Zachary Grey explains that Shakespeare's *"jingles, puns,* and *quibbles"* derive from the false taste of his time; King James I himself, and Bishop Lancelot Andrewes, were not above using such "low (but then fashionable) kind of wit." As late as 1774 William Richardson recounts at length the disabilities under which Shakespeare labored and urges that we pity rather than censure him; but that nevertheless, in considering his tragedies, "a standard must be established, by which our judgments are to be determined." Richardson perfectly exemplifies the historical critic's

---

absolutely; it is otherwise a valuable study. See also: G. M. Miller, *The Historical Point of View in English Literary Criticism from 1570–1770* (Heidelberg: C. Winter, 1913); D. M. Foerster, *Homer in English Criticism: The Historical Approach in the Eighteenth Century* (New Haven: Yale University Press, 1947); René Wellek, *A History of Modern Criticism: 1750–1950,* vol. 1, *The Later Eighteenth Century* (New Haven: Yale University Press, 1955), pp. 26–30, and on Johnson, pp. 101–4.

3. Miller, *Historical Point of View,* p. 17. It is worth noting that T. S. Eliot, *On Poetry and Poets* (New York: Farrar, Straus, and Cudahy, 1957), p. 187, decides that the absence of relativistic methods "contributes to the singular merit of this Preface"—because Shakespeare is in fact incomparable.

view: we must understand the dramatist's situation, but we must preserve standards.[4] The differences between this, and that of the "progressive" (hardly relativistic) critics, is merely one of degree. Thomas Blackwell, for example, in his *Life and Writings of Homer* (1735) relies on historical evidence (and a handsome amount of conjecture) much more extensively than had been commonly done, and he certainly takes this evidence into consideration when passing judgment. Still, in his comparison of Homer with the moderns he appeals clearly to extrinsic standards of excellence; these standards allow him to praise Homer's depiction of the simple passions, but at the same time to prefer the moderns' treatment of landscape to his. Thus he is necessarily measuring Homer against absolute (however unspecified) criteria. A cluster of mid-century writers—Hurd, the Wartons, John Brown, Robert Wood in his *Essay on the Original Genius and Writings of Homer* (1769)—are much more interested in historical contexts than Gildon or Grey, but they, too, are in the main principled and judicial critics.[5]

To a degree, these new interests attracted Johnson. Nine years before the *Preface* he wrote: "It is the great excellence of Shakespeare, that he drew his scenes from nature, and from life. He copied the manners of the world then passing before him, and has more allusions than other poets to the traditions and superstition of the vulgar; which must therefore be traced before he can be understood." This is straightforward historical criticism; a knowledge of the past can *explain*. But two other comments are pertinent. In his *Miscellaneous Observations on . . . Macbeth* (1745) he writes: "In order to make a true estimate of the abilities and merit of a writer, it is always necessary to examine the genius of

4. Gildon, quoted in Marks, *Relativist and Absolutist*, pp. 83–84; *Remarks on Mr. Mason's Elfrida* (London, 1752), pp. 59–60; Zachary Grey, *Critical, Historical, and Explanatory Notes on Shakespeare*, 2 vols. (London, 1754), 1: vii–ix; William Richardson, *Cursory Remarks on Tragedy* (London, 1774), pp. 37–39. Cf. George Lyttelton, *The Works* (London, 1774), p. 403. In France, only G. Alexandre de Méhégan's *Considérations sur les révolutions des arts . . .* (Paris, 1755) shows a strong sense of historical perspective; his object, he says, is to study the influence of civilizations and the arts on each other. Nevertheless, he has rigorous standards; it is clear that to understand all is not to pardon all.

5. Blackwell in *Eighteenth-Century Critical Essays*, ed. Scott Elledge, 2 vols. (Ithaca: Cornell University Press, 1961), 1: 447. Thomas Warton, *Observations on the "Fairy Queen,"* 2d ed., 2 vols. (London, 1762), 2: 87, urges us to place ourselves in Spenser's "situation and circumstances."

his age, and the opinions of his contemporaries." Nearly thirty-five years later, in his *Life of Dryden*, he insists: "To judge rightly of an author we must transport ourselves to his time, and examine what were the wants of his contemporaries, and what were his means of supplying them. That which is easy at one time was difficult at another."[6] The phrases "to make a true estimate," "to judge rightly," together with that in the *Preface*, "to be rightly estimated," suggest a very close connection indeed between historical investigation and critical evaluation. Still, the proper question to ask is, how heavily will Johnson weigh his historical data when he comes to make his final judgment? Again, it is a matter of emphasis; we must first consider his own and his fellow critics' views of the Elizabethan Age and the influence it exercised on Shakespeare's work.

For Johnson, Shakespeare's age "was yet struggling to emerge from barbarity." Learning was being cultivated, but it was cultivated by only a few. Moreover, "nations, like individuals, have their infancy." The populace were as yet incompetent to judge properly of literature; like children, they naturally preferred the remote and wonderful, having "no taste of the insipidity of truth." Strange and fantastic events only could hold their attention; and to be popular, an author was required to cater for such unsophisticated taste. Condescension to the Elizabethans had of course been a long-standing prerogative of the Augustan poet and scholar. Dryden criticizes the impurity of Shakespeare's and Fletcher's language and explains: "But the times were ignorant in which they lived. Poetry was then, if not in its infancy among us, at least not arrived to its vigour and maturity: witness the lameness of their plots," etc. Pope describes the meanness of Shakespeare's audience: in tragedy they loved the strange and unnatural, bombast and verbosity. Of the late sixteenth century William Warburton laments: "Public Taste was in its Infancy; and delighted . . . in the high and the turgid." But Leonard Welsted's *Dissertation concerning the Perfection of the English Language* (1724) most perfectly promotes this view:

> It is not, unless I mistake, much more than a century, since England first recovered out of something like barbarism, with respect to its state

6. *Works*, 7: 53 (*Proposals for Printing the Works of Shakespeare*); ibid., 7: 3 (he preserves this in his opening note on *Macbeth*); *Lives*, 1: 411.

of letters and politeness. The great rude Writers of our nation, in early times, did indeed promise what the English genius would one day be capable of, when the refinement of our language, and other improvements, might afford favourable opportunities for the exerting of it; and at the Restoration it was, that Poetry and Polite Arts began to spring up. In the reign of William the Third, the founder of English Liberty, they acquired great strength and vigour, and have continued to thrive, gradually, down almost to our times.[7]

However, both the confidence and condescension of a Welsted were soon to be shaken severely, though not utterly eradicated. Thomas Hayward's preface to his collection of poetic "beauties," *The British Muse* (1738), is a singularly stalwart defense of the Elizabethan Age and its language. He vigorously criticizes Edward Bysshe's similar collection for its omission of Shakespeare. This, Hayward believes,

is but an indifferent compliment to the *readers of our age*, and seems, in making them sacrifice dignity of wit, and energy of sense to sound and colour, to be placing them upon a level with some of our modern fine ladies, who estimate their admirers by their dress and equipage, and not their merit and understanding.

Earlier collections, he points out, have tended to ignore dramatic poetry as too contemptible for inclusion, but the English have an extraordinary genius for tragedy, and this genius especially

7. John Dryden, *Essays*, ed. W. P. Ker, 2 vols. (Oxford: Oxford University Press, 1926), 1: 165; Pope in *Eighteenth-Century Essays on Shakespeare*, ed. D. N. Smith (Oxford: Oxford University Press, 1963), p. 46; Warburton in ibid., pp. 95–96; Leonard Welsted, *Works in Prose and Verse* (London, 1787), p. 121. See also: Shaftesbury, *Characteristicks*, 5th ed., 3 vols. (London, 1732), 1: 242: the earliest and easiest style to achieve is the miraculous and pompous, for children delight first in the marvelous; Peter Whalley, *An Enquiry into the Learning of Shakespeare* (London, 1748), pp. 17, 72 (on Othello's account of his adventures to Desdemona); John Dennis, *The Critical Works*, ed. E. N. Hooker, 2 vols. (Baltimore: Johns Hopkins Press, 1939–43), 2: 197; *Some Remarks on the Tragedy of Hamlet* (London, 1736), pp. 8–9; John Upton, *Critical Observations on Shakespeare*, 2d ed. (London, 1748), p. 27; William Guthrie, *An Essay upon English Tragedy* (London, [1747?]), p. 9; Richard Hurd, ed., *Q. Horatii Flacci epistolae ad Pisones, et Augustum*, 3 vols. (London, 1766), 1: 43, 210 (implicitly); Charles Batteux, *Les beaux arts réduits à un même principe* (Paris, 1747), p. 73.

manifested itself in the Elizabethan Age.[8] It was the likes of Hayward, rather than Welsted, who were to take the field by the fifties and sixties. In 1756 Theophilus Cibber can praise the Elizabethan period as an era of revived learning and intelligence naturally conducive to the boundless genius of Shakespeare. Writers like Spenser and Ariosto, says Thomas Warton, did not "live in an age of planning." They "engage the fancy" by bold images, etc., while nowadays, when "critical taste is universally diffused," we require order and design; yet by Spenser our heart is pleased, if our head is not. By the time Warton had assumed the formidable task of writing an *History of English Poetry*, his attitude was far from that of Bysshe or Welsted. The golden age of English poetry was the Elizabethan: "It certainly may not improperly be styled the most poetical age of these annals."[9]

Of all mid-century critics, Richard Hurd most earnestly devoted himself to reviving admiration for those very qualities dismissed by Johnson as the progeny of an adolescent taste. The purpose of his *Letters on Chivalry and Romance*, published three years before the *Preface*, is to demonstrate that gothic culture and manners, in yielding more fertile materials for the poetic fancy, are superior to the classical. Less well known, perhaps, are his two dialogues *On the Age of Queen Elizabeth*, written in 1759. The English of

8. Hayward, ed., *The British Muse* (London, 1738), p. xvi. Gildon's collection, he goes on to concede, might have rectified Bysshe's deficiency, but although Gildon includes some Shakespeare, he fails to include enough. Hayward himself confesses he has not represented authors prior to *The Mirror for Magistrates*, being "afraid to venture them in this refined aera of our language, till his readers might be prepared by the poetry of an intermediate age to relish the wholesome force and native beauties of older times, notwithstanding their antiquated garb and manners" (ibid., p. xxi).

9. T. Cibber, *Dissertations on Theatrical Subjects* (London, 1756), p. 123; Warton, *Observations on the "Fairy Queen,"* 1: 15–16; and his *History of English Poetry*, 3 vols. (London, 1840), 3: 395. On the whole, Warton seems to regard the age as a sort of mean between barbarism and excessive refinement, "when genius was rather directed than governed by judgment, and when taste and learning had so far only disciplined imagination, as to suffer its excesses to pass without censure or control, for the sake of the beauties to which they were allied" (*History of English Poetry*, 3: 403). In his zeal to defend the Elizabethans, Guthrie, *Essay upon English Tragedy*, p. 31, inclines perilously toward relativism: what Frenchmen censure as low wit may be held by Englishmen to be genuine; and similarly "an Englishman under King George, and one under Queen Elizabeth . . . would have very opposite sentiments, with regard to Shakespear's low wit."

that period, he believes, was most suitable for poetry: "It was pure, strong, and perspicuous, without affectation." Then too, the "prosaic genius of philosophy and logic" had not yet discouraged its use of inventive and audacious figures. The Elizabethan Age may pass for golden, he declares, "notwithstanding what a fondness for this age of baser metal may incline us to represent it." By the time of *Chivalry and Romance* he can deplore the triumph of reason over the poets' *"lying wonders"* and issue his famous lament: "What we have gotten by this revolution . . . is a great deal of good sense. What we have lost, is a world of fine fabling." Typically, Mrs. Montagu is assiduous to reiterate Hurd's praise: in the Elizabethan Age "philosophy had not mitigated the austerity of ignorant devotion, or tamed the fierce spirit of enthusiasm." Thus through the late fifties and sixties precisely those aspects of the age regarded by earlier critics as childish and rude became esteemed as wild and imaginative, especially apt for such a poetic genius as Shakespeare's. But the difference between a Welsted and Hurd is not that the one is an absolutist and the other a relativist; rather, the one is a conservative neoclassicist, and the other what we must call, until a less teleological term is available, a pre-Romantic. When he prepared his edition of Horace, a decade earlier, Hurd had been much more traditional, but he has not so much abandoned old standards as acquired new ones. He is not extolling Elizabethan poets because he has suddenly seen them relative to their age, but because they evince characteristics which he has come to favor. Ultimately, the principal difference between Welsted and Hurd—besides that of quality—is that Welsted enjoys Dryden, while Hurd prefers Spenser.[10]

The distinction between relativist and absolutist, then, is perhaps impertinent to our study of Johnson. Like Hurd, he was acquainted with Elizabethan authors, and like Hurd he appreciated the excel-

10. Richard Hurd, *The Works*, 8 vols, (London, 1811), 3: 210–13; 4: 350; Elizabeth Montagu, *An Essay on the Writings and Genius of Shakespeare* (London, 1769), p. 143. The debate across the Channel followed similar lines. As late as his *Appel à toutes les nations* (Paris, 1761), p. 39, Voltaire pours contempt on the Elizabethan audience and the taste which was then corrupting works of art; see also his *Letter to the Academy* (*Oeuvres complétes*, 70 vols. [Paris, 1785–89], 49: 329). Yet cf. Abbé La Blanc, *Letters on the English and French Nations*, 2 vols. (Dublin, 1747), 1: 58: the English language began to decline before it reached its highest excellency, but "under Queen Elizabeth . . . it came nearest to this excellency."

lence of their English. As is well known, in the preface to his *Dictionary* he praises pre-Restoration works as *"the wells of English undefiled,* as the pure sources of genuine diction." He extols the language of Hooker, the Bible, Bacon, Raleigh, Spenser, Sidney, and Shakespeare, terming these works the "ground-work of style." "From the authors which rose in the time of Elizabeth," he says, "a speech might be formed adequate to all the purposes of use and elegance." From Shakespeare specifically he would take "the diction of common life."[11] Johnson must not be classified with the Bysshes, against whom Hayward railed and for whom both the age and its language were barbarous. It is not to the language of the Elizabethans that he takes exception, but to their taste; for while Hurd regretted losing the poets' "lying wonders," Johnson's own taste could never permit him to regard the "luxurious wonders of fiction" as superior to the "insipidity of truth." Unlike Hurd, he had standards which an understanding of the age, and even an enthusiasm for its language, were unable to change, howsoever these may have tempered them.

Having described the taste of the age, Johnson discusses its influence on Shakespeare's works. The looseness of his plots, again, is considered first, and where Johnson had earlier censured them, he now proceeds, as a good historical critic, to *explain* why they were what they were. They were taken largely from popular novels, chronicles, or ballads, whose stories were crowded with incidents and familiar to many. Johnson then distinguishes between the spectacular and the aesthetic qualities of a play. An infant society is initially attracted to pomp, the visually impressive, and only as it matures does it develop a relish for poetic beauties: "As knowledge advances, pleasure passes from the eye to the ear, but returns, as it declines, from the ear to the eye." Hence Shakespeare favored bustle and visual excitement; he knew how to please in this way, and regardless of whether this delight is natural, or a prejudice which he has helped to instill in us, we continue to prefer such action and vigor to cold if elegant declamation.

Earlier assessments of Shakespeare seldom fail to consider the influence of his age upon the irregularity and spectacle of the plays. In the late forties Johnson's friend William Guthrie paints a traditional picture of the reign of Henry VIII; the entertainments of

11. *Oxford Works,* 5: 39–40.

the people were not then dramatic, but were discovered in "justs and tournaments, in pageants, in largesses, and in conduits running with wine and hyppocrus." Henry, uninterested in more polite diversions, gave no encouragement in that direction, nor did Edward or Mary. Elizabeth, to be sure, began to encourage patrons of the drama, but the plays remained very rude. "While the stage was thus over-run with ignorance, impertinence, and the lowest quibble, our immortal Shakespeare rose." Shakespeare did all that he could, and though he was constrained to provide the people with marvelous trifles, at least he ennobled them: "Pomp, when introduced, was attended by poetry, and courage exalted by sentiment." But as his houses were full, he attempted no real reformation; and the "regularity of Johnson, the genteel manner of Fletcher" finally brought the stage near to perfection. Two decades later, Mrs. Montagu is still excusing Shakespeare's faults because of his period —"when learning was tinctured with pedantry; wit was unpolished, and mirth ill-bred." His plays were "to be acted in a paltry tavern, to an unlettered audience, just emerging from barbarity." That her condescension almost equals Welsted's, though they could hardly be more dissimilar in most respects, demonstrates the near-unanimity of neoclassicism on this point.[12]

Johnson's complaint against Elizabethan taste and its deleterious effect on Shakespeare is therefore not exceptional. However, he is no less an historical critic than Hurd: both use their historical understanding of the age to explain certain characteristics in the authors of that period. The difference is that Hurd is attracted by these characteristics as newly imaginative, while Johnson dismisses them as merely immature. They both have standards of judgment, but their standards are not the same. Hurd, now an Enlightenment critic, writes as a partisan for the good old primitive times of

12. Guthrie, *Essay upon English Tragedy*, pp. 8–12; Montagu, *An Essay on Shakespeare*, pp. 10, 19. The *Universal Spectator* castigates the taste of both the past and the present, for to it "no doubt we owe the Parade of Battles and Coronations, and the low Interludes of Clowns and Peasants in the immortal Shakespear" (reprinted in *Gentleman's Magazine* 9 [March 1739]: 136). See also: *Critical Review* 8 (July 1759): 87 for similar sentiments; and Hanmer, *Eighteenth-Century Essays on Shakespeare*, p. 86; James Ralph, *The Touch-Stone* (London, 1728), p. 83. On Johnson's notion of pleasure passing from the eye to the ear and back again, cf. Pope's *First Epistle of the Second Book of Horace*, lines 312–13: "(For Taste, eternal wanderer, now flies/ From heads to ears, and now from ears to eyes.)"

simplicity and wonderment, whereas Johnson, the conservative, recognizes that in some things—particularly Hurd's despised "good sense"—society may have advanced, and that the man is fatuous who would exchange these things for less.

The dispute was not solely between those who praised Elizabethan extravagance as charming and those who denounced it as childish. Some went so far as to contend that that age, and all unsophisticated ages, were delighted with *plainness* rather than pomp, and that the stage became *more* spectacular and ornamental as society developed. On this matter, indeed, Johnson himself seems to have been undecided.[13] For the most part, though, he did not regard simplicity as characteristic of the period; he inclined rather to see a licentious wildness, a craving for visual sensationalism, and greater appetite for action than for poetry. The curious thing is that while he parted company with Hurd over the superiority of the Elizabethans' taste, he concurred with him in judging its influence on Shakespeare as by no means entirely pernicious. In the dedication written for Mrs. Lennox, Johnson says of his plots, with some sarcasm: "It was sufficient to recommend a Story, that it was far removed from common Life." But he adds that Shakespeare is actually indebted to this taste "for the licentious Variety, by which he has made his Plays more entertaining than those of any other Author." In his "General Observation on *Henry VIII*" he attributes the long success of that play to the "splendour of its pageantry."[14] And in the *Preface* itself, having expressed dissatisfaction with the looseness of the plays, he goes on to prefer their variety to cold declamation. To enforce this point, he undertakes a contrast which had been for some years a favorite of more liberal neoclassicists:

13. See: Thomas Wilkes, *A General View of the Stage* (London, 1759), p. 211 (on the Elizabethan age specifically), and Kames, *Elements of Criticism*, 3 vols. (Edinburgh, 1762), 1: 255–56 (who is speaking in general terms). In the *Life of Pope* Johnson says that cultures in an early stage are satisfied with "plain sense," but that "a saturated intellect soon becomes luxurious, and knowledge finds no willing reception till it is recommended by artificial diction. Thus it will be found in the progress of learning that in all nations the first writers are simple, and that every age improves in elegance" (*Lives*, 3: 239). However, Johnson is here concerned with stylistic matters, not with the *subjects* of early works—these, presumably, might be extravagant, while the style remains simpler and less complex than that of subsequent writers.

14. Charlotte Lennox, *Shakespear Illustrated* . . . , 3 vols. (London, 1753–54), 1: ix; *Works*, 8: 657.

he opposes the plays of Shakespeare to Addison's superlatively classical *Cato*. *Cato*, he says, is the production of judgment; it "affords a splendid exhibition of artificial and fictitious manners" in smoothly wrought verse. Shakespeare is, however, vigorous and inventive; he is concerned with human sentiments and human actions, and speaks to the heart. Addison "speaks the language of poets, and Shakespeare, of men. . . . we pronounce the name of *Cato*, but we think on Addison." This paragraph is in fact a variation on the theme of his "Drury Lane Prologue," written eighteen years before, where he traces the decline of English drama from the Elizabethan Age "till declamation roar'd, while passion slept."

On its performance in 1713 *Cato* had been applauded by Whig and Tory alike; but the attitude taken toward the play by critics was indicative of their aesthetic, if not necessarily their political views. In France, critics like Voltaire praised it highly. Addison was "the first Englishman who wrote a rational tragedy," he says, though he concedes that "young ladies" may not so much delight in it. Earlier criticism in England was equally generous. In 1731 the *Universal Spectator* traces the decline of the stage from the Restoration but observes: "Mr. *Addison* . . . at once, by his *Cato*, placed himself on a level with the greatest Authors, and restor'd in his Audience a just and true Taste of Poetry." [15] But by 1757 the tone is more frigid. The *London Chronicle* has a long review of *Cato* in that year which is perceptibly defensive in its praise: "However our Audiences in general are fond of Performances where the Passions are more intensely agitated than in this Piece, it must be allowed, in Spite of fashionable Criticism, that *Cato* . . . is the Work of Genius, and that such a Composition would do Honour to any Age or Country." The allusion to "fashionable Criticism" suggests rightly that some were aspersing the work. Just a decade before, the author of *An Examen of . . . The Suspicious*

15. Voltaire, *Works*, 38 vols. (London, 1778–81), 13: 140 (but cf. his more critical remarks in *Théâtre de Corneille*, 2: 576); *Universal Spectator*, reprinted in *Gentleman's Magazine* 1 (April 1731): 153. Jean Baptiste Boyer, *Réflexions historiques et critiques sur le goût* (Amsterdam, 1743), p. 62, praises *Cato* as being perfect and elegant, while at the same time avoiding declamation. Lewis Riccoboni, *An Historical and Critical Account of the Theatres in Europe* (London, 1741), pp. 174, 331–32, cannot understand why *Cato* has failed to reform the British stage.

Husband had written: "Mr. *Addison* is a great *Poet,* and his *Cato* is a noble *Poem—but further this Deponent sayeth not."* Joseph Warton considers the play "a fine dialogue on liberty," but a poor dramatic performance, "wanting action, pathos, and characters."[16] Other plays than *Cato* were arraigned on similar grounds; criticism in the fifties and sixties was increasingly concerned with spirit and naturalness over artificial, *poetic* beauties;[17] and it is hardly surprising that Johnson's own *Irene* was no more immune from these strictures than *Cato.*[18] That Johnson should contrast Shakespeare and Addison in this manner shows not that he is *avant-garde,* but that he is quite in step with current opinion.

In his next paragraph, and the last before he considers Shakespeare's learning and originality, Johnson elaborates metaphorically on his contrast with Addison. A regular writer is a garden "accurately formed and diligently planted," while Shakespeare is a forest "filling the eye with awful pomp, and gratifying the mind with endless diversity." The one is a cabinet of gems "minutely finished, wrought into shape," while the other is a mine "which

16. *London Chronicle,* no. 17 (5–8 February 1757); *An Examen of . . . The Suspicious Husband* (London, 1747), p. 45; Joseph Warton, *An Essay on the Genius and Writings of Pope,* 4th ed., 2 vols. (London, 1782), 1: 271. For similar criticism, see: Francis Gentleman, *The Dramatic Censor,* 2 vols. (London, 1770), 1: 459; Hurd, *Horatii epistolae,* 1: 80; and an editorial note in the Smollet edition of Voltaire (*Works,* 13: 142). Peter Smithers, *Life of Joseph Addison* (Oxford: Oxford University Press, 1954), pp. 255–68, discusses the great popularity of *Cato* and believes Dennis (in his *Remarks upon Cato)* to be unique in his adverse criticism among early critics; this is probably true. However, his contention that the fame of *Cato* continued to grow throughout the period must be seriously qualified by the instances of antagonistic criticism cited here; indeed, even before the first production of the play Pope had voiced such criticism (Joseph Spence, *Anecdotes* [London, 1820], p. 196).

17. See: *London Chronicle,* no. 12 (25–27 January 1757), and no. 32 (12–15 March 1757); *Critical Review* 8 (July 1759): 14. For G. E. Lessing, *Hamburgische Dramaturgie,* 2 vols. (Hamburg, 1769), st. xvii, Addison is "ein guter Kopf," but not a dramatist by nature. See also Montagu, *An Essay on Shakespeare,* p. 38: "Many Plays are little more than Poems rehearsed . . . of which the Poet remains the apparent hero."

18. E.g., Frances Burney, *Diary and Letters of Madame D'Arblay,* 2d ed., 7 vols. (London, 1854), 1: 123: "I went and shut myself up in a sweet cool summer-house, to read Irene;—which, indeed, though not a good play, is a beautiful poem." See also "Nicholas Nipclose," *The Theatres* (London, 1772), p. 30. Years later Johnson praises *Cato* but terms it "rather a poem in dialogue, than a drama" (*Lives,* 2: 132).

contains gold and diamonds in unexhaustible plenty, though clouded by incrustations, debased by impurities, and mingled with a mass of meaner minerals." If to Johnson's forest and mine we add a gothic cathedral, we shall have three of the most popular objects with which Shakespeare was compared to excuse or extol his irregularity. Pope, of course, in his own preface had compared Shakespeare to "an ancient majestick piece of *Gothick* Architecture," rude but various, strong and solemn, so that the whole strikes us, although the parts may be ill-placed. And Theobald in his preface conceived of Shakespeare as a "spacious and splendid Dome"; a thousand beauties strike the eye, "a gay Confusion of pleasing Objects, too various to be enjoyed but in a general Admiration." Earlier, Addison had compared his two classes of geniuses to a "Wilderness of noble Plants" on the one hand, and a formal garden on the other.[19] But by mid-century, critics, taking Addison's lead, seek rather for organic than architectural metaphors. Thus in David Mallet's poetical essay *Of Verbal Criticism* (1733) we find the antecedent of Johnson's mine: Shakespeare is excellent, "Yet is his sense debas'd by gross allay: / As gold in mines lys mix'd with dirt and clay." Johnson's cabinets appear in Corbyn Morris's discussion of Shakespeare's comedies (1744):

> Upon the whole, *Johnson*'s Compositions are like finished Cabinets, where every Part is wrought up with the most excellent Skill and Exactness;—*Shakespeare*'s like magnificent Castles, but not perfectly finished or regular, but adorn'd with such bold and magnificent Designs, as at once to delight and astonish you with their Beauty and Grandeur.

The forest metaphor becomes especially fashionable in the fifties and sixties.[20] But it is Mrs. Montagu who provides us with a really singular variation; she compares Shakespeare, not to a castle or cathedral, but to the "prodigious structures of Stone-Henge," which we admire because we cannot guess how they were raised. Like

---

19. Pope in *Eighteenth-Century Essays on Shakespeare*, p. 58; Theobald in ibid., p. 59; *Spectator*, ed. D. F. Bond, 5 vols. (Oxford: Oxford University Press, 1965), 2: 129 (no. 160). See also Joseph Trapp, *Praelectiones poeticae*, 3d ed., 2 vols. (London, 1736), 2: 177.

20. Mallet, *Of Verbal Criticism* (London, 1733), lines 51–52; Corbyn Morris, *An Essay towards Fixing the True Standards of Wit* (London, 1744), p. 36. See also: *Connoisseur* no. 125 (1756) and Daniel Webb, *Remarks on the Beauties of Poetry* (London, 1762), p. 79.

them, Shakespeare's works are "the greatest monuments of the amazing force of nature, which we ought to view as we do other prodigies, with an attention to, and admiration of their stupendous parts, and proud irregularity of Greatness." Whether this is a happy comparison other critics may decide; certainly it is interesting in the history of Romantic taste. She does not, it is true, avail herself of an organic figure, but in using Stonehenge, rather than a Gothic cathedral, she has chosen that which is infinitely more mysterious, primitive, and arcane than a mere medieval structure; Stonehenge, with its eldritch and magical connotations, is something almost elemental and prehuman, and hence much more suited than a few-centuries-old cathedral to represent, for the Romantic mind, Shakespeare's "amazing force of nature."[21]

Thus the gardens and forests, the cabinets and mines, were quite current by the time Johnson was writing. He manages them very effectively, but even the less erudite of his audience would have found them familiar; indeed, they would have expected them. His use of these metaphors hardly justifies the term *pre-Romantic*. Like Pope and Theobald, Johnson is simply defending a certain amount of naturalness and irregularity—and to do this, as I have argued with respect to tragicomedy, is not to discover a latent Romantic strain. It is the reliance on such god-words as *organic, force, energy,* and the like, that discriminates Montagu and Coleridge from Pope or Theobald. It is nevertheless curious that Johnson, who was ever so much less enthusiastic over the *age* than critics like Hurd or Mrs. Montagu, should have concurred so entirely with them on the virtue of Shakespeare's "wildness." Never much disposed to idealizing past ages and pretty much convinced that life, in essentials, is everywhere and in every time the same, he was not prepared to issue extravagant and exotic claims for any period. He was thus not interested in speculating at large about the Elizabethans. Still, Shakespeare obviously had qualities which an

21. Montagu, *An Essay on Shakespeare,* p. 11. Cf. Johnson's letter to Mrs. Thrale in 1783, where he calls Stonehenge "probably the most ancient work of Man upon the Island. Salisbury Cathedral and its Neighbour Stonehenge, are two eminent monuments of art and rudeness, and may show the first essay, and the last perfection in architecture" (*The Letters,* ed. R. W. Chapman, 3 vols. [Oxford: Oxford University Press, 1952], 3: 86). Johnson is also recorded as saying: "Corneille is to Shakespeare as a clipped hedge is to a forest" (quoted in *Works,* 7: 84 n.).

Addison wanted, and Johnson was willing to praise these. Underlying Hurd's celebration of the Elizabethan Age as especially *apt* for poetry is the conviction that it very much contributed to Shakespeare's success. But Johnson, who believed that an intelligent being could do practically anything well if he but applied himself, was doubtless more interested in the *man* than the *age*. And it is to the man that he now turns.

SHAKESPEARE'S LEARNING, GENIUS, AND ORIGINALITY

Johnson questions "whether Shakespeare owed his excellence to his own native force, or whether he had the common helps of scholastick education, the precepts of critical science, and the examples of ancient authours." He first refers to the tradition that the dramatist was generally unlearned, misquoting (in the first edition) Ben Jonson to the effect that Shakespeare "had small Latin and *no* Greek." This contemporary testimony, he believes, ought to be accepted unless evidence to the contrary is produced. He then presents the evidence offered by those who argue for Shakespeare's "deep learning": usually some passage or other which seems to find an analogue in the classics. But these passages, he decides, can as easily be accounted for on three possible grounds: Shakespeare took them from existing translations; they are mere "coincidences of thought"; or they are proverbial and were in general circulation at the time. On one or another of these grounds Johnson explains several curious similarities. He declines to determine the extent of Shakespeare's knowledge of modern languages, though he seems to believe that he was ignorant of them. As for Latin, he may have been able to construe, but could probably do little more. Johnson concludes: "I am inclined to believe, that he read little more than English, and chose for his fables only such tales as he found translated." His works, it is true, show much knowledge; but there were by that time many translations, and native arts had been so cultivated as to provide "a stock of knowledge sufficient for a mind so capable of appropriating and improving it."

In the main, Johnson accepts the consensus of earlier editors and critics. Rowe, Pope, and Theobald generally emphasize Shakespeare's lack of classical learning, as do Dennis and Gildon; however, Pope argues that he had much reading, if not learning, and

Theobald suggests he may have used translations.[22] But as early as 1725 Dr. George Sewell contends for more learning, there being (he finds) abundant evidence of Shakespeare's knowledge of Latin, Roman history, and heathen mythology. And by 1754 Zachary Grey declares that the poet's knowledge of Latin and Greek "cannot reasonably be called into question" because of the evidence of his exact imitation of ancient poets and historians, especially of Saxo Grammaticus in *Hamlet*. Whalley had cited Saxo as evidence a few years earlier, and he produces many parallel passages to prove Shakespeare's learning; just as Johnson cites Ben Jonson's famous comment to suggest that Shakespeare had *little* formal schooling, Whalley appeals to it to show that he had *some*.[23]

But by mid-century more scholars began to act on Theobald's hint and consider whether translations might be responsible for those passages in which classical learning was detected. In the forties and fifties several critics advance, but do not develop, this idea. Richard Farmer's *Essay on the Learning of Shakespeare* (1767) was the first to do so; it is the careful production of a scholar and antiquary, far better read than most of his contemporaries in Elizabethan literature. He first summons up contemporary or near-contemporary testimony as to Shakespeare's ignorance (Drayton, Digges, Suckling, Milton, etc.), then calls upon North's *Plutarch,* Golding's *Ovid,* and other pieces to account for his classical allusions, phraseology, and knowledge of mythology. It is an ably conducted and penetrating work which argues convincingly that Shakespeare's "*Studies* were most demonstratively confined to Nature and *his own language.*" In his own time Farmer was not significantly challenged. The reviewer in the *London Magazine* summarizes his proofs very efficiently and seems entirely to accept his conclusions. Richard Warner in 1768 calls his evidence presumptive rather than positive and believes that Shakespeare used certain Latin words in their

22. Rowe, Pope, and Theobald all in *Eighteenth-Century Essays on Shakespeare*, pp. 2–3, 50, 68–70; Dennis, *Critical Works,* 2: 430–31; Charles Gildon, *Works of Shakespear,* vol. 7 (London, 1710), pp. iii–iv. See also: Seward's preface to *The Works of Beaumont and Fletcher,* ed. Lewis Theobald, et al., vol. 1 (London, 1750), p. li, and Lennox, *Shakespear Illustrated,* 2: 240.

23. Sewell, *Works of . . . Shakespeare,* vol. 7 (London, 1725): x; Grey, *Critical Notes on Shakespeare,* 1: vii; Whalley, *Enquiry into Shakespeare,* pp. v–vi. Others defend Shakespeare's learning; see: Aaron Hill's *Prompter,* no. 92 (1735); Upton, *Critical Observations on Shakespeare,* pp. 3–8; an editorial comment in Smollet's edition of Voltaire (*Works,* 26: 209).

Latin sense. He thinks that Shakespeare understood as much Greek "as a school-boy, never suppos'd to be an idle one, might be allow'd to have done"; and that with respect to Latin "he *might,* or *he might not,* have had a tolerable at least, if not a competent, knowledge of that language." But Warner does not seriously question Farmer's conclusions, and indeed his discussion throughout is temperate and cautious to the point of insipidity.[24]

Johnson's opinion is therefore quite up-to-date; indeed, he stresses the importance of translations more than any other critic before Farmer. Johnson was not equivocal in his approbation of Farmer's work, whom he is said to have assured: "You have completely finished a controversy beyond all further doubt." Moreover, when Johnson visited Cambridge in 1765 he met Farmer at Emmanuel and they corresponded thereafter. Considering that Johnson was then working on the *Preface,* it is more than possible that they should have discussed this point; Johnson may even have read the *Essay* in an early draft.[25] But regardless, Johnson's assessment of Shakespeare's learning is the most enlightened and reasonable before Farmer's; and in fact it is superior to Farmer's in that he refuses to determine with such confidence against Shakespeare's knowledge of *any* Latin or Greek.

Johnson finally decides that "the greater part of his excellence was the product of his own genius." However, he moves on to a question which is still concerned with Shakespeare's learning: whether or not Shakespeare improved as he grew older and wiser. Johnson quotes Rowe's famous opinion that "Art had so little, and Nature so large a Share in what he did, that, for ought I know, the Performances of his Youth, as they were the most vigorous, and had the most fire and strength of Imagination in 'em, were the best." [26] But, Johnson counters:

24. Farmer in *Eighteenth-Century Essays on Shakespeare,* p. 201; *London Magazine* 36 (February 1767): 81–83; Warner, *A Letter to . . . Garrick* (London, 1768), pp. 16–18. *Critical Review* 23 (1767): 47–50, does have some strictures to which Farmer replied in the second edition the same year. On the use of translations, see also J. Holt, *An Attempte to Rescue That Auciente English Poet . . .* (London, 1749), p. ix, and Hurd, *Horatii epistolae,* 3: 173–74.

25. Northcote's *Reynolds,* quoted in *Life,* 3: 38–39 n. 6; see "Richard Farmer" in the *Dictionary of National Biography.* Johnson received information from Farmer years later for his *Lives of the Poets.*

26. Rowe in *Eighteenth-Century Essays on Shakespeare,* p. 4.

The power of nature is only the power of using to any certain purpose the materials which diligence procures, or opportunity supplies. Nature gives no man knowledge, and when images are collected by study and experience, can only assist in combining or applying them. Shakespeare, however favoured by nature, could impart only what he had learned; and as he must increase his ideas, like other mortals, by gradual acquisition, he, like them, grew wiser as he grew older, could display life better, as he knew it more, and instruct with more efficacy, as he was himself more amply instructed.

In discovering here his position in a long-standing controversy, Johnson has revealed as well his understanding of poetic creation and the poetic genius.

The controversy itself is simply stated and rather tedious to explore: If Shakespeare had been more learned, it was debated, would such knowledge have stifled his native fire and energy? As Johnson knew, Rowe had assumed the affirmative position at the beginning of the century. On the other side, Dryden had long before argued that Shakespeare's language, at least, so often ungrammatical and coarse, had improved with time and experience; and both Dennis and Gildon frequently assert that more learning and art would have made Shakespeare an even greater poet. Gildon, though he praises highly Shakespeare's natural abilities, denies outright that learning "could either have curb'd, confin'd, or spoil'd the natural Excellence of his Writings." Though some minor poets may break immediately into a great reputation, then decline, nevertheless "all the Poets, that have without Controversy been Masters of a great Genius have rose to Excellence by Degrees"; thus "we ought to look into *Shakespear's* most imperfect Plays for his first."[27] But Rowe's position commanded a following more abundant and vociferous. Virtually undiversified with new insights, the line of argument runs from Rowe's *Life* (1709) to Young's query exactly half a century later: "Who knows whether *Shakespeare* might have thought less, if he had read more?" Such works as William Duff's *Essay on Original Genius* (1767) bestowed a scientific respectability on Rowe's conjecture. In both a society and an individual, Duff believes, the sciences have a slow and gradual development, while works of art "are impetuous, and attain their

27. Dryden, *Essays*, 1: 203; Dennis, *Critical Works*, 2: 4, 7, 14 (see note, 2: 428–31); Gildon, *Works of Shakespear*, 7: iii–iv, and 309–11.

utmost perfection at once." Learning inhibits originality and encumbers the mind of a poet: Milton's use of the scales to foreshadow Satan's fall, for example, is unhappy; if he had not known Homer, his own imagination might easily have led him to describe the fight itself, and this would have been preferable. Thus Shakespeare is a natural genius who neither requires knowledge nor would be improved by it. The following from the *Critical Review*, appearing the same year as the *Preface*, suggests how common this view had become:

> Shakespear . . . was one of those self-taught genius's which nature rarely produces, or, at most, once an age. His poetry was *inspiration* indeed, and he was, as Pope observes, truly an *original*. He seems to have discerned mankind by intuition—to have seen through human nature at one glance—*master* of every passion.

The cult of originality, then, conspired with the new theories of genius and poetic composition to preserve the credibility of Rowe's casual and conjectural comment.[28]

Johnson's epistemology is generally Lockian, and this alone would have prohibited him from adopting such theories of original genius. Ultimately, he says, the power of the mind can be traced to memory, which collects and distributes images. The imagination or invention "selects ideas from the treasures of remembrance, and produces novelty only by varied combinations." Thus the mind, even of a genius, must first have time and occasion to store up images before the imagination will have sufficient material on which to operate. For this reason, Johnson concluded of the poetry of St. Kilda: "It must be very poor, because they have a very few images." Boswell replies that genius may be shown by its ability to combine the images. But Johnson: "Sir, a man cannot make fire but in proportion as he has fuel. He cannot coin guineas but in proportion as he has gold." At the end of the tour of the Hebrides Johnson

---

28. Young, *Conjectures on Original Composition*, ed. E. J. Morley (Manchester: Manchester University Press, 1918), p. 36; Duff, *An Essay on Original Genius*, ed. John L. Mahoney (Gainesville: Scholars' Facsimiles & Reprints, 1964), pp. 260–96; *Critical Review* 19 (January 1765): 5. See also: Welsted, *Works*, p. 141; Theobald, *Eighteenth-Century Essays on Shakespeare*, p. 68; Lennox, *Shakespear Illustrated*, 2: 240–41; *Works of Beaumont and Fletcher*, 1: li–lii; Hurd, *Horatii epistolae*, 3: 120; Joseph Baretti, *Discours sur Shakespeare* . . . (London, 1777), p. 22.

praises the journey as having produced an "accession of new images." Imlac, one recalls, finds the Happy Valley less tedious than the others only because "I have a mind replete with images, which I can vary and combine at pleasure." This understanding of poetic creation informs the *Lives of the Poets* as well.[29] Learning, then, especially that to be acquired by a poet, requires time, observation, and reflection, as Imlac's arduous preparation for his craft demonstrates. Johnson says in a sermon: "Knowledge is to be attained by slow and gradual acquisitions, by a careful review of our ideas, and a regular superstructure of one proposition on another; and is, therefore, the reward only of diligence and patience." Most learning, however, occurs when young; writing to Mrs. Thrale in 1775, he contends that a mature scholar

> seldom makes with regard to life and manners much addition to his knowledge, Not only because as more is known there is less to learn, but because a mind stored with images and principles, turns inward for its own entertainment, and is employed in sorting those ideas which run into confusion, and in recollecting those which are stealing away, practices by which wisdom may be kept but not gained. The merchant who was at first busy in acquiring money, ceases to grow richer, from the time when he make it his business only to count it.

The concluding mercantile metaphor nicely illustrates Johnson's attitude: we acquire wisdom much as we acquire money. Nor does his belief that more learning occurs when young contradict his conviction that the mind requires time to develop: the mind is simply limited in what it can retain, and hence there comes a point when it is less capable of digesting new information as it is interested in reinvigorating the old. But perhaps most suggestive are his remarks on *Evelina*. He comments to Mrs. Thrale that no man could have written a book so young as Fanny Burney has done. Mrs. Thrale suggests Pope and *Windsor Forest*. But Johnson replies:

---

29. *Works*, 2: 137–38 (*Idler* no. 44); *Life*, 5: 228–29 (*Tour to the Hebrides*), and 405; *Oxford Works*, 1: 228 (*Rasselas*, chap. 12). See also: *Lives*, 3: 94, 359; and cf. his note on *Henry V* (*Works*, 8: 541) where he observes that Shakespeare's imagination was "crowded with a tumultuary confusion of images" which he thought, while they were yet "unsorted and unexamined," he could bring into his over-all design.

"Windsor Forest", though so delightful a poem, by no means required the knowledge of life and manners, nor the accuracy of observation, nor the skill of penetration, necessary for composing such a work as "Evelina:" he who could ever write "Windsor Forest," might as well write it young as old. Poetical abilities require not age to mature them; but "Evelina" seems a work that should result from long experience, and deep and intimate knowledge of the world.

In a sense, then, Johnson might well have agreed that "poetical abilities" themselves are not susceptible to cultivation; "he who could ever write" a work like *Windsor Forest* could write it at any time. But the fact remains that the fuel—the materials for such abilities to work upon—must be accumulated, and, assuming that learning does not of itself cramp such abilities, the poet must be supposed to grow better as he grows older and wiser.[30]

Having determined the relationship between learning and genius, Johnson attempts to identify those characteristics which arise from natural as distinguished from acquired abilities: "There is a vigilance of observation and accuracy of distinction which books and precepts cannot confer; from this almost all original and native excellence proceeds." These qualities reduce to two: acute observation of mankind and of the physical world. The new philosophy, Johnson tells us, had not yet been developed; Shakespeare was ignorant of those attempts to analyze the mind, to trace the springs of vice and virtue, the relationship of cause and effect, which have so extensively refashioned the late eighteenth-century world. "Mankind was not then to be studied in the closet; he that would know the world, was under the necessity of gleaning his own remarks, by mingling as he could in its business and amusements." Shakespeare, furthermore, overcame the disadvantages of his birth and obtained "an exact knowledge of many modes of life. . . . he had none to imitate, but has himself been imitated by all succeeding writers." He was a penetrating observer, too, of physical nature; because he could not take his descriptions from other books, he was

30. *Oxford Works*, 9: 365 (Sermon 8); *Letters*, 2: 80 (cf. 2: 381); Burney, *Diary and Letters*, 1: 199. Johnson's epistemology is far too complex a subject to examine here; see Jean H. Hagstrum, *Samuel Johnson's Literary Criticism* (Chicago: University of Chicago Press, 1967), chap. 1 passim, and pp. 53–55, 86–96, and also Rodman D. Rhodes, "*Idler* no. 24 and Johnson's Epistemology," *Modern Philology* 64, no. 1 (1966): 10–21, who draws intelligent distinctions between Locke and Johnson.

compelled to read the book of life. "Shakespeare," Johnson concludes, "whether life or nature be his subject, shows plainly, that he has seen with his own eyes; he gives the image which he receives, not weakened or distorted by the intervention of any other mind; the ignorant feel his representations to be just, and the learned see that they are compleat." Johnson's phraseology strikingly resembles Armstrong's in 1758: "True genius may be said to consist of a perfect polish of soul, which receives and reflects the images that fall upon it, without warping or distortion." But critics had so described Shakespeare for nearly a century:

> He was the man who of all modern, and perhaps ancient poets [Dryden writes in *An Essay of Dramatic Poesy*], had the largest and most comprehensive soul. All the images of Nature were still present to him, and he drew them, not laboriously, but luckily; when he describes any thing, you more than see it, you feel it too. Those who accuse him to have wanted learning, give him the greater commendation: he was naturally learned; he needed not the spectacles of books to read Nature; he looked inwards, and found her there.

Johnson reproduces part of this paragraph in his *Preface*, and indeed most eighteenth-century accounts of Shakespeare's genius are footnotes to it, though they are notes which, like Milton's Satan, become voluminous and subtle. Pope says of Shakespeare in 1725: "He is not so much an Imitator, as an Instrument, of Nature; and 'tis not so just to say that he speaks from her, as that she speaks thro' him." His accomplishments are wonderful considering his "lack of education or experience in those great and publick scenes of life which are usually the subject of his thoughts: So that he seems to have known the world by Intuition, to have look'd thro' humane nature at one glance." Some twenty-five years later William Guthrie asserts: "It is not Shakespear who speaks the language of nature, but nature rather speaks the language of Shakespear. He is not so much her imitator, as her master, her director, her moulder. Nature is a stranger to objects which Shakespear has rendered natural." Guthrie is following Pope closely here, but note the difference. Pope says that Shakespeare "is not so much an Imitator, as an Instrument, of Nature." For Guthrie he is neither her imitator nor her instrument, but rather, her master and molder. Anticipating, though without his whimsy, Wilde's paradox that nature imitates art, Guthrie says that it is she rather that imitates Shakespeare. Both Pope and Guthrie, in their zeal to praise the dramatist, are moving away from mimetic conceptions of art, and both, in slightly different ways, contribute to a theory of genius which was to triumph among the Romantics. Shakespeare is nature's *instrument* in that he opens his mind to be irradiated by her light; he is a genius without a set character: a passive conduit, in effect, through which the energies of nature are presumed to pulse. Yet at the same time he *molds* her in a way that merely imitative artists cannot. The true poetic genius both *expresses* and *captures* her most perfectly. Before 1750 this conception is but faintly foreshadowed by such criticism as Pope's, but it soon achieves popularity after this time.[31]

What Dryden and Pope were content to describe as Shakespeare's acute and spirited observation is developed by mid-century critics into something quite different: the natural genius's transcendence of the self and sympathetic identification with his creatures. Guthrie provides us with an early and remarkable example:

> The genius forgetting that he is a poet wraps himself up in the person he designs; he becomes him; he says neither more nor less than such a person, if alive and in the same circumstances would say; he breathes his soul; he catches his fire; he flames with his resentments. The rapid whirl of imagination absorbs every sensation; it informs his looks; it directs his motions. Like Michael Angelo, who, when carving any great design, wrought with an enthusiasm, and made the fragments of the marble fly around him, he is no longer himself.

Mrs. Montagu says that Shakespeare "seems to have had the art of the Dervise . . . who could throw his soul into the body of another man, and be at once possessed of his sentiments, adopt his passions, and rise to all the functions and feelings of his situation." Kenrick terms this praise an "elegant eulogy" and develops a tortuous and labored "refinement" on the theory. Defining the true dramatic genius in 1770, Hiffernan says: "In the

---

31. John Armstrong, *Miscellanies*, 2 vols. (London, 1770), 2: 135; Dryden, *Essays*, 1: 79–80; Pope in *Eighteenth-Century Essays on Shakespeare*, pp. 44–46; Guthrie, *Essay upon English Tragedy*, p. 11. Cf. *The Covent-Garden Journal*, ed. G. E. Jensen, 2 vols. (New Haven: Yale University Press, 1915), 1: 288, and Paul Hiffernan, *Dramatic Genius* (London, 1770), p. 9: "He tow'rs above the imagery of Nature,/ That wond'ring stares at his creative powers!" Whalley, *Enquiry into Shakespeare*, pp. 53, 81, and Hurd, *Horatii epistolae*, 3: 18–19, 28, offer the usual praise of Shakespeare's accurate descriptions of life and manners.

hour of composition he is no longer himself. Enthusiasm irradiates his glowing fancy, and operates an immediate transition of the poet into each character he draws." [32]

This notion, perhaps more than any other, effected a profound change in traditional conceptions of the psychology of composition; it laid the groundwork for the theories of Coleridge especially, and prepared the way for Keats's famous definition of the poetical character and his "negative capability." [33] A. O. Lovejoy thus glosses the meaning of these new beliefs: the "artist's task is to imitate, not simply Nature's works, but her way of working, to enter into the spirit of the universe by aiming, as it does, at fullness and variety without end." This, according to Lovejoy, is the superiority of "romantic diversitarianism" over neoclassical "uniformitarianism." The newer theories promote

> as both an aesthetic and a moral aim for the individual, the effort to enter as fully as possible into the immensely various range of thought and feeling in other men. It thus made for the cultivation, not merely of tolerance, but of imaginative insight into the points of view, the valuations . . . of others; and this not only as a means to the enrichment of one's own inner life, but also as a recognition of the objective validity of diversities of valuation.[34]

32. Guthrie, *Essay upon English Tragedy*, pp. 18–19; Montagu, *An Essay on Shakespeare*, p. 37; William Kenrick, *Introduction to the School of Shakespeare* (London, 1774), pp. 9–10; Hiffernan, *Dramatic Genius*, p. 90. See also Richardson, *Cursory Remarks*, p. 75. In the fifties and sixties this idea is developed quite as explicitly in French criticism; for three remarkable examples, see: Louis Racine, *Remarques sur les tragédies de Jean Racine*, 2 vols. (Paris, 1752), 2: 399; Méhégan, *Considérations sur les révolutions*, pp. 184 ff; Jean-François Marmontel, *Poétique françoise*, 2 vols. (Paris, 1763), 1: 69. And cf. Lessing (in J. G. Robertson, *Lessing's Dramatic Theory* [Cambridge: Cambridge University Press, 1939], pp. 450–55).

33. See: *Shakespeare Criticism, 1623–1840*, ed. D. N. Smith (London: Oxford University Press, 1964), pp. 220–21 (Coleridge), 306 (Hazlitt); John Keats, *Letters*, ed. H. E. Rollins, 2 vols. (Cambridge: Harvard University Press, 1958), 1: 386–87; W. J. Bate, *Negative Capability: The Intuitive Approach in Keats* (Cambridge: Harvard University Press, 1939), and his "Sympathetic Imagination in Eighteenth-Century English Criticism," *ELH* 12 (1945): 144–64. This understanding of genius, together with its application specifically to Shakespeare, has become entirely jejune by the time it appears in Aleister Crowley's *Moonchild* (1929), chap. 2.

34. Arthur O. Lovejoy, *The Great Chain of Being* (New York: Harper and Row, 1960), pp. 303–4.

Despite Lovejoy's commendation, however, one supposes that Johnson would have viewed such an aesthetic and moral aim only with repugnance. Keats writes of the poetical character:

> It has no self—it is every thing and nothing—It has no character . . . it lives in gusto. . . . It has as much delight in conceiving an Iago as an Imogen. What shocks the virtuous philosopher, delights the camelion Poet. . . . It is a wretched thing to confess; but it is a very fact that not one word I ever utter can be taken for granted as an opinion growing out of my identical nature—how can it, when I have no nature?[35]

This is sentimentalism at its most assiduously "tolerant," disdaining to distinguish between an Iago and an Imogen. But Johnson correctly diagnosed Boswell's problem—that he had no character—and urged him to form his as soon as possible (a piece of advice which Boswell, the perpetual assumer of rôles, was unwilling or unable to heed). For Johnson, to have character meant necessarily having *a* character, having an identity which was partly responsible for shaping its destiny and which would be judged by God. It would be difficult to find a more telling contrast between neoclassicism and Romanticism than that discovered between Imlac's description of a poet in the tenth chapter of *Rasselas* and Keats's ecstatic portrayal of the negatively capable Apollo at the end of *Hyperion*. In *Rasselas* the poet, by striving to *learn* all things, becomes a moral legislator; in *Hyperion*, by *entering into* all things, he becomes divine: "Knowledge enormous makes a God of me." Yet Apollo is melancholy, and unhappily given to shrieks and raving. Lovejoy may diagnose his condition as universal sympathy and tolerance, but to others it may look very like despair.

Other critics, while less extravagant in their claims for poetic genius, were nevertheless laying considerably more stress on originality. Johnson expressed surprise that anyone could take Edward Young's *Conjectures on Original Composition* (1759) as revolutionary or even novel, and his surprise was justified: Young merely pronounced more emphatically what many had been saying for some years.[36] But even these less enthusiastic aestheticians seem

35. Keats, *Letters*, 1: 387 (no. 118).

36. See: William Melmoth, *Letters . . . by . . . Sir Thomas Fitzosborne* (London, 1769), pp. 20–22; Arthur Murphy, *The Gray's-Inn Journal*, 2 vols. (London, 1756), 1: 105–9 (this may not be by Murphy: see 2: 336); Armstrong, *Miscellanies*, 2: 168; Webb, *Remarks on the Beauties of Poetry*, p. 65. In French criticism

to have exercised little influence on Johnson. Hurd's attitude (at least before he had become quite so enamored of the Elizabethans) is typically neoclassical and probably most closely reflects Johnson's own: "The superiority of Homer and Shakespeare to other poets doth not lie in their discovery of *new sentiments or images,* but in the forceable manner, in which their sublime genius taught them to convey and impress *old ones.*" As he says later: "The objects of imitation, like the *materials* of human knowledge, are a common stock, which experience furnishes to all men. And it is in the *operations* of the mind upon them, that the glory of *poetry,* as of *science,* consists. . . . from hence alone is the praise of *originality* to be ascertained." Johnson devotes his *Adventurer* no. 95 to the nature of originality and the difficulty of attaining it. Like Hurd, he defines it primarily as arrangement and style; it is by varying the disposition that an author may dress old thoughts pleasantly and effectively. Moreover: "the mutability of mankind will always furnish writers with new images, and the luxuriance of fancy may embellish them with new decorations." Elsewhere he is even doubtful about this last point; in *Rambler* no. 169 he finds that one of the reasons the ancients are superior to the moderns is "merely by priority, which put them in possession of the most natural sentiments, and left us nothing but servile repetition or forced conceits." Most truths are "too important to be new," and Johnson did not imagine that his contemporaries could discover very many which satisfied the requirements both of importance and novelty.[37]

But despite this skepticism, Johnson commonly emphasizes the excellency of first-hand observation and original description. He states confidently in *Rambler* no. 154: "No man ever yet became great by imitation. Whatever hopes for the veneration of mankind must have invention in the design or the execution; either the effect must itself be new, or the means by which it is produced." Imlac, in his celebrated description of the poet, repeats the assertion that "no man was ever great by imitation"; the poet must investi-

---

see: Le Blanc, *Letters on the English,* 2: 30, 96, and especially 1: 286–87; Jean Terrasson, *La philosophie applicable à tous les objets de l'esprit* . . . (Paris, 1754), p. 145; P. F. Le Tourneur, *Shakespeare traduit de l'anglois,* vol. 1 (Paris, 1776): lxxvii–lxxviii, lxxxii.

37. Hurd, *Horatii epistolae,* 3: 55, 73–74; *Works,* 2: 429; 5: 132. Joseph Warton, *Genius and Writings of Pope,* 2: 24, expresses the conservative attitude toward the value of originality.

gate all knowledge, search nature for images, "be conversant with all that is awfully vast or elegantly little"; he must know "all the appearances of nature." In his practical criticism, Johnson consistently distinguishes those books which are copies or imitations from those which are truly original. Thus he praises the metaphysicals for at least having "to read and think," rather than merely borrowing or imitating; although admittedly they also exemplify the opposite danger of "a voluntary deviation from nature in pursuit of something new and strange." In a letter to Boswell he compliments the *Corsican Journal* as rising "out of your own experience and observation." On the other hand, Boswell's *History*, he says, is satisfactory, but "borrowed from without . . . copied from books," while in the *Journal* "You express images which operated strongly upon yourself." This distinction occurs regularly in the *Lives of the Poets*.[38] Concerning Shakespeare's original genius, then, Johnson is reasonable, if restrained. Without compromising his own very traditional doubts about the possibility of genuine originality, and without adopting sentimental and relativistic theories, he is able at once to appreciate Shakespeare's first-hand observation, and yet to place a proper emphasis on the importance of learning. Blake pronounced, not very vatically, some years later: "The Man who says that Genius is not Born but Taught—Is a Knave."[39] It is not extraordinary that Johnson should appear in Blake's catalogue of knaves as well as idiots. But for Johnson the mind, whatever intrinsic qualities it may possess, must ideally be cultivated. It is an ignorant belief, though not held only by ignorant people, that learning and poetry are at odds.

Having commenced his historical criticism by investigating the influence of the age on Shakespeare, and having then examined Shakespeare himself, Johnson concludes by considering the influence of Shakespeare on his country and its language. "Perhaps it would not be easy to find any authour, except Homer, who invented so much as Shakespeare, who so much advanced the studies which he cultivated, or effused so much novelty upon his age or country."

38. *Works*, 3: 233; 1: 221; *Lives*, 1: 21, 35; *Letters*, 1: 230. See also *Lives*, 3: 216; 1: 457; and cf. 3: 298–99; 1: 291–92; 3: 66. In his *Life of Browne* he describes the *Vulgar Errors* as "a work, which . . . arose not from fancy and invention, but from observation and books" (*Oxford Works*, 6: 482).

39. *Poetry and Prose of William Blake*, ed. Geoffrey Keynes (London: Nonesuch Press, 1927), p. 987.

Johnson ascribes to Shakespeare the "form, the characters, the language, and the shows of the English drama." He quotes Dennis's opinion that Shakespeare was the inventor of dramatic verse, professes doubt on this point, but agrees that Shakespeare "is the first who taught either tragedy or comedy to please," all the earlier pieces having been forgotten. Unless Spenser shares the honor, Shakespeare was the first to smooth and soften the English language: "He endeavours indeed commonly to strike by the force and vigour of his dialogue, but he never executes his purpose better, than when he tries to sooth by softness." Thus to Shakespeare Johnson attributes three achievements: he refined the drama and made it more agreeable; he possibly invented the looser, dramatic blank verse; and he definitely improved its smoothness—all serve to enforce his initial proposition that no one has invented so much except Homer.

The comparison of Shakespeare with Homer had become not only commonplace but trite by Johnson's time.[40] Like Homer, he was original because he had no alternative: all critics postulate the utter rudeness and insignficance of English drama before Shakespeare. The author of *Some Remarks on the Tragedy of Hamlet* (1736) praises him all the more for having had so little to build upon: "Thus much we must observe, that before his Time there were very few (if any) Dramatick Performances of any Tragick Writer, which deserve to be remembered; so much were all the noble Originals of Antiquity buried in Oblivion." He is echoed by the anonymous author of *Miscellaneous Observations on the Tragedy of Hamlet* in 1752. Shakespeare "first revived, or more properly form'd the Stage." By his judgment, imagination, and "a perfect Knowledge of human Nature, without the least Assistance from Art, he dispell'd those condense Clouds of Gothic Ignorance which at that Time obscured us." French criticism follows a similar vein.[41] But till mid-century little attention seems to have been

40. E.g., Pope in *Eighteenth-Century Essays on Shakespeare*, p. 44; Whalley, *Enquiry into Shakespeare*, p. 15; Duff, *Essay on Original Genius*, p. 287; these are most explicit. See also: Dennis, *Critical Works*, 2: 4 (*Genius and Writings of Shakespeare*); *Works of Beaumont and Fletcher*, 1: lxxv; Upton, *Critical Observations*, p. 135; John Hippisley, *A Dissertation on Comedy* (London, 1750), p. 40.

41. *Some Remarks on Hamlet*, p. iii; *Miscellaneous Observations on the Tragedy of Hamlet* (London, 1752), pp. 7–8; and see also: Dryden, *Essays*, 2: 17; Upton, *Critical Observations*, p. 98; Warton, *History of English Poetry*, 3:

given to the degree to which Shakespeare may have refined English poetry. For most critics, an adequate history of metrics did not extend beyond Pope's ritualistic invocation of Waller and Denham.[42] But by 1758 Armstrong is willing to praise Shakespeare for having the "most musical Ear of all the *English* Poets. . . . his wildest Licenses seldom hurt the Ear; on the contrary, they give his Verse a Spirit and Variety, which prevents its ever cloying." Three years before the *Preface* Webb asserts: "Shakespear, when he attends to it, is not only excellent in the mechanism of his verse, but, in the sentimental harmony, equal if not superior to, any of our English poets." Hence Johnson on these points is current but conventional. Like other mid-century critics, he values Shakespeare's versification at a higher rate than earlier critics did.[43]

Johnson concludes this section of the *Preface* by balancing his praise with a few strictures. Much of our esteem, after all, derives from "custom and veneration" as well as from judgment; and with this we are returned to the problem which opened the *Preface:* How do we achieve a proper and just evaluation? We tend to regard Shakespeare's beauties rather than his faults, "and endure in him what we should in another loathe or despise." He has in fact "corrupted language by every mode of depravation." No play of his, perhaps, if believed to be by another writer, "would be heard to the conclusion." Shakespeare himself was to blame for this, since he did not strive to do more than would please his own audience. He was not concerned with posterity "or had any further prospect, than of present popularity and present profit." He attempted to make no collected edition, or to rescue pieces in danger of being lost. These omissions of his have cooperated with the general complexity of his style and the incompetence and ignorance of the early players and copiers to reduce his texts to their present chaotic state.

401; La Place, *Le théâtre anglois,* vol. 1 (London, 1746), p. vi; Riccoboni, *Account of the Theatres in Europe,* p. 166; J. B. A. Suard, *Variétés littéraires,* vol. 1 (Paris, 1768), p. 51; Le Tourneur, *Shakespeare traduit,* 1: ii–iii.

42. E.g., the brothers Warton generally ignore Shakespeare's versification altogether; Joseph does give Spenser some credit for smooth verse, but Thomas will hardly even do that (J. Warton, *Genius and Writings of Pope,* 2: 351–53; T. Warton, *Observations on the "Fairy Queen,"* 1: 113–34).

43. Armstrong, *Miscellanies,* 2: 164; Webb, *Remarks on the Beauties of Poetry,* pp. 31–32 (cf. pp. 48–49).

Others had noted that we tend to revere Shakespeare excessively, and tolerate in him what we would not in another. Goldsmith, for example, wishes that many of his scenes might be forgotten and urges us to ask ourselves whether we would approve some of the things we see in revived pieces "if written by a modern poet." He suggests that the spectator "will find that much of his applause proceeds merely from the sound of a name and an empty veneration for antiquity." That Shakespeare neglected posterity was also a common complaint. As Pope had said years before, Shakespeare wrote for "gain, not glory," and "grew Immortal in his own despight." Johnson himself comments to this effect in the notes when dealing with some carelessness or other.[44]

Like those examined in the previous chapter, Johnson's opinions here are neither idiosyncratic nor progressive. As an historical critic he shows a strong sense of perspective, but no real inclination to regard his own standards as merely relative. This is especially evident when he describes the Elizabethan Age. His is an intelligent discussion, but it is plainly condescending in a way that the Wartons', Hurd's, and even a minor figure like Guthrie's are not. Hurd, while not a relativist, does apply new standards in judging Spenser, but one senses, on Johnson's part, little dissatisfaction with the old ones. That he contrasts Shakespeare favorably with Addison, and summons up the usual metaphors to defend his wildness and irregularity, indicates, on the other hand, that his standards were far from those of the petrific Rymer, or even Dennis. Johnson's assessment of Shakespeare's learning is particularly satisfactory and, in attending to the importance of Elizabethan translations, fully up-to-date. His account of Shakespeare's genius, judged against that of the Gerards, the Duffs, and even the Guthries, could not be called *avant-garde*. It is especially instructive to compare him with Duff. *An Essay on Original Genius* appeared two years after the *Preface;* like his fellow Scotsman Gerard (whose *Essay on Taste,* it will be remembered, came out in 1759), Duff tries there to construct a theory—in his case to justify contemporary cults of primitivism.

---

44. Oliver Goldsmith, *An Enquiry into the Present State of Polite Learning,* p. 132 (cf. *Works of Beaumont and Fletcher,* 1: xv–xvi); Pope, *First Epistle of the Second Book of Horace,* lines 71–72. See also Warburton in *Eighteenth-Century Essays on Shakespeare,* p. 89; Edward Capell, *Introduction to Works of Shakespeare,* vol. 1 (London, 1768), p. 2; and Johnson's "Notes to Shakespeare" in *Works,* 7: 336, 417; 8: 550.

Just as Gerard had attempted to furnish a systematic account of what the sentimentalists were content to call taste, so Duff, by a sociological examination into the nature of primitive societies, would enumerate the "causes" why primitive cultures—and unlearned individuals—are precisely those most capable of energetic originality. Thus in Duff, as in Gerard (and, in moral philosophy, Diderot), an ostensibly scientific investigation is conducted in order to demonstrate an essentially sentimental theory. Again, the sentimentalist and positivist unite. But Johnson's understanding of the operation of the mind rendered unaccountable the notion of a full-fledged genius without learning, just as originality itself was for him unaccountable except in terms of disposition, the rearranging of existing materials. The empiricism of Locke, united with the neoclassical understanding of *invention*, necessarily excluded Johnson from the company of those who celebrated primitive geniuses or who seriously compared the poet to the divine and omnisympathetic creator. Finally, coming full circle, the eternal standards, never forgotten, exhibit themselves again in Johnson's enumeration of those several qualities irrationally praised in Shakespeare but rightly found intolerable in others; these, however, do not prevent him from assessing judiciously Shakespeare's contributions to drama and the English language.

Johnson, then, is not a relativist but an absolutist in the most fastidious sense. From such a position it is as possible to perceive and approve the excellencies of an earlier age as it is to value that element of truth in other religions than one's own. Some condescension is inevitable, and from this the relativist, presumably, would be free (save that he condescends to all absolutists). But this condescension is not incompatible with understanding and even approbation; and thus, with a rational and unenthusiastic confidence in his own age, did Johnson understand and approve.

Chapter VI

Johnson and His Age

It remains to gather together the strands. What relationship does in fact obtain between the *Preface,* taken as a whole, and its milieu? What final judgment can we form of the *Preface* as itself a work of art? What, ultimately, does it tell us about the quality of Johnson's criticism? To answer the first question, rather than producing a number of generalizations, I should prefer to explore, quite specifically, the critical response of Johnson's contemporaries; hopefully, some of the strands hitherto isolated will make a final and more *patterned* appearance as they manifest themselves in Johnson's critics. I shall then consider the style and structure of the *Preface,* and conclude with some observations on Johnson and the art of criticism.

THE REVIEWERS

Willam Kenrick produced the longest and (uncharacteristically) the most intelligent review, which appeared in the *Monthly Review* for October and November, 1765.[1] Kenrick opens with a mournful disquisition on the difficulties of a Shakespeare editor, the number of problems he must encounter and disappointments endure: "From the present Editor, it is true, we hoped better things. But what shall we say?" In that ironically cautionary style of which Kenrick was a master, he supposes that either indolence or possibly ignorance may have caused the notes to be (as he insinuates) the unrewarding morsels of useless erudition that they are. Proceeding to the *Preface,* he discovers in the first several pages "little . . . but trite and common-place reflections . . . delivered in that pompous style which is so peculiar to himself, and is so much admired by some kind of readers." He quotes extensively and approves of

---

1. All quotations from this review will be from *Monthly Review* 33 (October 1765): 285–301; (November 1765): 374–89.

Johnson's favorable criticism, although he comments, with respect
to tragicomedy: "We do not feel the force of this reasoning [that
frequent alternation of passions is natural]; though we think the
critics have condemned this kind of drama too severely." But he
is particularly eager to dispute the insufficiency of Shakespeare's
moral plan:

> But if it be admitted, as our Editor actually admits, that a system of
> social duty may be selected from his writings, and that his precepts and
> axioms were virtuous; we may justly ask, whether they are less so for
> dropping casually from him? Must a writer be charged with making a
> sacrifice of virtue, because he does not professedly inculcate it? Is
> every writer *ex professo* a parson or a moral philosopher?

A poet, he believes, will be moral enough who diverts the world
without making it worse. Johnson, he continues, elsewhere excuses Shakespeare because of his ignorance of poetical composition;
why does he not excuse him here? Shakespeare was apparently
unaware that a poet should write like a philosopher—and a good
thing, too, thinks Kenrick. By not observing poetic justice, he
produced "a strict imitation of nature; and Shakespeare is the Poet
of Nature. . . . He did not presume to limit the designs of providence to the narrow bounds of poetical justice; but hath displayed
the sun shining, as it really does, both on the just and the unjust."
If Johnson defends Shakespeare's violation of the rules because he
was ignorant of them, and if Johnson defends tragicomedy because
it is like (sublunary) nature, why cannot we defend Shakespeare's
want of poetic justice on the same grounds? Kenrick's objections
are shrewd, if not entirely just; for as we have seen, Johnson
elsewhere *did* argue that art should show life as we must expect
it to be. Johnson would of course have been quick to reply that
moral truths are more important than literary rules, and hence to be
guarded more jealously.

Kenrick makes little attempt to justify Shakespeare's faulty
plots or his imperfect style and language; he offers the usual exten-
uation that the age was both rude and tasteless. He reproduces the
"quibble" paragraph and remarks that Johnson clearly "takes full
as much delight in starting and hunting down a poor conceit as
he affirms Shakespeare did." His indignation is especially excited by
the passage where Johnson, having criticized the dramatist's "cold

declamation," imprudently suggests that "Shakespeare hardly escapes without the pity or resentment of the reader." Kenrick demands specific examples, and declares with all the righteousness of an offended bardolator: "Were we disposed to be as harsh and severe on the learned Annotator, as the Annotator himself hath been on his GREAT, INIMITABLE Author, we might here appeal to the public, to decide which of them most demands our *pity* or merits our *resentment*."

The unities and dramatic illusion elicit the most ingenuity from Kenrick: "We cannot, on the principles of common-sense, conceive, how any dramatic Writer can be justly said to have preserved the unity of action, who hath confessedly shewn no regard to those of time and place." He first accuses Johnson of irrelevance: "The dramatic unities if necessary, are necessary to support the *apparent probability,* not the *actual credibility* of the drama." The spectators are not literally deceived, but are partly so; thus the drama must be probable to entice our senses, even though our judgment may not be fooled in the least. As always, Kenrick is alert to discern inconsistencies; he notes that after Johnson proves that the drama is incredible, he turns around and says it *is* credited—"with all the credit due to a drama." At this point Kenrick reveals his own near-sentimentalist position: the affected spectator does not reflect at all on the scene before him; he does not compare the fiction with the original or consider that he may be exposed to the misfortunes shown on the stage. "The audience are moved by mere mechanical motives; they laugh and cry from mere sympathy at what a moment's reflection would very often prevent them from laughing or crying [at] at all. . . . we neither fancy the players nor ourselves unhappy. . . . we are . . . merely passive, our organs are in unison with those of the players on the stage, and the convulsions of grief or laughter are purely involuntary." We do not know a play is fiction, and our pleasure proceeds from the "transient sense of pain . . . excited in us by sympathy, instead of actually and durably feeling it ourselves." The audience do not literally *believe* the drama to be real, but they believe enough to inhibit reflection. "We are moved by sympathy, and to this end the appearance, the imitation, of distress, even though we are conscious, in reflection, that it is no more than an imitation, is yet sufficient." The drama appeals to the sentiment, while the understanding "enters into a compact, as it were, to keep holiday." Therefore the unities, in the interests of probability, ought to be preserved. In preferring sympathy and voluntary delusion to reflection, Kenrick is perfectly in accord with sentimentalist doctrine; he perceives the apparent inconsistency in Johnson's denial of dramatic illusion, and his own account of that phenomenon, though somewhat disorganized, is remarkably thoughtful.

Kenrick takes strong exception to the "play read" passage, affirming that there is "a wide difference between the auditor of a drama and the reader of a narrative." His point is that one cannot represent as much on the stage as might be read in the same time: "It is indeed impossible for the action represented to seem to be longer than the actual time of the representation; for . . . it is the senses, and not the imagination, that is immediately employed on the representation." Disagreeing with Johnson, he asserts that we *observe,* and do not *contemplate,* a drama. Here Kenrick, while he continues to be ingenious, ceases to be convincing. It is self-evident that a play three hours long cannot contain actions which in themselves take longer than three hours; yet it *can* represent much more than could occur in three hours by condensing episodes, causing events to pass between the scenes or acts, etc. A spectator accepts these conventions, just as a reader accepts others; this is all that Johnson intends. Considering the emphasis Kenrick places on illusion, it is surprising that he should be so obtusely literalistic here; obviously, the imagination is employed, as well as the senses, in seeing a play, though perhaps not to so great a degree as in reading a book. Here one must suppose Kenrick to have been misled as much by his own fervor to criticize as by Johnson's rather too emphatic language. He concludes his discussion: "It appears, on the whole, that the unities are essential to the drama, though not in that degree as hath been asserted by the critics; so that the result of Dr. Johnson's enquiries concerning them, is as erroneous as his supposition of the necessity on which they were founded." He then quotes extensively the paragraphs on Shakespeare's learning, genius, age, lack of regard to posterity, all with little comment; but he closes the review on a curious and not imperceptive note:

> There runs, indeed, through the whole of this preface, such a mixed and inconsistent vein of praise and censure respecting others; and of boasting and excuse regarding himself, that we think we discover it

to be the production of a wavering pen, directed by a hand equally wearied and disgusted with a task injudiciously undertaken, and as indolently pursued.

Kenrick's review is the most thorough that Johnson received; it is often shrewd and occasionally acute, at times displaying Johnson as a vacillating and unprincipled Whig. On such subjects as poetic justice and dramatic illusion it is both clever and sensible, rightly catching Johnson out in some possible inconsistencies. As a sentimentalist, Kenrick illustrates how a critic, much influenced by *avant-garde* aesthetics, could become all the more an ardent champion of the rules; for although he is "advanced" in his understanding of poetic justice and delusion, he is almost as aggressive in his defense of the unities as Rymer.

The observations in the *Critical Review* are of less import, but occasionally interesting.[2] Like Kenrick, the reviewers say they had expected much from Johnson's edition: "Mr. Johnson has at last brought the child to light; but alas! in the delivery it has received so many unhappy squeezes, pinches, and wrenches, that the healthful constitution of the parent alone can prevent it from being lame and deformed for ever." In commenting on Johnson's introductory remarks about the test of time, they draw an incomprehensible distinction between taste and feeling, affirming that one must judge Shakespeare by the latter, which, unlike taste, is the same everywhere; these comments point up the lucidity of Johnson's discussion of literary consensus when compared with that of most of his contemporaries. On Shakespeare's "general characters" they disagree: "Shakespeare has succeeded better in representing the oddities of nature than her general properties" (citing Falstaff, Malvolio, Benedick, Caliban, as being not at all species). But they do agree that Shakespeare knew human nature and that he has no heroes. They regret that Johnson condescended to consider the objections of a Dennis, a Rymer, or, "more contemptible than both, a Voltaire." Johnson ought rather to have *defended* Shakespeare against their strictures than to have *apologized* for him. Where, they ask, *is* Claudius's intoxication exhibited, and why accept the charge that Menenius is a buffoon? They censure his simile ("the painter neglects the drapery") as infelicitous, for they are unaware of "any

2. All quotations will be from *Critical Review* 20 (November 1765): 321–32; (December 1765): 401–11.

eminent painter ever neglecting the drapery of his figures, if he intended they should be cloathed." Less obtusely, they criticize his defense of tragicomedy, not as unsuccessful in itself, but as paying insufficient consideration to Shakespeare's structural skill; the plays, after all, are not "a daily news-paper" which, like life, jumble everything promiscuously together. They are unimpressed with Johnson's complaint that Shakespeare lacked a moral plan; and in his enumeration of Shakespeare's other faults they find "beyond what the greatest enemies of his author have ever urged to his dispraise"—surely Johnson is not serious! They then quote extensively and approvingly from Johnson's remarks on the unities and illusion; these are "worthy Mr. Johnson's pen." They urge, however, that anyone who has seen Barton Booth in *Othello* knows very well the difference between reading and witnessing a play. His opinions about *Cato*, they decide, are not new. They find little else disagreeable and profess that they do not mean to insinuate that the piece is "without merit; we think, some parts of it are well wrote, and if the reader will indulge us a pun, with a *truely* critical spirit, tho' not in the *true* spirit of criticism." Nevertheless, they affirm that in examining the *Preface* they have "differed from him who differs from (we believe) all Englishmen in the ideas of Shakespeare's genius and merit."

The subsequent installments of this review examine Johnson's notes very thoroughly, complaining particularly of his slender knowledge of the Elizabethan Age; their consideration of the *Preface* itself is therefore markedly less comprehensive than that in the *Monthly*. Unlike Kenrick, they endorse his opinions on the unities and theatrical delusion. In challenging the accuracy of Voltaire's criticism and in objecting to some of the implications of Johnson's defense of tragicomedy, they are rather acute. But perhaps most interesting is their disagreement with Johnson over Shakespeare's general characters; by praising the *oddities* in Shakespeare, they manifest the tendency of progressive critics to prefer the humorous and eccentric—the specific—to the universal. Finally, the reviewer's undisguised astonishment over Johnson's conventional criticism of Shakespeare's faults shows how pervasive and fashionable "Shakespeare idolatry" had become. To compare the two reviews is to validate the accuracy of at least the first half of Johnson's opinion, expressed in his interview with King George III, "that the

Monthly Review was done with most care, the Critical upon the best principles." [3]

William Kenrick, aptly described by the *Dictionary of National Biography* as the "enemy of every decent and successful person," was apparently unsatisfied with the censorious but relatively inoffensive *Monthly* review which is probably his. In the same year he offered a *Review of Dr. Johnson's . . . "Shakespeare,"* the purpose and tone of which are adequately conveyed by the rest of its title: "in which the Ignorance, or Inattention of that Editor is exposed, and the Poet defended from the Persecution of his Commentators." Johnson ignored this work, which is such a composition of malignity that the modern scholar is well advised to follow his example. Kenrick is concerned with the notes, not the *Preface,* and a violent contest is waged throughout between the innocent and vilified genius of the great bard, and the petulant, hypercritical, and ignorant censures of Johnson.[4]

To return to less polemic reviews, George Colman's *Notes to Mr. Johnson's Edition of Shakespeare* appeared in the *St. James's Chronicle* the very morning the *Preface* was published.[5] Like the *Critical Review,* he believes that Johnson was too lenient with Dennis's complaints (because Menenius is *not* a buffoon). The defense of tragicomedy is termed a "very sensible and spirited vindication," but he rebukes Johnson for being "infinitely too strong" on Shakespeare's faults. Of the "quibble" paragraph he asks: "Has not Mr. J. been as culpably fond of writing upon Quibble, as Shakespeare in persuing it? and is not his laboured paragraph upon quibble as puerile as a remnant of a schoolboy's declamation?" Besides, he adds, all Shakespeare's age shared this fault. Colman praises his remarks on the unities as containing "much good sense, sound criticism, and fine writing," but he wishes that Johnson had "rather maintained the character of a

---

3. *Life*, 2: 40.

4. Of this work observes the *Monthly Review* 33 (December 1765): 457: "Mr. Kenrick is, in controversy, what the North-American Indians are in war; and comes armed with a tomahawk and scalping knife, to slay, and to strip the slain." And the *Critical Review* 20 (November 1765): 332, reproaches him for adopting the notion of the Tartars, "that by killing a man of eminence he becomes possessed of all his good qualities."

5. All quotations will be from George Colman, *Prose on Several Occasions,* 3 vols. (London, 1787), 2: 59–69.

reasoner, than assumed that of a pleader." He condemns extreme
violations of the unities and suggests that Johnson ought to have
considered *how far* these rules might be transgressed. This is the
extent of Colman's criticism: orthodox, reasonable, and unexciting.
The appearance of Johnson's edition, and especially the *Preface,*
seems to have aroused considerable interest, but the other reviews
of 1765 are meager, satisfied merely to quote long extracts from it.[6]
The next few years, however, produced several further assessments
and discussions.

The *Annual Register* for 1765 takes a neutral and retrospective
glance at some of the criticisms. The reviewers rejoice to concur
with the other critics in praising Johnson's "General Observations"
on the plays; there is unanimity as to their excellence. But this

> is far from being the case with regard to his preface, to which many
> objections have been raised; but most of them on such different
> accounts, that they serve only to justify the common observation con-
> cerning the great difficulty of equally pleasing all tastes. For our part,
> we think, that, if there is any fault in this piece, it is the almost para-
> doxical manner into which Mr. Johnson has contrived to throw his
> sentiments. Read first, what he says of Shakespeare's beauties, and you
> will be apt to think he can have no blemishes . . . . Read first, what
> he says of his blemishes, and you be equally apt to conclude, that he
> can have no beauties.[7]

They quote copiously from the sections on the unities and Shakespeare's general characters.

The tone and manner of Johnson's pejorative criticism excited
more irritation than that evinced by the *Annual Register.* Herbert
Lawrence, in his *Life and Adventures of Common Sense* (1769),
says that though Johnson "is very Candid and honest in his

---

6. *St. James's Chronicle,* nos. 718–20 (8–10, 12–15 October 1765) carried
Colman's review; portions of this review were used by: *Public Ledger* no. 1803
(15 October 1765), and *London Magazine* 34 (October 1765). *Gentleman's Magazine* 35 (October 1765): 479, quotes from the *Preface,* giving only cursory praise.
Lloyd's Evening Post, nos. 1288–94, prints the *Preface* with no commentary, only
terming it "as masterly a production as any in the language of this country."
London Chronicle, nos. 1375–77, quotes long extracts with no further comment
than that it is "elegant and copious." A letter signed by "Crito" in *Owen's
Weekly Chronicle,* no. 405 (28 December 1765) severely criticizes the notes.

7. *Annual Register* (London, 1766), pp. 312–13.

Declarations and Opinions, he advances them in so Cinical a
Manner, and shows such Contempt of the Person whose Work he
is criticising, that it carries along with it the Appearance of
Envy, which must create him many Enemies." The congenial
James T. Callender, in his *Deformities of Dr Samuel Johnson*,
terms the *Preface* "an incoherent jumble of reproach and pane-
gyrick." Like Kenrick, he is exasperated by Johnson's suggestion
that Shakespeare "seldom escapes without the pity or resentment
of the reader": "The Doctor himself is an object of pity. Shakespeare has been in his grave near two centuries—His life was innocent—His writings are immortal. To feel resentment against so
great a man because his works are not every where equal is an
idea highly becoming to the generosity of Dr Johnson." He advises
that we blush at Johnson's remarks about the insignificance of
love, finds that the edition was "received with general disregard,"
and that the *Preface* itself was "the particular butt of censure."
Obviously, Callender went to school to Kenrick; but, absorbing
his malignant irascibility, failed to achieve his acuity and wit.[8]

But Mrs. Montagu, the same year as Herbert Lawrence, speaks
highly of the *Preface,* and Dr. Thomas Campbell pronounces "that
the preface and notes were worth the whole subscription money."
Murphy calls it a "tract of great erudition and philosophical criticism." That very judiciousness which excited the wrath of Kenrick
is for Boswell its greatest merit: "A blind indiscriminate admiration of Shakspeare had exposed the British nation to the ridicule
of foreigners"; by candidly admitting the faults, Johnson has done
more good than all the panegyrists.[9] In France the *Preface* soon
acquired an extraordinary reputation. A translation appeared in
the *Gazette Littéraire* the same year, and in 1769 J. B. A. Suard
printed some "Observations sur Shakespeare, tirées de la Préface
[de] M. S. Johnson." The real beginning of its popularity, however,
can be discovered in P. F. Le Tourneur's introduction (1776) to his

8. *Life and Adventures of Common Sense,* quoted in R. G. Noyes, *The
Thespian Mirror* (Providence: Brown University Press, 1953), p. 55; Callender,
Deformities of Dr. Samuel Johnson, 2d ed. (London, 1782), pp. 39–47, 82 (this
work has been erroneously attributed to John Callander).

9. Elizabeth Montagu, *An Essay on the Writings and Genius of Shakespeare*
(London, 1769), pp. 14–15; Campbell, quoted in *Johnsonian Miscellanies,* ed.
G. B. Hill, 2 vols. (Oxford, 1897), 2: 358; Murphy in ibid., 1: 474; Boswell in
Life, 1: 496–97.

Shakespearean translations, an essay which is largely a patchwork of passages from Rowe, Warburton, Theobald, Hanmer, Sewell, and Johnson. He invariably selects, as "le plus intéressant," the liberal passages: Johnson on dramatic illusion, the unities, Shakespeare's genius, the ability to draw from his writings "un système complet de sagesse économique & civile," etc. Of Johnson's censures he quotes very little. Baretti's immodest borrowings from the *Preface* in his *Discours sur Shakespeare* (1777) have been mentioned in chapter 3.

But nothing better illustrates the immediate and real influence of the *Preface* than the introduction to Richardson's (or Taylor's) *Cursory Remarks on Tragedy* (1774), which is given over largely to controverting Johnson's conclusions about the unities and illusion. For the most part, Richardson assumes the sentimentalist position: "fiction must put on the air of truth, for to feel we must first believe, and to what we refuse our credit, to that likewise shall we refuse our tears." [10] Hence, the unities are necessary. He cites Johnson's objections, but like Kenrick in the *Monthly*, contends that the objection "is not only to the impossibility, but to the impropriety of changing the place." This leads him into a tedious and ungainly discussion, the point of which being that we can tolerate so much, but not too much, improbability; if one presumes to show us drops of sweat from the archangel Michael, we should disbelieve, but if he continued to show us other fantastic things, our disgust would grow. Having furnished us with this felicitous image, Richardson concludes of Johnson:

> In good truth the doughty critic seems disposed to treat us as lord Peter did his brothers, who, because they were willing for the sake of domestic harmony and their own convenience, to allow that a crust of bread was excellent mutton . . . affirmed, that it was likewise a beer-glass of claret. The two brothers, stagger'd at the first, but quite confounded at the latter assertion, determined to be silent, and not to argue the point with a person so unreasonable, and of a disposition so untractable.

Returning to the question of delusion: If it does not exist, he inquires, why the scenery, why all the skill of Garrick? He admits

10. *Cursory Remarks on Tragedy* . . . (London, 1774), p. 2; all further quotations will be from pp. 3–29.

that the spectator does not take a play for reality from beginning to end, but verisimilitude must be preserved nevertheless: a play, like a landscape painting, "the more it resembles reality, the more it will please, the more merit will it have." Like Kenrick, he modifies the sentimentalist position: though we are not literally deluded, we are partly so, hence, a certain amount of verisimilitude is required.

He then devotes ten pages to confuting Johnson's reflective theory: that we fancy ourselves, not the players, unhappy for a moment, and that we lament the possibility, rather than suppose the presence, of misery. No, says Richardson, when I see Lear in the rain, I cannot fancy myself unhappy since I am no king, am not old, have no daughters, etc. As for "lamenting the possibility"— since I have no children, I cannot lament the possibility of losing what I do not possess. Disclosing his own essentially sentimentalist position, Richardson then asserts that "the mind is rather passive than active"; it perceives, and must have corresponding sensations. Furthermore, he says, Johnson's belief is "clearly false" that the delight of tragedy proceeds from our consciousness that it is fiction. The pleasure consists in knowing that we are free of such calamities, and in the pity we feel for those who we believe are enduring them; the pleasure ultimately arises "from the intimate alliance between pleasure and pain." Richardson's analysis is confused and inept, far inferior to Kenrick's, although rather like it; yet it testifies to the weight which Johnson carried. Richardson is most annoyed by Shakespeare's lack of verisimilitude; hence, if Johnson's observations were allowed to stand unopposed, much of the Shakespeare criticism in Richardson's book would necessarily fall. Thus an introduction of twenty-nine pages is devoted to a contradiction of the central portions of the *Preface*. As one might expect, his strictures against Shakespeare are much more severe than Johnson's: another indication that Johnson's adverse criticism is not so extreme as the *Critical*, for example, seems to believe.

What Johnson himself thought of his work is uncertain; as to what he did *not* think of it, we have some indications. "To tell the truth," he writes to Joseph Warton 9 October 1765, "as I felt no solicitude about this work, I receive no great comfort from its conclusion; but yet am well enough pleased that the public has no further claim upon me." To Sir John Hawkins, who had ventured to praise the edition, he replies: "I look upon this as I did upon the Dictionary: it is all work, and my inducement to it is not love or desire of fame, but the want of money, which is the only motive to writing that I know of." These comments were made, to be sure, with reference to the entire edition. However, when an anonymous lady was so audacious as to term his *Preface* superior to Pope's: "I fear not, Madam . . . the little fellow has done wonders." Thus the Shakespeare, like the *Dictionary*, was dismissed with "frigid tranquillity."[11]

More than any other part, the reviewers and early critics were interested in the passages on illusion and the unities; it is not surprising that in the section of "Essays" in the *Annual Register* these only were selected for reproduction. The *Critical Review* and Colman (with some reservations) approve, as later do Mrs. Montagu and Le Tourneur in France; while the *Monthly Review* and the author of *Cursory Remarks* vehemently disagree, affirming a certain element of delusion and the necessity of the unities. It is worth remarking that both Kenrick in the *Monthly* and Richardson in the *Cursory Remarks* qualify their sentimentalist theories by conceding that dramatic delusion is extremely transient and volitional. We have noticed that some critics expressed themselves far too indiscreetly or imprecisely about this phenomenon, and it is at least arguable that Johnson's manly denial compelled them to refine their theories. Other parts of the *Preface* occasion about equal comment, and can best be summarized in catalogue form:

Both the *Monthly* and the *Critical:*
    are skeptical of his remarks on tragicomedy;
    defend Shakespeare against the charge that he wrote without
      a moral plan—he is sufficiently moral;
    criticize his opening paragraphs on taste (though not very clearly
      or intelligently);
    object to the "play read" paragraph.
Colman and the *Monthly* ridicule the "quibble" paragraph.

11. *The Letters*, ed. R. W. Chapman, 3 vols. (Oxford: Oxford University Press, 1952), 1: 177; Hawkins's *Life of Johnson*, quoted in *Life*, 1: 319 n.; *Johnsonian Miscellanies*, 1: 183–84. See Arthur Sherbo, *Samuel Johnson, Editor of Shakespeare, With an Essay on The Adventurer*, Illinois Studies in Language and Literature, vol. 42 (Illinois: University of Illinois Press, 1956), p. 7, on Johnson's dislike of his task.

Callender and the *Monthly* are enraged by the "pity and resentment" remark.

Colman and the *Critical* regret that Johnson failed to defend Shakespeare properly against Dennis, Rymer, and Voltaire.

The *Critical* alone objects to Johnson's observations on the dramatic characters; Shakespeare excelled in *particular* characters.

Both the *Monthly* and the *Critical,* Colman, and—if fanaticism may
be admitted as evidence—Kenrick and Callender, believe Johnson
to have been generally too severe and unrelenting a critic.

In several of the reviews (especially the *Monthly,* the *Critical,* and
Colman's) there is a sense, either explicit or implicit, that the
Preface has not measured up to expectation.

Some of his contemporaries, then, found him too liberal regarding the unities, others too conservative on Shakespeare's faults. To
generalize, the reviewers seem to have received the *Preface* with
the same deficiency of enthusiasm with which it was offered to them,
although the copious extracts reproduced by the journals and news-
papers suggest that it was much read and discussed. Seldom is
something praised in it as being genuinely new; yet the novelty of
his opinions on tragicomedy and the unities is sometimes remarked,
and only one reviewer quarrels with his comments on Shakespeare's
general characters. In short, the *Preface* was received by contemporaries as are so many pieces of substantial merit: it was neither
dismissed as merely repetitive nor acclaimed as apocalyptic. Certainly, it is instructive to contrast the public reception of the *Preface*
with the furor produced by Macpherson's *Ossian* three years earlier;
it is instructive, that is to say, in the mysterious movements of taste.
Just as certainly, Johnson's critics, indeed Johnson himself, would
have heard with astonishment B. Thiel's discovery a century later
that the *Preface* "inaugurates a new era not only in the aesthetical
criticism, but also in the literary-historical treatment of Shakespeare's works," and that the forces it unleashed culminated in the
"reestablishment of Shakespeare's full authority."[12] More properly,
the *Preface* concluded an old era, and, for nearly all of its critics,

12. B. Thiel, *The Principal Reasons for Shakespeare's Remaining Unpopular
Longer Than a Century Even in England* (Augsburg, 1874), p. 17.

seemed rather to challenge than to reinforce Shakespeare's recently acquired reputation.[13]

THE *PREFACE TO SHAKESPEARE*

The structure of the *Preface* is not complex. Sherbo's most interesting discovery in this connection is that none of the editors before Johnson includes an introductory discussion of taste or consensus: "each indicates immediately . . . that Shakespeare's position is secure and that he deserves extended criticism." None, in other words, is prepared to undertake a general consideration of the nature of a classic. But aside from this, Sherbo believes that by 1765 the general formula for a preface to Shakespeare had been established; the editor was expected to comment on Shakespeare's faults and virtues, describe his own editorial position, account for the dramatist as a *lusus naturae,* dwell on his force of imagination,

13. For references praising Shakespeare before 1765, see R. W. Babcock, *The Genesis of Shakespeare Idolatry, 1766–1799* (Chapel Hill: University of North Carolina Press, 1931), p. 199 n. I cite in addition the following laudatory items appearing before the *Preface*: T. Cooke, *Epistle to the Countess of Shaftesbury* (London, 1743), passim; *An Examen of . . . The Suspicious Husband* (London, 1747), pp. 20–39; Arthur Murphy, *The Gray's-Inn Journal,* 2 vols. (London, 1756), 1: 24, 144, 259–63: "*Shakespear* is a kind of established Religion in Poetry, and his Bays will always flourish with undiminished Verdure"; *Monthly Review* 20 (April 1759): 317: Kenrick, reviewing Wilkes's *General View of the Stage,* indicates just how trite encomiums on Shakespeare and Garrick had become: they "appear to us extreamly needless and disgusting. Mr. Wilkes might almost have told his Readers, that Homer was the greatest poet, and Roscius the most admired actor of antiquity, as to have launched out into futile and worn-out eulogies, on the most celebrated bard and comedian among the moderns." How audacious, then, of Johnson six years later to offer Kenrick other than eulogies! An article on "The Ballance of Poets" in *Museum* 2 (1746): 165–69, ranks twenty foreign and English writers on a zero to eighteen scale under a number of categories. Under "Critical Ordonnance" (structure) Shakespeare and Ariosto rank lowest with zero, but Shakespeare is rewarded with a top score of eighteen under "Pathetic Ordonnance" (creating moving incidents), "Dramatic Expression" (excellence in delineating character), "Incidental Expression" (excellence in portraying manners), and "Moral." Only he and Homer have a grand eighteen in the "Final Estimate." Sherbo, *Samuel Johnson, Editor of Shakespeare,* pp. 56–57, cites a number of adverse criticisms in this period to demonstrate the moderate quality of Johnson's strictures. As I have indicated in chap. 4, I agree that his criticisms are relatively mild, but in the light of such adulation as that recorded above, one can understand why even those less fanatically devoted to the dramatist than Kenrick (who christened his son William Shakespeare) would find Johnson severe.

and the like.[14] It is possible, however, to be more particular than this. As I have suggested in the previous chapter, the first and by far the more substantial section of the *Preface* (the only section considered in this book) opens and closes on a similar theme: the comparative rather than the absolute merit of art. The initial paragraphs postulate this principle, then justify a critical investigation of the plays themselves; and it is reaffirmed toward the end to justify an examination of the age and the natural abilities of Shakespeare. Between these two spots of theorizing is contained Johnson's judicial criticism. Johnson first praises Shakespeare for his language, his character delineations, and his tragicomedy; he is the poet of nature, although this *nature* carries with it diverse connotations. And he then censures him for his insufficient morality, imperfect plot-structure, faulty or inappropriate language—for his failure, in short, to *improve* enough upon nature. Johnson follows this with a defense of his violation of the unities and an attack on illusion. Then, having discussed the beauties and faults of the plays themselves, Johnson reiterates his initial argument—literary excellence is comparative—and progresses to an account of the age and of Shakespeare's genius. In this part the same symmetry prevails: Shakespeare is first judiciously praised for that irregularity which was the consequence of his age and for the originality of his genius; then his negligences and defects are enumerated. This concludes the first and larger section of the *Preface;* the second section, not analyzed here, evaluates previous Shakespeare editors and establishes the principles and purposes of Johnson's own editorial policy. Thus the form of the first section is both logical and lucid: (a) the establishment of Johnson's fundamental aesthetic principles; (b) an examination, positive and negative, of the plays; (c) a reaffirmation of his aesthetic position; and (d) an examination, positive and negative, of Shakespeare's genius and age, and the influence which each exercised upon the other.

The style of the *Preface* affords a much more fertile field for speculation and analysis—more than there is opportunity to cover here. In general, it is what one expects from Johnson's writings at this stage of his career; there is the customary Latinate diction and deliberate paralleling of sentence structure, with little evidence of the rather sparer, less factitious style which was to characterize

14. Sherbo, *Samuel Johnson, Editor of Shakespeare,* pp. 51–52.

the *Lives of the Poets.* As so often with Johnson, there is a greater
abundance of metaphorical language than a first reading suggests,
and for the most part the figures, though hardly novel, are appropriate. Thus he compares natural and enduring passions to rock,
and particular personal habits to sand: "The sand heaped by one
flood is scattered by another, but the rock always continues in
its place. The stream of time, which is continually washing the
dissoluble fabricks of other poets, passes without injury by the
adamant of Shakespeare." We are not remarkably surprised by
the figure, but it is perfectly satisfactory; and if one but consider
the geological relationship between sand and rock, the metaphor
becomes yet more significant. All human experiences, too, may
be reducible to an elementary substance, but some, because they
are truly pervasive, will endure the corrosions of time; and these
the great poet must select for his subjects. Objects such as these
drawn from physical nature are used twice more in the *Preface.*
First, they are employed to describe Shakespeare's dialogue and
characters:

> Shakespeare's familiar dialogue is affirmed to be smooth and clear, yet
> not wholly without ruggedness or difficulty; as a country may be emi-
> nently fruitful, though it has spots unfit for cultivation: his characters
> are praised as natural, though their sentiments are sometimes forced,
> and their actions improbable; as the earth upon the whole is spherical,
> though its surface is varied with protuberances and cavities.

These images are rather more audacious, but they convey Johnson's
thought well enough. His second use—the comparison of Shakespeare to a forest and a mine—has already been discussed and is
quite conventional and appropriate.[15]

Johnson also uses manufactured objects to illustrate his point.
Estimating Shakespeare from particular passages only, he says,
is like trying to judge a house from a single brick. He later compares a formally perfect play to a citadel representing all the
orders of architecture; and he combines the two realms of the
physical and the manufactured in his contrasting of a natural mine
with "cabinets . . . wrought into shape." The various metaphorical
mutations through which Johnson in one paragraph compels the

15. *Works,* 7: 70–71, 84. See W. B. Carnochan, "Johnsonian Metaphor and
the 'Adamant of Shakespeare,'" *Studies in English Literature* 10 (1970): 541–49.

poor quibble to pass stand out remarkably from the general tenor of the *Preface;* they draw attention to themselves most decidedly, and in this, as we have learned from the ridicule of Kenrick and Colman, they were thought to offend against chaste, classical taste. Again mixing the natural with the artificial, Johnson uses a river, a mountain, and a building to exemplify the distinction between absolute and comparative qualities, as he uses Peruvian and Mexican palaces when he returns later to that theme. All these figures are in the main appropriate, but never surprisingly so, and seldom even extremely so. Is estimating Shakespeare from a single passage in fact like judging a house by one of its bricks, of which all, unlike the variety of Shakespeare's passages, are presumably identical? Is the relationship between a natural character and his occasionally rugged speech nicely represented by the contrast between a spherical earth and its relatively minor "protuberances"? It is all very well to compare the purpose of a play (to instruct and delight) with that of a citadel (to repel the enemy); but though the metaphor is consistent, does it "illustrate and ennoble the subject" as Johnson himself required of perfect similes? And of course before the "quibble" paragraph modern criticism, at least, must indeed sink down in reverential silence. I am far from suggesting that these metaphors are inept, but only that they are sometimes confusing, and seem often to be the product of contrivance rather than a source of enlightenment.[16]

Johnson is happier when he avoids attempting the direct and is content with the submerged or implicit metaphor; of this device he who wrote "Still drops some joy from withering life away" was surely one of the masters in our language. Consider, for example, the following sentence.

> This therefore is the praise of Shakespeare, that his drama is the mirrour of life; that he who has mazed his imagination, in following the phantoms which other writers raise up before him, may here be cured of his delirious ecstasies, by reading human sentiments in human language; by scenes from which a hermit may estimate the transactions of the world, and a confessor predict the progress of the passions.[17]

16. Paul Fussell, *The Rhetorical World of Augustan Humanism* (Oxford: Oxford University Press, 1965), is more sympathetic; on the brick metaphor, see p. 196, and on the citadel, p. 200.

17. *Works,* 7: 65.

Here is a passage abundant with connotative figures, extraordinarily suggestive and expressive, yet with an inner consistency. Shakespeare is the seer of truth, whose revelations exorcise the unnatural spectres invoked by inferior wizards and liberate the deluded reader from his meretricious enchantment. But what I have written is directly metaphorical and such as a wretched imitator of Carlyle or Coleridge might have produced. Johnson does not vitiate the validity of his image by making it explicit. Here the meaning is both "illustrated and ennobled" by figurative embellishment, but not distorted. This technique may be found as often in a short as a long period: "The mind, which has feasted on the luxurious wonders of fiction, has no taste of the insipidity of truth." It is partly through the ubiquitous use of connotative verbs ("feasted") and figurative substantives ("luxurious wonders") that Johnson makes his prose animated, vivid, and inimitably communicative; these devices, harnessed to the service of Johnson's own natural genius and penetration, prevent the *Preface* from being a dull reiteration of what oft was thought. Macaulay hazarded the opinion that "the preface, though it contains some good passages, is not in his best manner." This is fair enough, providing one remembers that what is not in Johnson's best manner may yet be something to which Macaulay would aspire in vain.

How then, in fine, do we gauge the worth of the *Preface to Shakespeare?* Received without much enthusiasm at the time, it does not seem to have gained significant popularity throughout most of the nineteenth century,[18] though by 1875 Thiel, as we have seen, could describe it in such revolutionary terms as surely would have provoked a smile or a sarcasm from its author. Yet in 1944 Joseph Wood Krutch comments that "the *Preface* came to be pretty generally accepted as the best statement yet made concerning the nature and the extent of Shakespeare's achievement." The same year, T. S. Eliot judges the *Preface* to be "very fine." Walter Jackson Bate in 1955 calls it "pioneer," "one of the most decisive documents in the entire history of criticism," recommends it as "still one of the best general discussions of Shakespeare," and quotes

18. See Sherbo, *Samuel Johnson, Editor of Shakespeare*, pp. 49–50; J. Klein, "The History of Johnson's *Preface to Shakespeare*, 1765–1934" (M.A. thesis, McGill University, 1936). The influence of the *Preface* on Continental Romantic critics was considerable, though by them it was sometimes misread, or read in parts.

with approval Adam Smith, who had described it as "the most
manly piece of criticism ever published in any country." Just one
year later, however, Arthur Sherbo is perceptibly less enthusiastic:

> Some of the ideas in the Preface were current in the periodicals of
> the time; most were pretty much common property. . . . Johnson's
> superior command of language enabled him to say more strikingly and
> more memorably what his predecessors had said before him, but the
> belief, still persistent in some critics, that Johnson had something new
> to say on Shakespeare in the Preface must be discarded.

Sherbo says also that "any effort to use the Preface as evidence of
an individual, or particular, critical system is necessarily false" since
the *Preface* is "highly derivative" from other sources. He is taking
to a still further degree D. N. Smith's more generous opinion that
there "is little new matter in his Preface. . . . Its importance lies
mainly in its being a conclusive summing up by a strong, wise, and
impartial mind, of a prolonged discussion."[19]

Sherbo's phrase "superior command of language" describes inade-
quately, I should say, Johnson's achievement, but his conclusions
must in part be accepted. Bate errs in calling the *Preface pioneer,* for
although it is many good things, it is simply not that. On the other
hand, he also calls it *decisive,* and this is precisely the word.
The *Preface* neither erects new ramparts nor opens new veins, but
rather decides, or defines, for neoclassical criticism its final estimation of Shakespeare; just so, in a few years, were the *Lives of the
English Poets* to decide the position of neoclassicism with respect to
many of its own writers.[20] The cliché that the *Preface* is a "great

19. Krutch, *Samuel Johnson* (New York: Harcourt, Brace, & World, 1963),
p. 282; Bate, *The Achievement of Samuel Johnson* (New York: Oxford University
Press, 1955), p. 41; Sherbo, *Samuel Johnson, Editor of Shakespeare,* pp. 60, 62.
See ibid., pp. 125–28, for an exhaustive chart of those remarks in the *Preface*
anticipated by earlier critics. While modern scholars have sometimes questioned
the originality of the *Preface,* few have endeavored to discredit wholesale its
ideas. Peter Gay asserts, as an *obiter dictum,* that it has "every virtue save one,
the virtue of being right" ("Carl Becker's Heavenly City," in *Carl Becker's
Heavenly City Revisited* [n.p.: Archon Books, 1968], p. 51). But possibly Professor
Gay is treating us to a little Voltairean iconoclasm.

20. I use "decide" *sub specie aeternitatis,* of course, and do not mean to
suggest that all contemporary neoclassicists were *decided* by Johnson's writings;
some critics were to disagree even more vehemently with portions of the *Lives*
than with the *Preface.* But from our perspective we are justified in taking

summing up" is true as most clichés are true—as a not utterly invalid oversimplification. On the following issues I should judge Johnson neoclassical, though as we have seen there were bona fide neoclassicists who disagreed with him on some of them: the test of time or consensus, poetic justice, Shakespeare's faults, his genius and originality, the Elizabethan Age. On the unities, dramatic illusion, and Shakespeare's general characters he is less easily classified. His arguments here are so individualistic, at times so idiosyncratic, that I should call them possibly neoclassical only because they are certainly not pre-Romantic. On tragicomedy he is his own man— both classicists and progressives attacked it. Thus the *Preface*, in *orientation* at least, is neoclassical. But Sherbo's observation is significant that none of the other prefaces contains an introductory discussion of consensus and the nature of a classic; for this indicates the distinctive quality of Johnson's neoclassicism. It is flexible and empirical, but at the same time never neglects the necessity of investigating fundamentals or establishing principles. Johnson uses the words of neoclassicism and thinks in its contexts; but he is nevertheless unintimidated by the unities or the false and strait-laced decorum of Rymer or Voltaire, unreluctant to defend the validity of tragicomedy and the originality of Shakespeare's genius. To say that the *Preface* is a great summing up, or that it differs from earlier criticism because of Johnson's "superior command" of English, is to affirm what is at once true and insignificant. Neo-classicism was far too various to be summed up in a meaningful way; nor is it Johnson's rhetoric alone that distinguishes him from the Dennises, Whalleys, and Hurds, though none of these were contemptible critics. W. J. Bate writes, with the *Preface* specifically in mind: "So the criticism of Johnson proceeds through

---

Johnson's position as "definitive." Donald Greene and other scholars have protested the use of such loose terms as *neoclassic* or *Romantic*. Yet I have employed these handy and familiar words regularly in this study, and have relied upon them in the concluding remarks which follow. In discriminating between the two, I take as a reference point P. H. Frye's enumeration of Romantic qualities: "A susceptibility to irregular beauty, a fondness for the striking and the unusual even at the expense of regularity and order, a preference for fascinating detail above symmetry and proportion, a predilection for the coruscations of style—for the glittering word and phrase, for the exotic and exquisite epithet, for everything that touches and thrills and dazzles, a hunger for sensation" (*Romance and Tragedy* [Lincoln: University of Nebraska Press, 1961], p. 35).

the tradition of neo-classic theory that had grown up since the Renaissance; but he accepts it as a pivot on which to revolve rather than a frame to limit the horizon."[21] We are apt, not merely from "Johnson idolatry," to consider this a more equitable judgment than Sherbo's. The *Preface* is, perhaps, "highly derivative," but so, as the neoclassicists never failed to remind us, was Shakespeare. The relationship of the *Preface* to conservative contemporary criticism and to that which went before is not so much a summing up as a final development. It is important to know that Johnson intelligently praises Shakespeare's characters; it is also important to know that he does so for radically different reasons from those of Mrs. Montagu four years later. It is significant that he admires Shakespeare's genius, and no less significant that his admiration is not that of his contemporaries Gerard or Duff. In short, it is necessary to see that although there will be excellent Shakespeare criticism after Johnson, there will be little more excellent Shakespeare criticism *like* Johnson's. And this—the unique merit of the *Preface* —Johnson's contemporaries, least of all, could be expected to perceive.

In this study I have intended as much to contemplate the age as to scrutinize Johnson, for it is only by looking at the age that we can finally assess his contributions in the *Preface*. The sentimentalist and positivist (or rationalistic) movements engendered by the seventeenth century could not but exercise a real if imponderable influence on art and criticism. Johnson, like Swift and Burke in their ways, not systematically or even deliberately, preserved for criticism a more traditional and comprehensive *reason* against the incursions of both. Indeed, "Johnson and the Sentimentalists" might have served as a title for the present study, though one must be wary of imposing too reductive a paradigm upon so various a century as this. To the controversy over taste, and Johnson's discussion of consensus, the paradigm is most easily applied. The sentimentalists and positivists agreed to accept taste as one of the determinations of literary excellence, the former content to consider it a feeling, the latter wishing to develop it into a science. Yet the one alternative does not exclude the other, for they both proceed from the same assumption: that artistic merit is first perceived subjectively; thus the same critic, as we have

21. Bate, *Achievement of Samuel Johnson*, p. 218.

seen, might equally affirm that taste is ineffable, but that it could be systematized to a degree. But Johnson concentrates on consensus alone, the collective wisdom of the ages; only this provides us with *some* certainty external to our sensibilities. If we are honest with ourselves we may find that it is this testimony, *first,* that convinces us of even Shakespeare's greatness; in any event, our sensibilities have a curious way of aligning themselves with it at last. In his initial definition of literary excellence Johnson has excluded impressionistic elements with a rigor which even the empirical and pragmatic Hume could not equal. Thus he founds his criticism on experience and consensus, and not at all on Gerard's a priori Newtonian reason or Dubos's mere feeling. Criticism is neither a science nor a sentiment, but an art.

That it is an instrumental art becomes more apparent in his discussion of Shakespeare's characters and tragicomedy. Here the paradigm must be expanded to include not only the sentimentalists, but also those rationalistic neoclassicists who, like the positivists, were eager to systematize the materials of existence. The sentimentalists, in their emphasis on realism and sympathy, would have confounded art and life, while the rationalistic critics, with their inflexible notions of decorum, would have removed it altogether from life as we know it. Moreover, the two agreed to reject tragicomedy, the rationalists on generic, the sentimentalists on psychological grounds. But in both instances Johnson uses criticism as an instrument, not to identify art with life or to separate it from life, but to penetrate to the real principles which underlie it. His criticism is uncircumscribed by a priori notions about decorum, the genres, or the sensibility. On these matters Johnson is at his most individualistic; here it is particularly improper to call the *Preface* "highly derivative."

Johnson is more traditional on the unities, dramatic pleasure and illusion, poetic justice. Here our paradigm assumes perhaps its most conventional form, with the emerging, sentimentalist theories arrayed against those conceptions of art which I have termed reflective but which, under one name or another, had been part of Western criticism since Aristotle. As a reflective critic, Johnson is not remarkable in his objections to the unities or his desire for a more evident moral plan in Shakespeare's works. On illusion his argument is more tortuous and seemingly contradictory, yet the elements of reflective theory are clearly evident. We are reasoning beings; our pleasure and our edification proceed from reflecting on a work of art as intelligent creatures, not from being galvanized into sympathy or pity. Here, too, the sentimentalists would have identified art with life; but if art offers us nothing different from life, why should we bother with it to begin with? Art is a commentary on life as well as its mirror; it must provide us with materials over which to reason.

Johnson's theories of poetic genius return us to something of our initial paradigm. By relegating everything to taste, the sentimentalists could, if they were so disposed, deny the very possibility of principled criticism; or they could suggest that once this mysterious entity is better understood, criticism might attain scientific certainty. So now, by such terms as *genius, native fire, inspiration*— all pushed to their most extreme and ambiguous meaning—they could obscure completely the nature of the act of poetic composition; or, like Duff, they could endeavor to explain this mystery on systematic and a priori grounds. But Johnson is unintimidated by the word *genius* and unencumbered by Duff's sociological and psychological principles. For him the poet is neither some passive aeolian harp through which the gusts of nature blow nor an inspired creator in any sense really analogous to God. The first conception is as bemeaning as the second is blasphemous. Johnson looks at the poet and discovers a man: as he grows he learns, and as he learns more he can probably tell us more. Johnson's understanding of the poetic genius may be generally Lockian, but it is not Locke as systematized by Hartley, Gerard, or Duff.

The premise of sentimental theories is that our sensibilities— personal feelings—are authoritative to a degree not supposed by earlier philosophies. The consequence for criticism is that it ceases to be a subordinate and instrumental art and becomes an art rather like poetry itself; it is itself a participation in the creative act. Thus, Johnson's judiciousness could hardly be expected to survive along with the "reverential tone" which, Coleridge decreed, was the true test of Shakespearean criticism; nor is reason very compatible with the oracular rhapsodies of Carlyle: "We called Dante the melodious Priest of Middle-Age Catholicism. May we not call Shakspeare the still more melodious Priest of a *true* Catholicism, the 'Universal Church' of the Future and of all times?"[22] To such hierophantic criticism, governed as it is by the principles of sensibility, the neoclassicist was unequal. If by the Age of Johnson we really mean the age of the Montagus and Morganns, then the *Preface* was written for a later, less reverential time. Its discerning judgments have promoted Shakespeare's reputation more ably than all the panegyrics: so Boswell argued in 1791; and with the lapse of years we may apply his opinion as properly to Johnson's reputation. Wherefore Krutch and Bate can say of the *Preface,* what surely cannot be affirmed of Carlyle's fuliginous effusions, that it remains one of the most authoritative and durable discussions of Shakespeare. In our present age, when the "universal churches" have shown themselves to be a diffuse and nerveless humanism, and when the lust for novelty or academic advancement throws annually into our libraries innumerable "new perspectives" on Shakespeare, the ingenuous criticism of Johnson appears ever more pertinent, whether that criticism be of literature or human life. "There are truths which, as they are always necessary, do not grow stale by repetition."

22. Carlyle, "The Hero as Poet," in *Shakespeare Criticism, 1623–1840,* ed. D. N. Smith (London: Oxford University Press, 1964), p. 368. We may remember, too, Herder's rhapsodic portrait of Shakespeare atop a rocky summit surveying the surging sea of life.

Appendix A

Shakespeare's Supernatural Characters

Johnson praises Shakespeare's dramatic characters as men who speak and act as we might do under similar circumstances; and this, he continues, is true not only of his realistic characters, but of his imaginary ones as well.

> Even where the agency is supernatural the dialogue is level with life. Other writers disguise the most natural passions and most frequent incidents; so that he who contemplates them in the book will not know them in the world: Shakespeare approximates the remote, and familiarizes the wonderful; the event which he represents will not happen, but if it were possible, its effects would, probably, be such as he has assigned; and it may be said, that he has not only shewn human nature as it acts in real exigencies, but as it would be found in trials, to which it cannot be exposed.[1]

Shakespeare's ability "to familiarize the wonderful" had been commended, with remarkable continuity, from Dryden's time. After 1750, however, interest shifts from the propriety and consistency of the supernatural characters to their novelty and to the fertility of the genius that was required to produce them. The earlier attitude is embodied in Dryden's explanation of Caliban, the most popular and extraordinary of Shakespeare's creations. He grants that Caliban seems to be a person "not in Nature"; but just as the imagination forms a centaur from a horse and a man, so Shakespeare's monster is the combination of an incubus and a sorceress; moreover, he is furnished "with a person, a language, and a character, which will suit him." Dryden articulates the usual opinion of Shakespeare's imaginary characters, making two points to which neoclassical critics were often to recur: that the

1. *Works*, 7: 65.

creation of a Caliban requires merely the *joining together* of heterogeneous ideas—an explanation perfectly in agreement with
Lockian epistemology—and that such a being must be possessed
of a language consistent with his character—"propriety." [2] Addison
calls rather more attention to Shakespeare's genius, but he says
nothing that would be discordant with the Lockian view: "It shews
a greater Genius in *Shakespear* to have drawn his *Calyban*, than
his *Hotspur* or *Julius Caesar:* The one was to be supplied out of
his own Imagination, whereas the other might have been formed
upon Tradition, History, and Observation." Addison later praises
Shakespeare's skill in the "Fairy Way of Writing" and adds:
"We cannot forbear thinking [his imaginary persons] natural, tho'
we have no Rule by which to judge of them, and must confess,
if there are such Beings in the World, it looks highly probable
they should talk and act as he has represented them." Addison's
highest praise is that of Johnson's: that the characters, though
impossible, are *probable.* They cannot exist, but if they did exist
they would probably behave as Shakespeare has them do.[3] *Probability,* then, is to be defined, not by looking to "real life," but
by considering the internal consistency and plausibility of the
characters themselves. To be sure, as Addison warns us, this is a
more perilous task than comparing characters with counterparts
in life: "we have no Rule by which to judge." This is expressly
pointed out a little more than a year after the *Preface* by the
reviewer of a dramatic romance called *Cymon.* There are, he decides, "works of Fancy" and "imitations of life"; the advantage
of the former is that if propriety is violated

2. John Dryden, *Essays,* ed. W. P. Ker, 2 vols. (Oxford: Oxford University
Press, 1926), 1: 219 (*Preface to Troilus and Cressida*). Rowe in his preface also
praises Caliban as a character "mighty well sustain'd," and expresses the by
then commonplace notion that Shakespeare had not only created a new character, but *"had also devis'd and adapted a new manner of Language for that
Character"* (*Eighteenth-Century Essays on Shakespeare,* ed. D. N. Smith [Oxford:
Oxford University Press, 1963], pp. 13–14).

3. Addison and Steele, *The Spectator,* ed. D. F. Bond, 5 vols. (Oxford: Oxford
University Press, 1965), 2: 586–87 (no. 279); 3: 573 (no. 419). See also *Some
Remarks on the Tragedy of Hamlet* (London, 1736), p. 2; J. Holt, *An Attempt
to Rescue That Auciente English Poet* (London, 1749), pp. 16–17; John Upton,
Critical Observations on Shakespeare (London, 1748), p. 91; Joseph Baretti,
Discours sur Shakespeare (London and Paris, 1777), p. 70. Cf. John Hippisley,
A Dissertation on Comedy (London, 1750), p. 36; Walpole, preface to the first
edition of *Otranto.*

it is a propriety of which very few can judge, and of which, for that reason, few can detect the violation. This advantage is wanting to imitations of life; they are immediately brought to the standard, and compared with their originals, with which almost every one is sufficiently acquainted to form a general judgment of the imitation.[4]

For Addison and the reviewer—and Johnson—it is a question of propriety and decorum; and what Addison is really concerned about is that we have no *external* rule by which to assess fanciful creations. Sublunary nature is irrelevant; we must bring to bear on them a more intellectual nature whose values are consistency and coherence. By the 1760s this had become an ordinary solution to the problems posed by a Caliban: such characters must have an internal unity and order. In effect, this is a logical extension of Horatian propriety and decorum: if the characters possess an internal probability—then a propriety has been preserved, even though it is a propriety that cannot be measured against external standards.[5]

But critics like Joseph Warton, Duff, and Mrs. Montagu, although equally enthusiastic about Shakespeare's imaginary beings, are less concerned with such prosaic matters as consistency and decorum. Warton directly contradicts Dryden's theory of the creation of Caliban: he is a product strictly of the imagination, Shakespeare having received "no assistance from observation or experience"; elsewhere he praises Shakespeare's fairy creatures as having been drawn, not merely with decorum, but also with "wildness of imagination." [6] Mid-century critics are often more impressed with the extravagance and creativity of Shakespeare's genius than with his propriety. Duff, for example, regards imagination as the most essential quality of genius, praising it primarily for its "plastic power of inventing new associations of ideas, and of combining them with infinite variety . . . to present a creation of its own, and

4. *Gentleman's Magazine* 37 (January 1767): 31–32.

5. See particularly John Gregory, *A Comparative View of the State and Faculties of Man* (London, 1765), p. 136 (in 1761) and Richard Hurd, *Works*, 8 vols. (London, 1811), 4: 324 (1762) for interesting discussions. And see also Charles Batteux, *Les beaux arts réduits à un même principe* (Paris, 1747), p. 110, who appeals explicitly to Horace and Quintilian.

6. A. Chalmers, ed., *The British Essayists*, vol. 25 (London, 1817), p. 31 (*Adventurer* no. 97); J. Warton, *Essay on the Genius and Writings of Pope*, 2 vols. (London, 1782), 1: 235.

to exhibit scenes and objects which never existed in nature." Only the "wildest and most exuberant imagination" will succeed in creating supernatural beings, and in such creation Shakespeare succeeded capitally. This imagination "sketches out a creation of its own, discloses truths that were formerly unknown, and exhibits a succession of scenes and events which were never before contemplated or conceived."[7]

But although Johnson can praise the imaginative creation of new worlds and beings,[8] he is not to be grouped with these critics. Johnson's conception of the imagination is taken up in chapter 5; here it is sufficient to say that his is a traditionally Lockian notion and quite unlike Duff's. For Johnson, memory, which collects and distributes images, is the fundamental power of the mind. The imagination "selects ideas from the treasures of remembrance, and produces novelty only by varied combinations."[9] He would certainly have agreed with Burke that "the power of the imagination is incapable of producing any thing absolutely new; it can only vary the disposition of those ideas which it has received from the senses."[10] Johnson's conception is what Coleridge was to bemean as *fancy,* a combinative faculty, whereas Duff's clearly anticipates Coleridge's definition of imagination, a virtue possessing real affinities with the divine act of creation. Dryden himself would have had little difficulty in understanding and approving of Johnson's opinion; indeed, I can see little disagreement between Johnson and the "father of English criticism" on this point. Not only does Johnson disbelieve that the imagination can really create anew, in the notes he denies to Caliban what even Rowe and other early neoclassicists had thought him to possess: "a new Manner of Language." "His diction is indeed somewhat clouded by the gloominess of his temper and the malignity of his purposes [John-

7. Duff, *An Essay on Original Genius,* ed. J. L. Mahoney (Gainesville: Scholars' Facsimiles & Reprints, 1964), pp. 7, 140–41, 89–90; Duff (p. 55) similarly praises Pope's sylphs. J. G. Cooper's *Tomb of Shakespear* (London, 1755) presents an extensive and romantic eulogy of Shakespeare's supernatural characters, as does Mrs. Montagu in a most interesting section of her *Essay on the Writings and Genius of Shakespeare* (London, 1769), pp. 135–62.

8. *Lives,* 1: 177–78 (Milton); and 3: 233–34 (Pope's sylphs).

9. *Works,* 2: 137 *(Idler* no. 44).

10. Edmund Burke, *A Philosophical Enquiry into . . . the Sublime and Beautiful,* ed. J. T. Boulton (London: Routledge and Paul, 1958), p. 17.

son concedes]; but let any other being entertain the same thoughts and he will find them easily issue in the same expressions."[11] Everything that Johnson was to say on this point had been said by Addison, Hurd, Gregory, and others (see notes 3 and 5). It is not his praise, as it is Duff's, that the characters are genuinely new (which is to say, among other things, particular and unique), but, what is just the reverse, that their dialogue is "level with life." For Shakespeare to have exhibited "objects that never existed" is admirable. But what is yet more remarkable for Johnson, he has *familiarized* them as well.

11. *Works*, 7: 123.

Appendix B

Love in the Drama

Criticizing those dramatists who depart from general nature, Johnson deplores the prominent position which they have accorded to love. By making love "the universal agent," he says, "probability is violated, life is misrepresented, and language is depraved. But love is only one of many passions, and as it has no great influence upon the sum of life, it has little operation in the dramas of a poet, who caught his ideas from the living world, and exhibited only what he saw before him."[1] Others have sketched, in general terms, the controversy over dramatic love.[2] Its opponents argued from moral or from generic suppositions: it was immoral to lay such stress on the operations of love, or love was a common emotion unbefitting the decorum of tragedy. Rymer's and Rapin's attacks are familiar and typical: they both object to love primarily because it renders the stage unheroic and effeminate; Rapin allows, however, that it is now "a usage so established" that he dare not oppose it. In mid-century the anonymous author of *Miscellaneous Observations on the Tragedy of Hamlet* (1752), so often and so unfairly censorious, rejoices, like Johnson, to praise its absence in Shakespeare: "*Love,* the usual Subject of modern Tragedies, our Poet has very wisely refused Admittance into his best Compositions; it is a Passion truly comic, and when introduced in Tragedy deserves our Contempt and Derision, rather than Pity or Compassion." The *Gray's-Inn Journal* for 1754 attributes the success of theaters—and public gardens as well—to the "love-sick Minds of Boys and Girls. . . . What numbers of *English* Tragedies have been sunk into an insipid Languor by the ineffectual Whim of Episodic Love?" At this same time, Hurd is making the generic

1. *Works,* 7: 63–64.

2. See: C. C. Green, *The Neo-Classic Theory of Tragedy in England during the Eighteenth Century* (Cambridge: Harvard University Press, 1934), pp. 29–30, 181–86; John Dennis, *The Critical Works,* ed. E. N. Hooker, 2 vols. (Baltimore: Johns Hopkins Press, 1939–43), 1: 438–39.

argument: the drama deals only with exalted passions, people of high rank, and important actions—"and this shews the defect of modern tragedy, in turning so constantly as it does on *love subjects.*" [3] Both criticisms are made as late as 1769 by Mrs. Montagu. On moral grounds she objects to "making the interest of the play turn upon the passion of love"—it panders to perverted tastes; and she also argues from the principle of decorum and genre: Voltaire introduced a love intrigue into the story of Oedipus, but tragedy, "thus converted into mere amorous ditty," prevents the dramatist from preserving the decorum of the characters (e.g., Corneille's Theseus neglects all of his duties for love). Probably influenced by Johnson, she also contrasts Shakespeare, who "does not confine himself to any particular passion," with the French, who so much emphasize love.[4] Dramatic love, then, may perhaps conduce to immorality, and will certainly divert one's attention from the truly tragic passions.

Champions of dramatic love are not numerous and invariably qualify their defenses. Louis Racine defends at length his father's use of love, and in 1775 William Cooke recommends love for a reason directly opposed to that which provoked Johnson's attack: love *is* universal and hence has a general effect on the spectators.[5]

3. René Rapin, *Reflections on Aristotle's Treatise of Poesie*, trans. Thomas Rymer (London, 1694), pp. 116–20 for the entire discussion; *Miscellaneous Observations on the Tragedy of Hamlet* (London, 1736), p. vii; Arthur Murphy, *The Gray's-Inn Journal*, 2 vols. (London, 1756), 2: 207–8; Richard Hurd, ed., *Q. Horatii Flacci epistolae ad Pisones, et Augustum . . .* , 3 vols. (London, 1766), 2: 167. See also James Ralph, *The Touch-Stone* (London, 1728), p. 56.

4. Elizabeth Montagu, *An Essay on the Writings and Genius of Shakespeare* (London, 1769), pp. 43–45, 82. For similar French criticism see: Charles Porée, *An Oration . . .* (London, 1734), pp. 64–74; *The Greek Theatre of Father Brumoy*, 3 vols. (London, 1759), 1: cx–cxviii.

5. Louis Racine, *Remarques sur les tragédies de Jean Racine*, 2 vols. (Paris, 1752), 1: 23 ff.; William Cooke, *The Elements of Dramatic Criticism* (London, 1775), pp. 42–45. Joseph Warton seems undecided on this point. In his *Essay on the Genius and Writings of Pope* (2 vols. [London, 1782], 1: 272–73) he objects to introducing love into all dramatic subjects, but admits a few paragraphs later that it is a universal passion "that will always shine upon the stage." Perhaps he is clearer in *Adventurer* no. 113: love, "from the universality of its dominion, may doubtless justly claim a large share in representations of human life; but . . . by totally engrossing the theatre, hath contributed to degrade that noble school of virtue into an academy of effeminacy" (A. Chalmers, ed., *The British Essayists*, vol. 25 [London, 1811], p. 129).

A great many critics, however, were prepared to defend a certain type of love as appropriate to tragedy. For some, proper dramatic love was defined quantitatively: a certain amount of love is acceptable, but not too much. Thus Dubos regrets that Racine reiied on love intrigues more excessively than Corneille, and that subsequent dramatists have followed his unhappy example; because we ought to admire and venerate tragic heroes, love should not have "un trop grand empire" over them.[6] Other critics were equally concerned with quantities of love, but reversed Dubos's position: if love is merely episodic, it is bad, but if it is truly fundamental to the plot, and pervading the action, it is not inadmissible. In his letter prefixed to *Mérope* (1744), Voltaire defends Racine's use of love and contends that if it is the foundation of the play, and "forms the principal interest," not a mere episode, it is acceptable. Love must be either tragic or insipid: "it should reign alone; it was never made for second place." And in 1752 Mason, appealing as usual to sentimental interests despite his superficial classicism, defends the moderns for giving love a principal share in the action: "For we were long since agreed, that, where Love does not degenerate into episodical gallantry, but makes the foundation of the distress, it is, from the universality of its influence, a passion very proper for Tragedy."[7] These several quantitative theories are not mutually exclusive. A perfectly orthodox neoclassicist might well reject love in all but the smallest amounts (it being an unheroic emotion) and at the same time agree that, in the interests of unity, love must be made the principal subject if it is to be used in any real degree; otherwise, it would be too diverting.

Critics were concerned with the quality of dramatic love as well. Gildon, for example, suggests that married love only is suitable for tragedy. William Egerton will permit "lawful and regular" love in tragedy, but he proscribes the illicit variety. La Motte

6. Jean Baptiste Dubos, *Réflexions critiques sur la poésie et sur la peinture,* 2 vols. (Paris, 1719), 1: 139. Cf. *Some Remarks on the Tragedy of Hamlet* (London, 1736), pp. 4–5.

7. Voltaire, *Works,* 38 vols. (London, 1778–81), 27: 249–50; William Mason, *Elfrida, a Dramatic Poem* (London, 1752), p. iii. Cf. Lewis Riccoboni, *An Historical and Critical Account of the Theatres in Europe* (London, 1741), pp. 297–98, and L. Sébastien Mercier, *Du Théâtre; ou nouvel essai sur l'art dramatique* (Amsterdam, 1773), pp. 288–89.

approves of love so long as the characters are animated by virtue; and Voltaire believes that love is bad only when it is "nothing more than gallantry" or, as sometimes in English drama, debauchery. But the rise of sentimentalism was to change the emphasis. Marmontel distinguishes qualities of love, not by their moral excellence, but by their emotional intensity; in general, love is the most theatrical, terrible, and touching of passions—not, however, cold gallantry, but truly furious and desperate love.[8] Finally, many critics regretted that love was so predominant in tragedy, laid the blame to the female audience, but decided that any attempt at reformation would be vain, and that at any rate, love *is* an important emotion.[9] To recapitulate, then, the objections to love are ultimately two: that it is immoral (or certain types of it are) and that it is "indecorous"—too low for the genre of tragedy. Some critics replied that love might be admitted in very slight degrees, or, if it is to be used extensively, it ought to be made fundamental to the action lest it divert our attention from the primary theme; in this case, however, it must not be flagrantly immoral.

C. C. Green cites Johnson's opinion along with Dennis's and Gildon's as though he were arguing, like them, that love is inappropriate to the tragic genre.[10] But we have already seen what Johnson thought of a decorum that excluded sublunary nature; if kings may be indecorous and swear or drink, why surely they may love! In fact, Johnson is not appealing to decorum. Nor is he here concerned very much with immorality, although he complains of that depravation of language which is the consequence of portraying amorous events. Thus, he does not make the tradi-

8. Charles Gildon, *The Complete Art of Poetry*, 2 vols. (London, 1724), 1: 200, 202; William Egerton, *Faithful Memoirs of . . . Mrs. Anne Oldfield* (London, 1731), p. 95; Houdart de La Motte, *Oeuvres de théâtre*, 2 vols. (Paris, 1730), 1: 29 (cf. 1: 138–39); Voltaire, *Critical Essays on Dramatic Poetry* (London, 1761), p. 31; Jean-François Marmontel, *Poétique françoise*, 2 vols. (Paris, 1763), 2: 187.

9. See, to a greater or lesser extent: Joseph Trapp, *Praelectiones poeticae*, 2 vols. (London, 1736), 2: 185–88; Voltaire, *Works,* 13: 142–43; 25: 4; P. A. de La Place, *Le théâtre anglois*, vol. 1 (London, 1746), pp. lxxxviii–cviii. Adam Smith, *The Theory of Moral Sentiments* (London, 1774), pp. 48–49, makes a curious defense of dramatic love: it is not in fact *love* which interests us, but the secondary passions (fear, shame, remorse, horror, despair) which a guilty love occasions. It is with these secondary passions, rather than with love itself, that we truly sympathize.

10. Green, *Neo-Classic Theory of Tragedy*, p. 185.

tional objections at all: he objects to love on the same grounds that he objects to exaggerated heroes and villains and superficially decorous monarchs: love is but a particular emotion and must not assume more than its proper share in an accurate delineation of general human nature. Love violates probability—hence Johnson rejects it, like Voltaire's decorum, by appealing to general nature. He would similarly have repudiated Richardson's belief, expressed nine years later, that because the tragedian must "copy nature in its influence over the heart and actions of man . . . to banish love would be to banish nature"; though to be sure Johnson is in the minority, and even he recognizes elsewhere the power and prevalance of love.[11] Behind his remarks in the *Preface,* possibly, is Dennis's conviction that Shakespeare better distinguished his characters than "any of his Successors have done, who have falsi-fied them . . . by making Love the predominant Quality in all."[12] But only Mrs. Montagu explicitly denounces love as merely a particular passion; and considering the extent of Johnson's in-fluence on her book, it may well be an echo of the *Preface* itself.[13] Johnson, then, though he concurs with the many who disapproved of excessive love in drama, does not do so for the usual moral or generic reasons. It is apparently the extreme and exaggerated use of love that Johnson deplores: like the undue emphasis on heroic qualities, it produces monsters, not men.

11. William Richardson, *Cursory Remarks on Tragedy* (London, 1774), pp. 78–79 (from a similar standpoint the 1825 Oxford editor of Johnson objects: love *is* truly a "universal passion"). On Johnson and love see: *Johnsonian Mis-cellanies,* ed. G. B. Hill, 2 vols. (Oxford, 1897), 1: 290; Frances Burney, *Diary and Letters of Madame D'Arblay,* 7 vols. (London, 1854), 1: 96; but in *Lives,* 1: 361, he opposes the "romantick omnipotence of Love" in *All for Love.*

12. Dennis, *Critical Works,* 2: 4.

13. Arthur Sherbo, *Samuel Johnson, Editor of Shakespeare, With An Essay on The Adventurer, Illinois Studies in Language and Literature,* vol. 42 (Urbana: University of Illinois Press, 1956), p. 5, suggests that Johnson may have been indebted to Joseph Warton's discussion of Shakespeare and love in *Adventurer* no. 113; this is very possible, although Warton's argument is more conventional.

Appendix C

A Play Read . . .

As I have indicated, the motive behind Johnson's refusal to distinguish between the experience of reading and seeing a play is quite intelligible: a spectator, like a reader, easily overcomes certain unrealistic conventions. Yet undeniably this equating of the two suggests to modern minds, as it did to some of Johnson's contemporaries, an insensitivity to theatrical representations; either he has expressed himself more strongly than his purpose warrants, or he is saying something which, without serious qualification, is patently absurd. To be sure, the art of acting was commonly depreciated in the first half of the eighteenth century, and it was also generally assumed that readers only were the proper judges of dramatic merit. "Since every Man who writes," says Dennis, "writes for the Publick, and not for a few; I resolve to have my own Opinion determin'd by that of the Publick. I appeal therefore from the Publick who neither did, nor could know the Play, to the Publick that will know it, that is, from the Spectators to the Readers."[1] Although such an apology would today prompt a smile, it was then quite usual to appeal to the closet reader who, playwrights sanguinely believed, had the time and temperament to appreciate the real virtues of a piece: its style, wit, and so forth. At least throughout the first two-thirds of the century, reviewers normally approached plays as books rather than as staged productions.

But a more modern note is sounded in Steele's preface to *The Conscious Lovers:*

1. John Dennis, *The Critical Works*, ed. E. N. Hooker, 2 vols. (Baltimore: Johns Hopkins Press, 1939–43), 1: 381 (Hooker's note, 1: 519–20, provides additional early eighteenth-century citations to this effect). And on actors see, for example, Nicolas Boileau-Despréaux, *The Works*, 2 vols. (London, 1712), 2: 75: "Thy Spirit [the playwright's] animates the moving Scene,/ For the best Actor's but a good Machine."

209

It must be remember'd, a Play is to be seen, and is made to be Represented with the Advantage of Action, nor can appear but with half the
Spirit, without it; for the greatest Effect of a Play in reading is to excite
the Reader to go see it; and when he does so, it is then a Play has
the Effect of Example and Precept.

The *Museum* in 1747 affirms the considerable difference between
a play read and a play acted, as do Brumoy and others in France.[2]
In England, Garrick was largely responsible for this quickened
interest in dramatic performances. Thus the author of *The Adventures of a Rake* (1759) observes:

> When the Skill of the Player is added to that of the Poet, and the one
> gives Utterance to the other's Conceptions, it is not the Actor or the
> Poet that we hear, 'tis the Character of the Drama that speaks to us. . . .
> *Shakespear's Macbeth* is scarcely intelligible to the Learned; Garrick's
> *Macbeth* lives, and is intelligible to the Vulgar. This proves to an evi-
> dent Demonstration, that acting any Piece is preferable to reading it.

One must not believe that the older view was extinct. Whalley
in 1748 praises the closet reading of Shakespeare, and eleven years
after, Goldsmith urges that plays be read rather than seen; but
his point (that we, reading, are more aware of the moral sentiments
and less excited by immoral scenes) testifies to the increasing power
attributed to stage productions.[3]

Johnson's own opinion of actors and the art of acting is notorious.
One thinks of that passage from the *Life* where Johnson vigorously
denies any merit to a player, "a fellow who claps a hump on his
back, and a lump on his leg, and cries *'I am Richard the Third.'* "
In the *Tour to the Hebrides* he explains that he failed to cele-

2. Steele, quoted in C. H. Gray, *Theatrical Criticism in London to 1795*
(New York: Columbia University Press, 1931), p. 42; *Museum* 3 (1747): 283. See
also: *The Greek Theatre of Father Brumoy*, 3 vols. (London, 1759), 1: vii: "Tragedy is not made to be read, she is all action"; Sébastien Mercier, *Du théâtre;
ou nouvel essai sur l'art dramatique* (Amsterdam, 1773), pp. 293–94; as a sym-
phony requires an orchestra, so a play requires actions and a stage. Cf. Houdart
de La Motte, *Oeuvres de théâtre*, 2 vols. (Paris, 1730), 1: 18; G. E. Lessing, *Hamburgische Dramaturgie*, 2 vols. (Hamburg, 1769), st. xxxvi.

3. *The Adventures of a Rake*, quoted in R. G. Noyes, *The Thespian Mirror*
(Providence: Brown University Press, 1953), p. 177; Peter Whalley, *An Enquiry
into the Learning of Shakespeare* (London, 1748), p. 77; Oliver Goldsmith, *An
Enquiry into the Present State of Polite Learning* (London, 1774), p. 130. Arthur
Murphy, *The Gray's-Inn Journal* (London, 1756), 2: 146, uses Garrick to argue
for the superiority of Shakespeare on the stage; and cf. 1: 239.

brate Garrick in his *Preface to Shakespeare* because "he has not made Shakespeare better known; he cannot illustrate Shakespeare." Elsewhere in the *Tour* he seems equally skeptical of the ability of actors to create any sort of illusion: "The appearance of a player, with whom I have drunk tea, counteracts the imagination that he is the character he represents. They say, 'See *Garrick!* how he looks to-night! See how he'll clutch the dagger!' That is the buz of the theatre." Johnson is at his most insufferably sarcastic in the *Life,* where Boswell inquires whether Garrick has not brought Shakespeare into notice: "Sir, to allow that, would be to lampoon the age."[4]

And yet Boswell assures us that he "had thought more upon the subject of acting than might generally be supposed."[5] One may point, for example, to his reasonable discussion of the differing talents of the poet and the actor in his *Life of Otway* or to his conversations with Mrs. Siddons and Kemble. As for the effect of staged productions, in the dedication which he probably wrote for John Hoole's *Cyrus* (1768) he confesses his fear that the merits of the play may not be so well perceived when read: "When I reflect how many circumstances contribute to please on the Stage, where every Thought or Expression is enforced with the graces of action and utterance, I cannot but be anxious lest the Reader should withhold that approbation in the closet which the Spectator testified in the representation."[6] Nor must two other considerations be overlooked: the barbarous and noisy conditions which prevailed in the playhouses,[7] and the popular declamatory style which Garrick, by his very superiority, made even more popular. It is probable that Johnson, at least for the last twenty-five years of his life, was neither an enthusiastic nor a frequent playgoer.[8] The dis-

4. *Life,* 3: 184; ibid., 5: 244–45; ibid., 5: 46; ibid., 2: 92.

5. Ibid., 4: 243.

6. *Samuel Johnson's Prefaces and Dedications,* ed. Allen T. Hazen (New Haven: Yale University Press, 1937), p. 62; and cf. *Works,* 8: 550.

7. There are many contemporary testimonies, but see especially the interesting observation of J. A. Rouquet in his *L'état des arts en Angleterre* (Paris, 1755), pp. 170–71.

8. That he was not a frequent spectator, see *Johnsonian Miscellanies,* ed. G. B. Hill, 2 vols. (Oxford, 1897), 2: 318; and unenthusiastic, *The Letters,* ed. R. W. Chapman, 3 vols. (Oxford: Oxford University Press, 1952), 1: 134: "I have frequented the theatre more than in former seasons. But I have gone thither only to escape from myself."

comfort which attended such events, together with his own imperfect sight and hearing, doubtless conspired to keep him away.
The latter point is particularly significant in understanding Johnson's attitude. He failed to praise Garrick, Murphy says, because
he "could not see the passions as they rose and chased one another
in the varied features of that expressive face." His own sensitive
recitations, Murphy adds, indicate that he regarded the stage as
too declamatory. Murphy recollects that "being in conversation
with Dr. Johnson near the side of the scenes during the tragedy
of King Lear: when Garrick came off the stage, he [sc. Garrick]
said, 'You two talk so loud you destroy all my feelings.' 'Prithee,'
replied Johnson, 'do not talk of feelings, Punch has no feelings.' "
Here Johnson seems at his most insensitive. But in Reynolds's
account of the same incident we can see that it has a far different
and much less unhappy implication. We discover in Reynolds
that Johnson had first denied to Garrick an excess of sensibility,
asserting that his trade "was to represent passion, not to feel it.
Ask Reynolds whether he felt the distress of Count Hugolino
when he drew it." The "Punch" passage follows, but it serves
only to enforce Johnson's real point: "Garrick left nothing to
chance; every gesture, every expression of countenance, and variation of voice, was settled in his closet before he set foot upon
the stage." [9]

Garrick, like Reynolds, is an artist, a deliberate craftsman: this
is Johnson's meaning. He is attacking, not the art of acting, but
those sentimental theories which supposed a sympathetic identification of the artist with his subject. Johnson's ridicule of actors
is perhaps a reaction to such cant. One might adduce, finally,
Johnson's reply to Percival Stockdale's question of whether or
not Garrick truly deserved all the adulation he had received. Johnson's answer is a direct contradiction of his reply to Boswell's
similar query in the Tour to the Hebrides. He responds affirm-
atively, crediting Garrick "for having seized the very soul of Shakespeare; for having embodied it in himself; and for having expanded
its glory over the world." [10]

9. Johnsonian Miscellanies, 1: 457; 2: 248.
10. Ibid., 2: 333.

Selected Bibliography

This is merely a reference list. It will enable the reader to identify those works, original sources and modern scholarship, which have been cited more than once, and in abbreviated form, in the notes. It includes only such works. Periodicals, except for those published as sets, have also been excluded. Titles have been shortened.

Abrams, M. H. *The Mirror and the Lamp*. Oxford: Oxford University Press, 1953.

Addison, Joseph, and Steele, Richard. *The Spectator*. Edited by Donald F. Bond. 5 vols. Oxford: Oxford University Press, 1965.

Aikin, J., and Aikin, A. L. *Miscellaneous Pieces in Prose*. London, 1773.

Armstrong, John. *Miscellanies*. 2 vols. London, 1770.

Babcock, Robert Witbeck. *The Genesis of Shakespeare Idolatry, 1766–1799*. Chapel Hill: University of North Carolina Press, 1931.

Baretti, Joseph. *Discours sur Shakespeare et sur Monsieur de Voltaire*. London and Paris, 1777.

Bate, Walter Jackson. *The Achievement of Samuel Johnson*. New York: Oxford University Press, 1955.

Batteux, Charles. *Les beaux arts réduits à un même principe*. Paris, 1747.

Boileau-Despréaux, Nicolas. *The Works*. 2 vols. London, 1712.

Boswell, James. *Life of Johnson*. Edited by G. B. Hill; revised by L. F. Powell. 6 vols. Oxford: Oxford University Press, 1934–50.

Boyer, Jean Baptiste. *Réflexions historiques et critiques sur le goût*. Amsterdam, 1743.

Brown, John. *A Dissertation on the Rise . . . of Poetry and Music*. London. 1763.

———. *Essays on the Characteristics*. 5th ed. London, 1764.

Brumoy, Pierre. *The Greek Theatre of Father Brumoy*. Translated by Charlotte Lennox. 3 vols. London, 1759.

Burke, Edmund. *A Philosophical Enquiry into the Origin of Our Ideas of the Sublime and Beautiful*. Edited by J. T. Boulton. London: Routledge and Paul, 1958.

Burney, Frances. *Diary and Letters of Madame d'Arblay*. 7 vols. 2d ed. London, 1854.

Chalmers, A., ed. *The British Essayists*. Vols. 23–25. London, 1817.

Chesterfield, Philip Dormer Stanhope. *Letters to His Son*. Edited by Oliver H. Leigh. 2 vols. New York: n.p., [1937].

Chetwood, W. R. *A General History of the Stage.* London, 1749.

Colman, George. *Prose on Several Occasions.* 3 vols. London. 1787.

The Companion to the Play-House. 2 vols. London, 1764.

Cooke, William. *The Elements of Dramatic Criticism.* London, 1775.

Cooper, Anthony Ashley. *Characteristicks.* 3 vols. 5th ed. London, 1732.

Corneille, Pierre. *Oeuvres complètes.* 2 vols. Paris, 1852.

Dacier, André. *Aristotle's Art of Poetry.* London, 1705.

d'Alembert, Jean le Rond. *Miscellaneous Pieces.* . . . London, 1764.

Davies, Thomas. *Dramatic Miscellanies.* 3 vols. Dublin, 1784.

Dennis, John. *The Critical Works.* Edited by Edward Niles Hooker. 2 vols. Baltimore: Johns Hopkins Press, 1939–43.

———. *Original Letters.* 2 vols. London, 1721.

Diderot, Denis. *Essais sur la peinture.* Paris [1795].

———. *Oeuvres de théâtre* . . . *avec un discours sur la poésie dramatique.* 2 vols. Amsterdam, 1772.

Dryden, John. *Essays.* Edited by W. P. Ker. 2 vols. Oxford: Oxford University Press, 1926.

Dubos, Jean Baptiste. *Réflexions critiques sur la poésie et sur la peinture* 2 vols. Paris, 1719.

Duff, William. *An Essay on Original Genius.* Edited by John L. Mahoney. Gainesville: Scholars' Facsimiles & Reprints, 1964.

Egerton, William. *Faithful Memoirs of* . . . *Mrs. Anne Oldfield.* London, 1731.

Elledge, Scott, ed. *Eighteenth-Century Critical Essays.* 2 vols. Ithaca: Cornell University Press, 1961.

An Examen of . . . *The Suspicious Husband.* London, 1747.

Fielding, Henry. *The Covent-Garden Journal.* Edited by G. E. Jensen. 2 vols. New Haven: Yale University Press, 1915.

Foote, Samuel. *The Roman and English Comedy Consider'd and Compar'd.* London, 1747.

Francklyn, Thomas. *A Dissertation on Antient Tragedy.* London, 1760.

Gentleman, Francis. *The Dramatic Censor.* 2 vols. London, 1770.

Gerard, Alexander. *An Essay on Taste.* Edited by Walter J. Hipple, Jr. Gainesville: Scholars' Facsimiles & Reprints, 1963.

Gildon, Charles. *The Complete Art of Poetry.* 2 vols. 2d ed. London, 1724.

———. *An Essay on the Art, Rise, and Progress of the Stage,* and *Remarks on the Plays of Shakespear.* In *The Works of* . . . *Shakespear.* Vol 7. London, 1710.

Goldsmith, Oliver. *An Enquiry into the Present State of Polite Learning.* London, 1774.

———. *Essays and Criticisms.* 3 vols. London, 1798.

———. *Miscellaneous Works.* Edited by J. Aikin. 5 vols. Baltimore, 1809.

Green, Clarence C. *The Neo-Classic Theory of Tragedy during the Eighteenth Century.* Cambridge: Harvard University Press, 1934.

Gregory, John. *A Comparative View of the State and Faculties of Man.* London, 1765.

Grey, Zachary. *Critical, Historical, and Explanatory Notes on Shakespeare.* 2 vols. London, 1754.

Guthrie, William. *An Essay upon English Tragedy.* London, [1747?].

Hagstrum, Jean H. *Samuel Johnson's Literary Criticism.* Chicago: University of Chicago Press, 1967.

Harris, James. *Three Treatises.* London, 1744.

Hartley, David. *Observations on Man.* 3 vols. London, 1791.

Hénault, C. J. F. *Nouveau théâtre françois.* Paris, 1747.

Hiffernan, Paul. *Dramatic Genius.* London, 1770.

Hippisley, John. *A Dissertation on Comedy.* London, 1750.

Home, Henry [Lord Kames]. *Elements of Criticism.* 3 vols. Edinburgh, 1762.

Hume, David. *Essays and Treatises on Several Subjects.* 2 vols. London, 1768.

Hurd, Richard. *The Works.* 8 vols. London, 1811.

———, ed. *Q. Horatii Flacci epistolae ad Pisones, et Augustum . . . .* 3 vols. 4th ed. London, 1766.

Johnson, Samuel. *The Letters.* Edited by R. W. Chapman. 3 vols. Oxford: Oxford University Press, 1952.

———. *The Lives of the English Poets.* Edited by G. B. Hill. 3 vols. Oxford: Oxford University Press, 1905.

———. *Samuel Johnson's Prefaces & Dedications.* Edited by Allen T. Hazen. New Haven: Yale University Press, 1937.

———. *The Works.* 9 vols. Oxford, 1825.

———. *The Yale Edition of the Works.* 8 vols. New Haven: Yale University Press, 1958–69.

Johnsonian Miscellanies. Edited by G. B. Hill. 2 vols. Oxford, 1897.

Kames. See Home.

La Motte, Houdart de. *Oeuvres de théâtre . . . avec plusiers discours sur la tragédie.* 2 vols. Paris, 1730.

La Place, P. A. de. *Le théâtre anglois.* Vol. 1. London, 1746.

Le Blanc, Jean Bernard. *Letters on the English and French Nations.* 2 vols. Dublin, 1747.

Lennox, Charlotte. *Shakespear Illustrated; or, The Novels and Histories on Which the Plays of Shakespear Are Founded.* 3 vols. London, 1753–54.

Lessing, G. E. *Hamburgische Dramaturgie.* 2 vols. Hamburg, 1769.

Le Tourneur, P. F. *Shakespeare traduit de l'anglois.* Vol. 1. Paris, 1776.

Lovejoy, Arthur O. *The Great Chain of Being.* New York: Harper and Row, 1960.

Lyttelton, George. *The Works*. London, 1774.

Marks, Emerson R. *Relativist and Absolutist: The Early Neoclassical Debate in England*. New Brunswick: Rutgers University Press, 1955.

Marmontel, Jean-François. *Poétique françoise*. 2 vols. Paris, 1763.

Mason, William. *Elfrida, a Dramatic Poem*. London, 1752.

Méhégan, G. Alexandre de. *Considérations sur les révolutions des arts....* Paris, 1755.

Melmoth, William. *Letters . . . by . . . Sir Thomas Fitzosborne*. 7th ed. London, 1769.

Mercier, L. Sébastien. *De la littérature et des littérateurs*. Yverdon, 1778.

———. *Du théâtre; ou nouvel essai sur l'art dramatique*. Amsterdam, 1773.

Miscellaneous Observations on the Tragedy of Hamlet. London, 1752.

Montagu, Elizabeth. *An Essay on the Writings and Genius of Shakespeare*. London, 1769.

Morris, Corbyn. *An Essay towards Fixing the True Standards of Wit*. London, 1744.

Murphy, Arthur. *The Gray's-Inn Journal*. 2 vols. London, 1756.

Noyes, Robert Gale. *The Neglected Muse*. Providence: Brown University Press, 1958.

———. *The Thespian Mirror. Shakespeare in the Eighteenth-Century Novel*. Providence: Brown University Press, 1953.

Porée, Charles. *An Oration in Which an Enquiry Is Made Whether the Stage Is . . . a School for . . . Virtue*. London, 1734.

Pouilly, L. J. L. de. *Theory of Agreeable Sensations*. London, 1749.

Racine, Jean. *Oeuvres*. 3 vols. Paris, 1755–60.

———. *Principes de la tragédie*. Edited by E. Vinaver. Manchester: Manchester University Press, 1944.

Racine, Louis. *Remarques sur les tragédies de Jean Racine*. 2 vols. Amsterdam and Paris, 1752.

Ralph, James. *The Touch-Stone*. London, 1728.

Ramsey, Paul. *The Lively and the Just*. Tuscaloosa: University of Alabama Press, 1962.

Rapin, René. *Reflections on Aristotle's Treatise of Poesie*. Translated by Thomas Rymer. London, 1694.

Remarks on Mr. Mason's Elfrida. London, 1752.

Reynolds, Joshua. *Discourses on Art*. Edited by S. O. Mitchell. New York: Bobbs-Merrill, 1965.

Riccoboni, Lewis. *An Historical and Critical Account of the Theatres in Europe*. London, 1741.

Richardson, William [or Edward Taylor]. *Cursory Remarks on Tragedy, on Shakespear, and on Certain French and Italian Poets*. London, 1774.

Richardson, William. *Essays on Shakespeare's Dramatic Characters*. London, 1784.

———. *A Philosophical Analysis and Illustration of Some of Shakespeare's Remarkable Characters.* 2d ed. London, 1774.

Robertson, J. G. *Lessing's Dramatic Theory.* Cambridge: Cambridge University Press, 1939.

Rymer, Thomas. *The Critical Works.* Edited by Curt A. Zimansky. New Haven: Yale University Press, 1956.

Shaftesbury. See Cooper.

Sherbo, Arthur. *Samuel Johnson, Editor of Shakespeare. With an Essay on The Adventurer. Illinois Studies in Language and Literature,* vol. 42. Urbana: University of Illinois Press, 1956.

Smith, Adam. *The Theory of Moral Sentiments.* London, 1774.

Smith, D. Nichol, ed. *Eighteenth-Century Essays on Shakespeare.* Oxford: Oxford University Press, 1963.

Some Remarks on the Tragedy of Hamlet. London, 1736.

Suard, J. B. A. *Variétés littéraires.* Vol. 1. Paris, 1768.

Terrasson, Jean. *La philosophie applicable à tous les objets de l'esprit et de la raison.* Paris, 1754.

Trapp, Joseph. *Praelectiones poeticae.* 2 vols. 3d ed. London, 1736.

Upton, John. *Critical Observations on Shakespeare.* 2d ed. London, 1748.

Voltaire, [F. M. A.] de. *Critical Essays on Dramatic Poetry.* London, 1761.

———. *Oeuvres complètes.* 70 vols. Paris, 1785–89.

———. *Works.* Edited by Tobias Smollett et al. 38 vols. "New Edition." 1778–81.

———, ed. *Théâtre de . . . Corneille.* 12 vols. [Geneva], 1764.

Warton, Joseph. *An Essay on the Genius and Writings of Pope.* 2 vols. 4th ed. London, 1782.

Warton, Thomas. *The History of English Poetry.* 3 vols. London, 1840.

———. *Observations on the "Fairy Queen."* 2 vols. 2d ed. London, 1762.

Webb, Daniel. *An Inquiry into the Beauties of Painting.* London, 1760.

———. *Observations on the Correspondence between Poetry and Music.* London, 1769.

———. *Remarks on the Beauties of Poetry.* London, 1762.

Wellek, René. *A History of Modern Criticism: 1750–1950.* Vol. 1, *The Later Eighteenth Century.* New Haven: Yale University Press, 1955.

Welsted, Leonard. *Works in Prose and Verse.* London, 1787.

Whalley, Peter. *An Enquiry into the Learning of Shakespeare.* London, 1748.

Wilkes, Thomas. *A General View of the Stage.* London, 1759.

The Works of Beaumont and Fletcher. Edited by Lewis Theobald, Thomas Seward, et al. Vol. 1. London, 1750.

Young, Edward. *Conjectures on Original Composition.* Edited by Edith J. Morley. Manchester: Manchester University Press, 1918.

Index

Abrams, M. H., 2, 9, 30 n

Addison, Joseph, 23, 60, 94, 99, 106, 108, 110, 113, 115, 155, 172; his *Cato*, 153–54; his genius compared w i t h Shakespeare's, 153; attacks poetic justice, 109, 121–22; on tragicomedy, 57–58; on tragic pleasure, 89–90; on Shakespeare's "fairy way of writing," 200–201

Adler, J. H., 84 n, 97 n

Adventures of a Rake, The, 210

Aikin, J., and A. L. Aikin, 40, 59 n, 88

Aldridge, A. O., 84 n

Ariosto, 148

Aristotle, 30, 34, 35, 60, 77, 91, 106, 109, 110, 111, 113

Armstrong, John, 6 n, 7, 74, 102, 164, 167 n, 171

Babbitt, Irving, 97

Babcock, Robert Witbeck, xi n, 2, 2 n, 73 n, 97 n, 187 n

Bacon, Francis, 150

Baretti, Joseph, 31 n, 89 n, 161 n, 183, 200 n

Bate, Walter Jackson, 84 n, 97, 110 n, 166 n, 191, 192, 193, 197

Batteux, Charles, 9, 21 n, 31 n, 32 n, 35 n, 81 n, 87 n, 133, 147 n, 201 n

Belle nature, la, 30 n, 56 n. *See also* Nature, general

Bentham, Jeremy, xv

Blackmore, Richard, 107

Blackwell, Thomas, 145

Blair, Hugh, 25, 42 n

Blake, William, 29, 71, 169

Boileau-Despréaux, Nicolas, 3, 91, 209 n

Bombast. *See* Language, propriety of

Booth, Barton, 179

Booth, Wayne C., 119, 125

Boswell, James, 161, 167, 182, 197, 211

Boulton, James T., 2, 12, 16

Bourgeois drama. *See* Domestic tragedy

Boyer, Jean Baptiste, 35 n, 76 n, 153 n

Bradley, A. C., 29

Brecht, Bertolt, 93

Bredvold, Louis I., xx n, 30 n, 56 n

Brown, James, xix n

Brown, John, 64 n, 76, 83 n, 112, 113, 119 n, 135, 137 n, 145

Brumoy, Pierre, 21 n, 42 n, 59 n, 85 n, 90 n, 91 n, 128, 129, 130, 136 n, 205 n, 210, 210 n

Burke, Edmund, xix, 11, 13 n, 16, 194, 202

Burney, Frances, 59 n, 154 n, 208 n

Bysshe, Edward, 148, 150

Caliban, 199–200, 201, 202

Callender, James T., 182, 186

Campbell, Thomas, x n, 182

Capell, Edward, 172 n

Carlyle, Thomas, 196–97

Carnochan, W. B., 189 n

Catharsis, 110–15, 123

Chaignean, William, 78 n

Characters: comic, 39–40, 40 n, 133; discrimination of, 44–46, 208; dramatic, chap. 2, sec. 1 passim (esp. 29, 32–47), 130–31, 178–179; supernatural, 199–203

Chesterfield, Philip Dormer Stanhope, 4th earl of, 32, 79 n, 87 n

Chetwood, W. R., 106 n

Chorus, 118; attacked, 82–84, 98, 113–14; defended, 75–76

Cibber, Theophilus, 106 n, 148

Cohen, Ralph, 84 n

219